HERB
ACEOUS

Published in 2003 by Murdoch Books®, a division of Murdoch Magazines Pty Ltd.

Murdoch Books® Australia
GPO Box 1203
Sydney NSW 2001
Phone: + 61 (0) 2 4352 7000
Fax: + 61 (0) 2 4352 7026

Murdoch Books UK Limited
Ferry House, 51–57 Lacy Road
Putney, London SW15 1PR
Phone: + 44 (0) 20 8355 1480
Fax: + 44 (0) 20 8355 1499

'Companion planting' and 'Medicinal herbs' written by Dr Judyth McLeod
'Introduction', 'Herb garden design' and special spreads written by Meredith Kirton
'Herb directory' written by Geoffrey Burnie and John Fenton-Smith
Additional text: Steven Bradley, Val Bradley, Geoffrey Burnie, John Fenton-Smith, Denise Greig, Lulu Grimes, Alison Haynes, Meredith Kirton and Kim Rowney
Recipes developed by the Murdoch Books Test Kitchen

Chief Executive: Juliet Rogers
Publisher: Kay Scarlett

Design Concept: Marylouise Brammer
Art Direction and Design: Alex Frampton
Editorial Director: Diana Hill
Project Manager/Photo Researcher: Sarah Baker

Copy Editor: Sue Wagner
Subeditor: Roland Arvidssen
Production: Fiona Byrne

National Library of Australia Cataloguing-in-Publication Data
    Herbaceous. Includes index. ISBN 1 74045 219 4. 1. Herbs. 2. Herb gardening. 3. Cookery (Herbs).
    4. Herbs – Therapeutic use. I. Baker, Sarah. 635.7

Printed by Toppan Printing Hong Kong Co. Ltd. PRINTED IN CHINA.

Note to readers

This book contains the opinions and ideas of its authors. It is intended to provide helpful and informative material on the subjects addressed in this book. It is sold with the understanding that the author and publishers are not engaged in rendering medical, health, or any other kind of personal professional services in this book. The reader should consult his or her medical, health or other competent professional before adopting any of the suggestions in this book or drawing inferences from it. The authors and publishers disclaim all responsibility for any liability, loss or risk, personal or otherwise, which is incurred as a consequence, directly or indirectly, of the use and application of any of the contents of this book.

HERBACEOUS

growing, harvesting + using herbs

Compiled and edited by Sarah Baker

MURDOCH
B O O K S

contents

INTRODUCTION   6

GROWING HERBS
cultivating   16
propagating   38
harvesting and storing   58
companion planting   70
herb garden design   88

USING HERBS
medicinal herbs   104
culinary herbs   124
cosmetic herbs   152
scented herbs   168
herbs for household use   182

HERB DIRECTORY   194

Index   250
Acknowledgments   256

No garden is complete without a few herbs — use them to add flavour and delight to food, to make cosmetics and herbal remedies, and as good companions and fragrant plants in the garden.

introduction

What is a herb?

To a botanist a herb is a plant that does not have a woody stem — that is, a plant that is not a tree or shrub. Its edibility is irrelevant. Gardeners have a different definition. To them, a herb is a plant that can be added to food or used for medicinal and household purposes, even if the plant in question is actually a shrub, such as rosemary, or even a tree, such as the bay tree.

The majority of herbs belong to three plant families — Lamiaceae/Labiatae, Umbelliferae and Compositae — but there are ten herb families in all. The most economically important family is the mint family (Lamiaceae/Labiatae), which includes herbs such as lavender, mint and rosemary.

With its fragrant flowers and heart-shaped leaves, sweet violet (*Viola odorata*) is an old-fashioned favourite. You can make an elegant dessert decoration with it by dipping the flowers in egg white, then dusting them with caster sugar.

A short history of herb cultivation

We could be forgiven for thinking that herbs are 'new age' but, in fact, the use of herbs goes back to the very beginning of humankind, and has undergone waves of popularity and understanding throughout the ages. As hunters and gatherers, we used and consumed wild plants, including herbs and spices. Long before recorded history, herbs were used for culinary and medicinal purposes.

Ancient times

The first documented evidence of the importance of herbs in the West is in the Sumerian and Egyptian civilisations. The Sumerians under Nebuchadnezzar II, King of Babylon 605–562 BC, are credited with building the legendary Hanging Gardens, one of the wonders of the ancient world. Unfortunately, there is no archaeological evidence that these gardens ever existed, but there are detailed descriptions of them in the writings of Strabo, a Greek geographer and geophysicist. Some of the plants that may have grown there include date palms, nut trees, olives, grapevines and fig trees.

The Egyptians imported herbs and spices along with the knowledge of their use from Babylon and India. Garlic, anise, caraway, saffron, coriander and thyme were used in foodstuffs, medicines, cosmetics, perfume and disinfectants, and in the process of embalming.

These traditions were picked up by the ancient Greeks. In about 500 BC, Herodotus listed about 700 herbs and their uses, many of which

According to Culpeper's *The Complete Herbal* (1649), both the bark and the ripe fruit of the mulberry (*Morus nigra*) are laxatives, while unripe fruit has the opposite effect, especially when dried.

The seeds of fennel (*Foeniculum vulgare*) once had many medicinal applications: they were used to treat flatulence, jaundice, gout and hiccups, and as an antidote to poisonous herbs or mushrooms.

remain valid today. In the first century AD, Dioscorides produced a herbal guide, which is still a reference in the practice of natural medicines. Hippocrates (c. 460–c. 375 BC), a Greek physician, was perhaps the first to practise medicine as a scientific method. He believed that in nature there was strength to cure disease, and he often used diet and herbs as the basis of treatment.

The medical inheritance eventually passed from Greece to Rome. Physicians in the Roman Empire used herbal remedies quite extensively. For example, the herb mandrake (*Mandragora officinarum*) was used in Roman times as an anaesthetic. When the legions of Rome marched through Europe, conquering and colonising, they took with them seeds and plants to cultivate for

their own use. Sage, fennel, betony, hyssop, borage, parsley, thyme and rosemary are just some of the herbs that were introduced into Britain by the Romans.

When the Romans landed in Britain, they found that the Druid sect had powerful priests with a deep understanding of natural remedies. The Druids collected various plants and animals, and used them to prepare concoctions for their patients. The oak tree was sacred to the Druids and the mistletoe (*Viscum album*) that grew on it played a special part in their rituals.

In the 17th century, **rue seeds** taken in wine were used as an antidote to poison.

The Dark Ages
During the Dark Ages (476–c. 1000 AD), after the invading barbarians tore down much of what the Romans had built, many of the monasteries and their gardens survived intact. The monks kept alive the Romans' knowledge of herbal remedies and treated those who lived outside the monastery walls. Some of the herbs they grew and used were poppies,

Wise women and witches

Women skilled in the medicinal uses of herbs were known as wise women or midwives. They assisted women in childbirth, and tended the sick, often using prayer or charms as well as herbs. But a failure to heal could result in accusations of witchcraft.

In Shakespeare's day, honeysuckle (*Lonicera periclymenum*) was known as woodbine.

burdock, marshmallow, houseleek, rue, lilies, fenugreek, savory, parsley, mint, cumin, fennel, iris and rosemary. Herbal medicines, many of which form the basis of today's liqueurs, were frequently mixed with wine to make them taste better. These recipes of digestive herbs were often taken to combat the chronic indigestion and flatulence caused by badly prepared food.

Medieval Europe

A growing sense of peace prevailed in the Middle Ages: kitchen gardens and orchards were now planted outside the castle walls. Favourite herbs included roses, iris, lilies, columbines, lavenders, dianthus, wild thyme, avens (*Geum urbanum*), borage, parsley, orach (*Atriplex patula*), honeysuckle and fennel. The first English herbal, published in 1551 by William Turner, was a scientific study of 238 native British plants. This provided the basis of two less rigorous works, the herbals of Gerard and Culpeper, both of which are still available today.

Tudor England

In the Tudor period in England, large houses often had a 'still room'. Wines, pot pourri, medicinal salves and burning perfumes as well as culinary preparations were all made there; plants with insecticidal or disinfectant properties were particularly in demand. The still room remained a feature of large English households until Victorian times.

The language of flowers

A tussie mussie or nosegay is a posy of flowers and herbs that conveys some meaning or purpose. Originally tussie mussies were intended to ward off disease, but their purpose evolved throughout the 18th century, and eventually came to spell out a message using the language of flowers. Most often this message was an expression of love for one's sweetheart, but it could also be other things, such as hate, grief or thankfulness. For instance, lemon balm was used to convey sympathy, violets for modesty, and forget-me-nots for true love.

According to the language of flowers, the sweet pea signifies everlasting pleasure.

The age of exploration

The 17th and 18th centuries brought about much change with the discovery of the New World, when plant hunters and spice merchants crisscrossed the globe with plants, including herbs, from many continents. It must have been an exciting time in the world of herbs. Large botanic gardens were set up to display this widening collection of plants from the New World, including nasturtiums and sunflowers. Seeds and recipes were brought back to Europe from America. With the help of the Native

The flower heads of the sunflower (*Helianthus annuus*) follow the sun as it passes across the sky.

Americans (whom we can thank for the deliciously refreshing Earl Grey tea flavoured by the oil of bergamot), much was learnt about native herbs and their use.

The naturalistic movement of the 18th century, which decreed that a garden should appear part of the natural landscape, led to the decline in importance of the physic gardens as medicine and botany drifted apart. Medicinal herbs retreated to the cottage garden. In rural areas, cottage owners kept gardens with many herbs and made home remedies, although this was mainly due to hardship, isolation, economic circumstances and lack of access to medicines, rather than fashion.

The modern era

By the 19th century, industrialisation had taken people away from their traditional livelihoods and sent them to work in the towns. They no longer had the room to grow herbs and so patent medicines and manufactured condiments took their place. In the early 20th century, herbs did regain importance in gardening through the work of gardeners like Vita Sackville-West and Gertrude Jekyll, but mainly for ornamental rather than medicinal purposes.

Genoa or sweet basil is the perfect accompaniment to vine-ripened tomatoes. It is also a good companion plant for tomatoes in the garden.

Today we mostly use herbs when cooking — even a pinch of dried herb from a supermarket can make a difference, but the same herb fresh from the garden can add a special savour and aroma that can elevate a dish from the banal and everyday to something special.

But don't confine your use of herbs to the kitchen. Explore their other uses — herbs are good companion plants, compost accelerators, pest repellents, dyes and ingredients for home-made cosmetics, perfumes, pot pourris and household cleaners.

The latest trend is rediscovering herbs and their use as a whole plant or essential oil rather than copying and isolating plant compounds. Herbs are credited with all sorts of medicinal qualities. In the past it was an essential part of a doctor's training to learn to distinguish beneficial herbs from useless and harmful ones, and these studies laid the foundations of modern botany. Some of the old prescriptions have been verified by modern science, and many modern drugs are still extracted from plants. The folklore attached to herbs is part of their charm, but don't dabble in herbal cures without seeking advice from your doctor or a reputable herbalist first.

Herbal medicine in the East

The Chinese have practised herbal medicine for 5000 years. One Chinese medical text, written in 2700 BC, lists 13 herbal prescriptions. The Chinese are noted for their knowledge and use of ginseng; many Chinese people believe that regular use of ginseng prolongs life.

In India, Ayurvedic medicine has many principles in common with the Chinese tradition — a holistic approach to health that emphasises the importance of balance and diet. The Muslim Empire of the 10th century (which stretched across Arabia, Persia, Spain and Africa), also developed traditional ways for using native herbs.

Gardening with herbs

It is traditional to grow herbs in a garden of their own, and if you have the energy and the space, a small formal herb garden can be very decorative. But if a formal bed doesn't appeal to you, plant a potted herb garden, or use herbs as companion plants among your flowers and vegetables. Experiment with colour, foliage and form to suit the style and conditions of your garden.

A formal bed in a traditional potager garden, where herbs, flowers and vegetables thrive together.

In medieval times, culinary herbs were grown with vegetables but medicinal herbs

GROWING

were kept separate to avoid tragic mistakes. Today herbs suit any garden design, from the rigid formality of knots and wheels to the rambling informality of a cottage

HERBS

garden, while the architectural forms of some herbs make them ideal potted specimens.

Everyone with access to an outdoor area should be able to grow a pot or two of herbs. You can plant them in a separate herb garden, either formal or informal, or among flowering annuals, perennials and vegetables.

cultivating

Soil and aspect

Many herbs originated in Mediterranean regions where the soil is often poor and stony. These herbs — lavender, sage and rosemary, for example — prefer a spot in full sun in reasonably well drained soil. When these herbs are 'grown hard' — that is, without additional fertiliser and without lots of water — they generally have a better flavour than those grown in supposedly ideal conditions. But tropical herbs — such as lemon grass, cardamom, ginger and turmeric — need rich, fertile soil. Consult the table on page 18, as well as the 'Herb directory' in the back of the book, and make sure you always check the required growing conditions before you plant.

If you live in a cold climate, lift mint and chives (shown here) in autumn, then pot them and place them in a heated greenhouse.

Purpose-built herb gardens, especially those in cool regions, may have brick or stone paths and walls, which help store and reflect the heat that most herbs enjoy. But in warm areas this is not necessary. So choose the warmest, sunniest spot in your garden for herbs, and make sure the soil is well drained. Open up heavier soils by digging in plenty of compost well before planting. If the drainage is still poor because your soil is heavy clay, import some fresh soil and make some raised beds.

Herbs for all soil types

Dry soil with good drainage	*Moderately moist soil*	*Wet soil*
Marjoram	Basil	Apple mint
Oregano	Bay	Mint
Rosemary	Bergamot	Pennyroyal
Sage	Borage	Peppermint
Summer savory	Burnet	Sorrel
Winter savory	Chervil	Spearmint
Thyme	Chives	
	Dill	
	Garlic	
	Lemon balm	
	Lemon grass	
	Parsley	
	Tarragon	

Lemon verbena (*Aloysia triphylla*) prefers a warm, humid climate and rich soil.

Have you ever wondered what the difference is between a herb and a spice? Herbs are the leaves of plants. Spices are produced from the other parts, such as flowers, seeds and roots.

Turmeric (*Cucurma domestica*).

Cardamom (*Elettaria cardamomum*) seed pods.

How to choose a good plant

1 First of all, check that the leaves are uniformly green.
2 Look for a specimen of balanced proportions, one that is neither lopsided nor top-heavy.
3 Check for any insect damage, weeds or fungus rots. Leave any contaminated plants alone.
4 Never buy a pot-bound plant. You can tell these from the roots growing out of the base of the pot or circling the surface. Don't hesitate to remove the pot to have a good look at the root system, but remember to replace it!
5 Don't be seduced by just the flowers; ask how long these last and picture what the plant will look like when they finish.

Get a quick start by buying seedlings of your favourite herbs in punnets, ready for planting out into the garden or in larger pots.

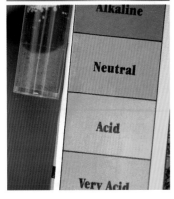

Testing soil pH

1 Place the soil sample in a tube (the tube should be about ⅕ full). Pour in water.

2 Shake the tube.

3 Let the sample settle. The colour change indicates whether the soil is alkaline or acidic. This test shows the soil is alkaline.

Soil pH

Gardening books often speak of the pH range. The pH is a measure of acidity and alkalinity, based on a scale of 1 to 14, with 1 being extremely acid and 14 being extremely alkaline. Test your soil to see if your plants are compatible with the pH. Many herbs require a range of 4.5 to 5.5 (acid). Most garden plants — including roses, bedding plants, annuals, mints, grasses and ferns — prefer slightly acid to neutral soils.

Nearly all members of the pea family (wisteria, peas, beans, sweet peas and clovers), iris, lilac, hydrangeas (where pink flowers are wanted) and many rockery plants and some herbs prefer alkaline soils with a pH range of 6.5 to 7.5.

Foliar feeding works regardless of soil pH and is handy in some cases. Use a watering can to pour diluted liquid fertiliser over the leaves so they can absorb the nutrients directly.

Feeding

When growing Mediterranean-style herbs, you should generally avoid adding manure and fertiliser, but if you have an acid soil, dig in some lime prior to planting. Dig in about 100 g (3½ oz) of lime or dolomite per square metre (square yard) or a little more if the soil has a high clay content.

Handy feeding hints

For herbs that require a nutrient-rich soil, follow these tips.

- Always fertilise when the soil is moist and water thoroughly after you have completed the application.
- If in doubt, apply fertiliser at half-strength twice as often.
- Plants don't use much food in winter, so don't bother feeding then. Spring, summer and autumn feeds generally provide better value.
- Nitrogen is responsible for leaf growth, but too much nitrogen can cause floppy growth and poor flowers.
- Phosphorus is vital for strong roots and stems. Light doses do bring some benefits.
- Potassium maintains the rigidity of plants, and is an important element in promoting flowering.

Pruning

The only pruning some kitchen herbs require is a little tip pruning. Regularly pinch out the tip shoot or bud to encourage bushy, compact growth. If you are growing herbs for cooking – such as marjoram, sage and thyme – then harvesting the tips every now and then may be all that is needed.

On the other hand, a shrub such as lavender should be pruned in late spring and autumn. If you don't cut back half the season's growth, the plant becomes woody and straggly. Make sure there is green wood below your cutting line, otherwise your lavender will not reshoot.

Hard prune salvia at the end of winter, and mulch it with manure for lush new growth in spring.

Growing herbs in containers

You can grow herbs in pots or plant several together in a large tub or a hanging basket. Group together plants that like the same conditions of sun, soil, feeding and drainage. Plant herbs that have a tendency to trail – such as oregano, thyme and prostrate rosemary – at the side of a large pot, and place upright herbs – basil, sage and sorrel – in the middle.

Add about 2 teaspoons of lime to the potting mix for a 20 cm (8 in) pot. Add more or less according to the size of the container. For herbs such as sage it may be worth incorporating some coarse sand into the mix so that the pot will drain rapidly.

Japanese parsley
(*Cryptotaenia japonica*).

Quality potting mixes contain water crystals. These act as a reservoir so that when the soil dries out, water can be absorbed from the crystals. Once you apply water the crystals are hydrated again. They continue the swelling and shrinking process, providing plants with water for up to six years. Use them at planting time.

Water the herbs well whenever they feel dry just below the surface. During windy summer heat you may need to water soft herbs such as basil, mint and parsley twice daily. However, many herbs are of Mediterranean origin and they prefer to dry out between waterings; it is easy to kill herbs such as rosemary by keeping them constantly moist.

Making a herb globe

If space is at a premium in your garden, fill a hanging container with a range of herbs. For this project, you'll need two hanging baskets (made from heavy-gauge wire and coated in plastic), chains, a hammer, a pair of pliers, an empty plant pot, sphagnum moss, herbs, premium quality potting mix containing water crystals and slow-release fertiliser, plywood, nails and plastic-coated wire.

1 Place one basket on top of a large empty plant pot. Line the lower half with a layer of sphagnum moss and press it firmly against the wire mesh, then add some potting mix to the same level.

2 Insert the first layer of herbs by passing them roots first through the mesh, so that the roots are resting on the potting mix and the tops of the plants are hanging down the sides. Line the top half of the basket with moss and potting mix as before. Insert the next layer of herbs and top up the potting mix until it is level with the rim. Place a square of plywood over the top of the basket then carefully turn it over to form a dome. Nail the basket rim to the plywood. Leave the basket in a sheltered place and water it regularly for two to three weeks. Prepare the second basket in the same way.

3 When the herbs are well rooted into the potting mix, place the domes on a flat surface and remove the nails. Carefully balance one dome, plywood side up, on top of an empty plant pot. Remove the plywood. Holding the plywood of the second dome in place, invert it over the first dome.

4 Slide out the plywood from the second dome and secure the two baskets together with plastic-coated wire. Attach hanging chains to the herb globe and hang it in a sunny position. Keep it well watered.

The most popular of all annual herbs is probably basil. Grow it in a rich, well drained soil and keep it watered during dry weather.

Top ten herbs

1   **Parsley.** The mostly widely grown herb, growing to 45 cm (18 in) from a thick taproot. Rich in iron and vitamins A, B and C, it is great in salads, soups, stuffing and garnishes. Legend has it that you have to be wicked to be able to grow parsley successfully. Replace your parsley plants by raising fresh seed when the existing plants begin to flower.

2   **Chives.** This perennial herb with fine, hollow leaves adds a delicate onion flavour to food and can be used as a companion plant for roses.

3   **Rosemary.** A woody shrub that loves full sun and dry conditions. It is perfect with lamb.

4   **Thyme.** A symbol of courage and vitality, this herb is used for flavouring egg and cheese dishes. It is mostly grown as an aromatic groundcover for a sunny spot.

5   **Dill.** This herb is great for use in pickling, with fish and in soups. It has attractive fine foliage and needs to be forced with lots of nitrogen fertiliser.

6   **Mint.** A herb that grows well in cool, moist areas, even shade, although it can become a pest if it likes the conditions too much. Mint can be used in drinks and salads and for flavouring the traditional favourite, roast lamb. (See 'Plant a mint garden' on page 28.)

7   **and 8 Marjoram and oregano.** These closely related, strongly flavoured herbs are excellent for flavouring soups and pasta dishes. They make a great groundcover in a sunny spot.

9   **Sage.** A close relative of ornamental salvia, with grey leaves that are useful for stuffing, as well as for flavouring soups, veal and poultry.

10 **Basil.** An extremely popular cooking herb for use in soups, tomato dishes and pasta sauces, basil is a summer-growing annual and needs replanting each spring. It is also an effective companion plant for tomatoes, as it repels whitefly and other pests.

Chocolate mint.

Bring your soil to life

Many gardeners put all their efforts into the above-ground parts of their garden, forgetting what is going on below soil level. Half of every plant lies beneath the soil, feeding and supporting the leaf and flower growth above.

To cater for your whole plant, it is important to understand soil, compost, mulching, fertilising and the organisms that make it all happen. There are three main factors in improving the soil in your garden: mulch, humus or compost, and fertilisers.

Indigenous to the Amazon rainforest, perennial coriander (*Eryngium foetidum*) grows best in a moist, shaded position. Rich in iron, carotene, riboflavin and calcium, it is used as a culinary herb in Asia and the Caribbean.

Tips for growing herbs

- Herbs grow naturally in many different soils and climates. Some thrive in extremely dry areas, others in tropical rainforests and temperate woodlands, so if you choose the appropriate herbs for the prevailing conditions you cannot go wrong.
- Most herbs prefer full sun and free-draining soil.
- Don't pick more than one-third of a young plant or more than half of a mature specimen at the one time. The more often you pick, the bushier and healthier herbs become.
- Don't overfertilise — there will be too much soft leafy growth at the expense of essential oils.
- Snails and insects like herbs too. Be vigilant and pick off grubs by hand, and trap snails with small saucers of beer (see page 45).
- To develop full flavour, most herbs should have at least five hours of sunlight a day or 16 hours under fluorescent lights (placed 5–10 cm, or 2–4 in, above the plants).

- Many herbs grow better when planted next to other herbs, but some will struggle in the wrong combinations. For example, mint hates growing near parsley. If your herbs aren't doing well, but they are growing in the right conditions, try planting some new neighbours.

Indoor growing tips

Herbs really grow best in full sun, so while temporarily growing them indoors is an option, don't expect them to last forever.

- Select a pot with plenty of drainage holes.
- Use a well drained potting mix suitable for shrubs.
- Incorporate a slow-release fertiliser at the highest recommended rate.
- Water with liquid fertiliser regularly if growth is slow.
- Give them as much direct sunlight as possible to build in flavour.
- Choose herbs that cope with some shade, such as mint and 5-in-1 herb (*Coleus amboinicus*), also known as Spanish thyme or Indian borage.

Mulch

Mulch provides a blanket layer over your soil. It is normally about 10 cm (4 in) thick. Mulch:

- regulates soil temperature, by keeping roots cool in summer and warm in winter;
- conserves moisture and cuts down on watering requirements by reducing evaporation from the soil surface and increasing water penetration; and
- controls weeds by preventing weed seeds from germinating.

Some organic mulches
Clockwise from top left: leaf litter, pine bark, teatree fines, plantation wood chip, eucalyptus fines and wood chip (stained redwood).

Mulches are available in many forms, both organic and inorganic. Various organic mulches are available commercially, in bags or in bulk. Choose one of premium quality to avoid introducing weeds or soil-borne diseases to your garden. Home-made compost can be used instead.

Common mint.

Worms

Worms are natural recyclers, converting vegetative matter into nutrient-rich worm castings. Once introduced, worms will multiply rapidly and increase the aeration and nitrogen content of the soil. Compost worms will eat their way through kitchen scraps and garden waste, and produce castings that can be used on the garden.

A worm farm full of compost worms is even better than a compost heap. A typical worm farm comprises three different layers: the top layer of paper scraps and organic matter, a centre layer where worms nest, and a bottom layer of castings (worm poo). Add food scraps to the top layer and, as the worms consume them, keep adding more food. Note, however, that worms do not like banana, citrus, onion or garlic.

As chambers fill with waste, empty them into the garden or into pots. If you occasionally pour water into the farm, it will filter through the worm castings and can be collected via a tap that allows you to drain off and use the liquid waste. Use this waste diluted 1:10 with water.

Some mulches — for example, lucerne and compost — have a high nitrogen content. These mulches improve the soil fertility, but they rot down quickly and so need to be replaced every few months. Never use peat moss as a mulch as it repels water once it is dry; instead, blend it into the soil and use it as a soil conditioner.

Inorganic mulches — such as black plastic, weed control mat, scoria and decorative gravels — are not really 'garden friendly': they add nothing to the soil structure, and once these mulches are in place, soil additives are difficult to incorporate. They tend to raise the soil temperature and some can even stop your soil from breathing, which may lead to serious problems.

Depending on the time of year at which you mulch, you can influence soil temperatures. For example, if you mulch at the end of autumn, you will keep the soil warmer for longer, while mulching in early spring will keep the soil cooler and prevent heat being trapped in summer.

Composting

Organic matter in the process of breaking down is referred to as humus or compost. This organic content brings your soil to life and is essential for sustaining living plants. Without organic matter your soil is 'dead'. The breakdown and decay of both animal and vegetable materials produces compost, which is rich in the essential elements for plant growth.

The composting process is a complex one, employing countless micro-organisms to bring about chemical changes in organic waste matter. These microscopic workers like plenty of air, a little moisture and heat in order to perform their composting duties; they also rely on a good carbon/nitrogen ratio. You can achieve this ratio in your compost heap by incorporating a balanced mix of wet (vegetables and grass) and dry (for example, leaf litter) ingredients, as well as by regularly turning the mix.

Adding compost to the garden is a natural way of aiding water retention and maintaining a rich, quality soil. Compost is, in effect, nature's miracle tonic. Composting can convert bulky 'rubbish' into a fertiliser that is of great benefit to the soil. If you add organic matter to your soil in the form of compost on a regular basis, even a poor soil can be transformed into a rich, friable organic loam, which in no time will be teeming with worms.

Spearmint.

Feature herb: mint

There are many species of mint, including apple mint, spearmint, eau de cologne mint, pineapple mint and pennyroyal. Mint repels most pests, especially fleas and beetles, which dislike the smell. Dried mint sachets in the wardrobe will freshen clothes and keep moths at bay. Fresh mint in the pantry will deter ants. Rub fresh mint leaves on your hands, neck and face to protect your skin from mosquitoes. Plant mints around a dog kennel or strew mint near animal cages to repel flies. Rub fresh mint around the eyes and mouths of horses or cows to discourage pesky flies.

Variegated apple mint.

Mint is the perfect companion plant for cabbages and tomatoes — it repels cabbage white butterfly, aphids and whiteflies.

If you already have mint growing in your garden, just dig up a runner with healthy roots and replant it.

Plant a mint garden

Mints have long been grown for their oil-rich leaves, which flavour teas, condiments and salads. The menthol improves digestion and has antiseptic and decongestant properties. However, mint can easily escape if you don't take steps to control it. To inhibit its spread, plant mint in a container, leaving a small ridge above soil level. Split established clumps in spring, and store roots in peat, compost or potting mix over winter in cold zones. For fresh leaves out of season, these can be forced in a conservatory or on a warm windowsill.

1 Place the mint in a pot and add potting mix.

2 Dig a hole and insert the pot of mint. The lip of the pot should protrude so that the runners won't easily spread into the surrounding soil.

3 All kinds of mint can be grown in this way, including the popular spearmint shown above. Mulch the pot and the surrounding soil, and keep it well watered.

Eau de cologne mint (*Mentha x piperita* var. *citrata*) releases a citrus scent when you brush past it.

Chocolate mint.

This pond is nestled among a variety of perennials, such as salvia.

Aquatic herbs

The allure and charm of a water feature is one of summer's underrated garden essentials. The water reflects light and cools the air, and moving water creates a peaceful ambience. Many people would love to have a water feature, but the thought of pumps, huge holes, liners and the like is off-putting. Installing a pond in the garden is also a fairly expensive business.

The easiest and cheapest way is simply to use a large pot. Wine barrels, stone and glazed pots, and plastic terracotta look-alikes are all suitable candidates. Really, you can use any large container, but you'll have to make sure the inside is waterproofed with a sealant and drainage holes are plugged up (a cork, sealant, epoxy putty or silica gel will do the job).

Most flowering aquatic plants like the sun, with lilies, water poppies, reeds, Louisiana iris and lotus all suited to a sunny spot. If you have a shady area, try dwarf papyrus, arum lilies, syngonium, sedges and water lettuce.

You can also use floating pond weeds, but these grow quickly, so either stock fish to keep them in check, or scoop out the excess regularly to give the other plants room.

Ponds take time to install but, once established, require less work than garden beds. Position is everything. Avoid placing ponds where overhanging branches will drop leaves and flowers and upset the biological balance. When selecting water plants, consider the position of your water feature. Arum lilies cope with shade, are long flowering and evergreen. Waterlilies don't like splashing water, need lots of sun and die down over winter, making them suitable for bigger ponds. Watercress prefers sun, or half sun.

The world's most popular aquatic plant is undoubtedly the waterlily, a perennial aquatic herb with both traditional and modern medicinal uses, such as a poultice for bruises. Native Americans made tea from the roots of *Nymphaea odorata* to treat coughs and stop bleeding.

You can use any container as a water feature but make sure you waterproof it with sealant first.

Growing waterlilies

There is a waterlily available to suit any climate, from tropical to cold zones. The miniature species *Nymphaea tetragona* (syn. *N. pygmaea*) is especially suited to pots. Very beautiful in flower, it is herbaceous, with the leaves dying back to a permanent rootstock as the weather cools. Rhizomes can be lifted during this dormancy, normally in late winter or early spring, and divided every two or three years.

You can grow waterlilies either in a large, shallow pond in the garden or in a pot on a deck or sheltered rooftop garden, as long as it is a sunny position. There are shorter stemmed waterlilies available that are perfect for pot culture. Select a tub or decorative pot, about 20–30 cm (8–12 in) deep and at least 50 cm (20 in) wide, without a hole. Lined half barrels are ideal.

Grow waterlilies in a wire mesh basket lined with peat or coconut fibre or in a pot. Add a pinch of slow-release fertiliser to the compost and insert the waterlily root system. (Too much fertiliser will result in algal blooms in the water.) Then gently settle the basket into the water on the bottom of the pot, or to a depth of about 50 cm (20 in) if you are planting in a pond.

Then keep the water clean; some fish will keep the mosquitoes at bay. After several weeks large leaves will appear, then huge, plump flower buds. Once waterlilies start flowering they keep blooming for months, and many are perfumed.

Waterlilies are popular and exotic herbs.

Floating aquatics

To keep the water clear and clean in your ponds, make sure you keep the sunlight off with a layer of floating aquatics that cover 70 per cent of the surface area. This will stop the algae from growing and keep your fish fed with their greens when you're away. Here, fairy moss (azolla) and other plants do the job.

Bog gardens

In poorly drained areas where the soil is constantly saturated, most deep-rooted shrubs and trees can't get quite enough air. Some herbaceous plants — such as *Gunnera*, *Alocasia*, cannas, arums and Louisiana iris — will flourish here, and look great teamed with ferns, sedges and some varieties of bamboo that also thrive in these conditions.

It always makes good sense to work with the conditions, so why not create a bog garden? They can look fantastic and display a wide range of flowering perennials that may be difficult to grow in hot, dry climates.

Planting waterlilies

1 A waterlily root with some new shoots.

2 Insert the waterlily root into compost, and mulch with pebbles.

Louisiana iris.

Go to a nursery that specialises in aquatic plants. The staff there will have the best advice and the widest range of waterlilies and other water plants.

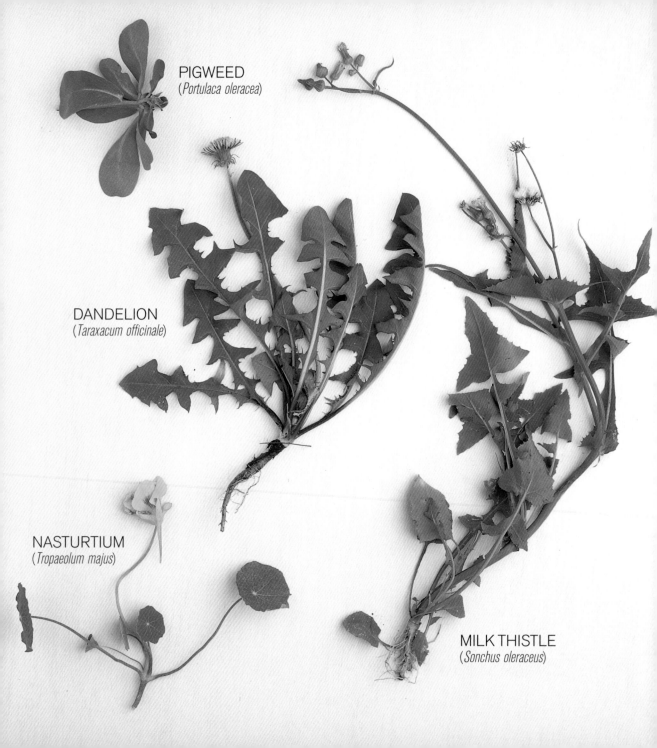

PIGWEED
(*Portulaca oleracea*)

DANDELION
(*Taraxacum officinale*)

NASTURTIUM
(*Tropaeolum majus*)

MILK THISTLE
(*Sonchus oleraceus*)

edible weeds

A weed is defined as an 'unwanted plant'. The tenacity of weeds is what sets them apart from other plants: drought, neglect, competition and poor soils don't seem to stop them. Harvest some of their strength and add them to your culinary repertoire. Use nasturtium, watercress, chicory and fennel in salads, and sauté milkweed, dandelion and plantain in butter and garlic.

CHICKWEED
(*Stellaria media*)

WATERCRESS
(*Nasturtium officinale*)

PLANTAIN
(*Plantago lanceolata*)

Problem-solving guide

Herb	Problem	Organic control	Chemical control
Apothecary's rose	Aphids, caterpillars and fungus diseases		Spray affected stems with combined insecticide/fungicide (usually sold as 'rose spray')
Basil	Beetles and slugs	Remove insects by hand. Set beer traps in damp soil among the plants	
Bay tree	Scale insects	Spray with insecticidal soap sprays	
Bergamot	Powdery mildew	Remove diseased plants immediately and dispose of them in the rubbish bin	
	Rust	Remove diseased plants immediately and dispose of them in the rubbish bin	
Celery	Snails, slugs, aphids and caterpillars	Inspect regularly and pick off insects by hand	If necessary, use a product with the lowest toxicity (pyrethrum, garlic or fatty acid based sprays)
Chervil	Aphids		Treat with appropriate sprays
Chives	Aphids in hot weather		Treat with appropriate sprays
Coriander	Bacterial wilt		Remove and burn affected plants
	Downy mildew		Treat with appropriate spray
Evening primrose	Self-seeds freely and so can create a major weed problem	Allow one plant to seed but collect the seed before it falls	
Feverfew	Slugs and snails	Beer trap	
	Caterpillars	Pick off and squash caterpillars when you see them	For a major infestation, spray with products containing *Bacillus thuringiensis*, a biological control that affects only caterpillars

Herb	Problem	Organic control	Chemical control
Garlic	Aphids	Rub them off by hand	
Herb Robert	Rust, mainly in warm, humid weather	Pick off infected leaves at the first sign of infection. Burn them or dispose of them in the rubbish bin	Spray with a fungicide
Horehound	Can be spread widely by seed	Remove the flower heads as soon as flowers fade	
Horseradish	Slugs and snails Caterpillars	Beer trap Pick off and squash caterpillars when you see them	For a major infestation, spray with products containing *Bacillus thuringiensis*, a biological control that affects only caterpillars
Lavender	Root-knot nematodes can arrest the flow of nutrients and water to the plant Leaf spot (yellowing leaves with whitish spots)	Companion planting with marigolds; improve drainage; remove diseased plants Move plants further apart to allow more air circulation; do not overwater leaves	
Lemon balm	Rust Powdery mildew Spider mite		Treat with fungal spray Treat with fungal spray Spray with insecticide
Lemon verbena	Spider mite and whitefly Powdery mildew	Hose leaves frequently; or spray with organic soap and pyrethrum Remove diseased plants	Treat with recommended chemical spray Spray with appropriate chemical
Lovage	Aphids Leaf miner maggots tunnel into leaves, causing white blotches	Hose vigorously; treat with organic spray Remove infected leaves	Treat with recommended insecticide
Marjoram	Damping off disease causes the plant to shrivel and die Aphids and spider mite	Keep beds warm and well drained, and use sterile seed mix Hose down	Treat with insecticide

Herb	Problem	Organic control	Chemical control
Mint	Mint flea beetle eats holes in the leaves and its larvae will eat into the roots of the plant	Keep weeds down and spread lime around the plant	
	Spider mite		Treat with appropriate spray
	Mint rust causes discolouring of leaves		Dust with sulphur
	Wilt causes leaves to brown and drop	Remove diseased plants and do not feed with high-nitrogen fertilisers	
Nasturtium	Aphids	Hose them off	Treat with appropriate spray
	Bacterial wilt and leaf spot	Don't cultivate while plants are wet; remove all diseased plants from the garden	
Oregano	Aphids, leaf miner and spider mite	Hose leaves; for bad cases, remove and burn the diseased plants	Treat with appropriate insecticidal sprays
	Root rot	Remove affected plants; rotate plants every 3 years	
Parsley	Parsley worm, root-knot nematode and carrot weevils	Practise crop rotation and destroy affected plants	
Purslane	Self-seeds readily	Remove flowers regularly to prevent unwanted spread by seed	
Rocket	Snails and slugs	Pick off by hand; lay beer traps	
	Can become an invasive weed	Prevent flowering except to provide seeds for resowing	
Rosemary	Mealy bug, scale, spider mite and whitefly	Treat with appropriate insecticidal sprays	
	Botrytis blight (fungal growth affecting all parts of the plant) and root rot	Improve drainage and remove yellowing leaves and dead flowers or badly infected plants	

Herb	Problem	Organic control	Chemical control
Rue	Fungus diseases of the leaves and root rot due to high summer heat, rain and humidity	Provide good drainage	
Sage	Slugs	Pick off by hand or lay a beer trap	
	Spider mites		Spray with appropriate insecticide
	Bacterial wilt	Remove affected plants before the disease spreads	
	Root rot	Provide good drainage	
Salad burnet	Root rot	Provide good drainage	
	Crown rot if conditions in winter are too damp	Provide good drainage	
Savory	Root rot sometimes affects winter varieties	Provide good drainage; rotate crops every 3 years	
Sorrel	Snails and slugs	Pick them off by hand; set beer traps	
	Leaf miner	Remove and destroy infected leaves	
Tarragon	Downy and powdery mildew	Remove affected plants and burn them	
	Root rot	Provide good drainage	
Thyme	Spider mite		Treat with recommended insecticidal spray
	Root rot	Provide good drainage	
Violet	Slugs and snails	Lay beer traps	
	Spider mites	Buy predatory mites to help control spider mites	
	Aphids	Treat with low toxicity pyrethrum, garlic or fatty acid sprays	
Watercress	Fungal diseases cause stems to rot and leaves to die	Remove infected plants	

So many herbs are easy to propagate from seeds or cuttings. But if saving seed you should weigh up the advantages — low cost, access to interesting new genetic material, and variation and variety — against the possible loss of particular characteristics (such as flower colour) that may change in the second generation, particularly in the case of annuals and biennials.

propagating

Seeds

A seed is a miniaturised plant, packed and stored within a protective coat, waiting for the perfect conditions that will give it its start in life. Some plants will easily self-seed, while others may need to be collected, treated, sown and transplanted. Seeds from dry seed heads can be shaken or rubbed from the plant, with any debris removed. In many cases, collecting seed heads from herbs in paper bags will help contain the seeds as they ripen and fall. The seeds of dill, angelica and coriander can be collected in this way.

Ocimum basilicum 'Red Rubin' tastes of sweet basil with cinnamon overtones. Sow it from seed into a warm soil — between 25°C (77°F) and 30°C (86°F).

All seeds have an optimum temperature range at which they germinate best. This range is mostly between 15°C (59°F) and 25°C (77°F), so spring and early autumn are generally the most appropriate times to sow seeds.

Herb seeds enclosed in fleshy fruits or berries, such as elder, need more vigorous treatment. First mash the fruit, then place the results in a jar with water, and shake. The pulp that floats to the top can be removed, leaving behind the seeds, which can then be dried and stored in paper bags.

Certain seeds need to be stimulated out of dormancy before they will germinate. Some cold climate herbs need an artificial cool time (called stratification) for germination to occur in milder climates. This is an adaptation to prevent seeds from germinating until the last of the cold weather is over, so that late frosts or snow don't harm the young seedlings. Other seeds respond to heat and smoke or drought. Hard seed coats can prevent plants from germinating by keeping out air and water, two vital ingredients in the process, and the seeds will therefore need to be chipped or rubbed with abrasive paper (a process called scarification) before sowing.

With your hand inside a large jar, mash the berries with your fingers. Add some water to the jar, replace the lid, and give the jar a good shake. The pulp should float to the top. Retrieve the seeds from the bottom of the jar, and dry them.

Hard seeds need to be scarified. Simply rub the seeds with some abrasive paper.

Once you have treated your seeds in the appropriate way, sow them in containers. Most seeds should be sown in a seed tray or in punnets initially, then pricked out and planted into larger containers as the seedlings develop.

When sowing very fine seeds, such as those of thyme, add fine dry sand to make spreading the seeds easier. Just tamp these seeds down slightly after sowing, rather than covering them over. Add sand to hairy seeds too, such as rose hip seeds, to stop them sticking.

Another way of separating seeds from the pulp is to place the fruit in a colander and push the pulp through the holes with your fingers. Hosing helps.

Slightly larger seeds can be sown straight from the packet or container. Draw a line (called a drill) with a pencil or stick, sow the seed, then backfill slightly. Most herb seeds can be handled like this, including seeds of chives, onions, parsley, salvia and viola. Even larger seed, such as those of nasturtium, can be sown directly into clumps.

Sowing large seeds in the garden

1 Rake a fine tilth in the garden bed.

2 Level the bed with a straight piece of timber.

3 Use the edge of the timber to create seed drills.

4 Plant the seeds in the drill. The distance between the seeds will vary according to what you are planting.

5 Backfill and water gently. Keep the soil moist until seedlings appear.

Pricking out, or removing seedlings from trays, can be done after the first set of true leaves appears (these develop after the baby pair of leaves, or cotyledons) and before the third set has arrived, to minimise root damage. The more leaves a seedling grows, the more roots it develops; transplanting might disturb these roots.

Always harden plants off before planting them out. A spell in an open, shaded position toughens them up and is particularly important if you have covered your seedling tray with glass to retain warmth and moisture. Try to gradually acclimatise the seedlings to cooler growing conditions, and watch that your seedlings don't dry out or get eaten by pests at this stage of their growth.

Recycled seed trays. Egg cartons are ideal seed propagation trays. The whole cup can be planted in the garden at the appropriate time. Just cut out the bottom.

Sow fresh seeds of the chestnut (*Castanea sativa*), as dried ones may not germinate. Although the chestnut has medicinal uses, always discard the fruit casing as it is poisonous.

Sowing herbs in pots

Many herbs grow well from seed, and packets of seeds are readily available from garden centres and most supermarkets. When you buy packets of seed, read the information on the packet to ensure that you are planting in the right season, and that the aspect and climate are appropriate. Most seeds germinate best in a warm place that is out of direct sun. Once the seedlings appear, gradually move the tray to a sunnier position and into more normal conditions.

You will need to buy some seed-raising mix and good quality potting mix. You can start seeds in any clean, flat container with adequate drainage. Plastic trays are ideal and are easy to wash clean. If you are reusing old containers, scrub them clean with a brush and a little detergent before potting to remove any disease pathogens.

There are both annual and perennial varieties of chamomile (*Anthemis nobilis* and *Chamaemelum nobile*) that can be grown from seed sown in spring. They need full sun and do not like a lot of fertiliser.

Sowing fine seeds

1 Place the seeds evenly in the drill.

2 Lightly cover the seeds.

3 Water in.

Steps to sowing

1 Use a seed-raising mix to fill clean punnets or seed trays. You can purchase this from a garden centre but it's easy to make your own. Use 2 parts of coarse washed sand to 1 part of peat moss or a substitute such as coconut fibre peat (cocopeat).

2 Bring the mix to within 2 cm (1 in) of the top of the tray and firm it down.

3 Gently sprinkle a few seeds over the surface and lightly press them into the mix so that the seeds come into good contact with it.

4 Finally, add a light sprinkling of mix on top of the seeds.

5 Carefully water the container with a fine spray, or soak the bottom of the container in a dish filled with water so that moisture will be drawn up into the mix. When the soil is completely moist, lift the container out of the dish and leave it to drain.

6 Keep the soil damp, but not wet, until seedlings emerge. This could occur within a week for fast-germinating seeds, but may take up to six weeks for parsley.

7 Once the seedlings have developed a few leaves and a root system, and are big enough to handle, transplant them into a pot or garden bed. It is best to do this in the cool of the day. Again, use a good quality potting mix if you are planting your herbs in pots, or into a garden bed that has been dug over with some organic matter added. Make a hole with your finger, just big enough to accommodate the seedling. Gently lower it into the hole and press the soil mixture around the roots.

8 Gently water the seedlings in; this will also settle the soil around the roots.

9 Place your potted herbs in a sheltered bright spot, away from direct sunlight, until they are well established.

The seedlings may need daily watering until they are established, then less frequent watering according to the weather, exposure and plant type. They should be established — that is, obviously strong and growing — after about 7–10 days. You can then begin to fertilise them with soluble plant foods, especially seaweed-based ones, a sprinkling of blood and bone, or pelleted poultry manure.

Herbs for pots

The following is a selection of popular herbs that are suitable for growing in pots.

Allium schoenoprasum (chives)

Chives can be propagated from spring-sown seeds but it is easiest to divide old clumps in late winter when the plants are still fairly dormant. Space them 2–5 cm (1–4 in) apart to allow for increase. Full sun, regular watering and fertiliser will ensure a regular supply for months. Chives are rarely attacked by insects, although aphids can be a problem.

Anethum graveolens (dill)

Sow seeds in spring 20–25 cm (8–10 in) apart. Dill seeds need full sun and wind protection, and may also need staking or support. Add lime to the potting mix. Allow the mix to dry out between waterings. Pick leaves as you need them but let the seed heads ripen before drying and storing them.

Bugs and snails

Watch out for bugs and snails. These pests can be quite a problem with seedlings, particularly in wet weather. You can protect new shoots with snail pellets, but if you're concerned for children or pets, hide the pellets in a piece of open pipe or inside an old terracotta pot. Snails love these places. Chewing caterpillars can also be a pest. Search for them, by torchlight if necessary, and destroy them. If you cannot find the pests, dust the plants with Derris dust on several consecutive nights.

Onion chives belong to the same family as onion, garlic, leek and shallot.

Try a beer bait. Place some beer in a bottle and half-submerge it in the soil so that the snails and slugs can get inside, but can't escape. Or use a shallow dish full of beer.

You can sow a lawn
with **chamomile** as it will
tolerate a little wear.

Anthemis nobilis (chamomile)

Sow chamomile seeds 15 cm (6 in) apart in spring, and
provide full sun, regular water and good drainage. Pick the
flower heads on a warm, dry day and spread them to dry.

Anthriscus cerefolium (chervil)

Sow chervil seeds in spring, and again in autumn in warm
districts, about 10 cm (4 in) apart. Chervil enjoys semi-shade
but is frost tender. It needs plenty of summer water. Pick the
leaves as you need them, or clip them before flowering and
hang them to dry.

Carum carvi (caraway)

Sow caraway in spring and again in autumn in warm areas.
Provide full sun and wind protection, as these plants are tall.
Space them 15–20 cm (6–8 in) apart. Water regularly but
don't keep the soil wet. When the seeds are ripe, cut off the
seed heads and dry them thoroughly before storing.

Coriandrum sativum (coriander)

Sow coriander seeds about 25–30 cm (10–12 in) apart in
spring, and again in autumn in warm areas. Coriander requires
full sun, wind protection and regular water to maintain growth.
It may need staking. You can pick the leaves often, but be
careful not to denude the plant. Collect the seeds when they
are dry and ripe.

Lemon grass is an untidy grower but you
can keep it presentable by trimming the
foliage back in spring.

Cymbopogon citratus (lemon grass)

You can start new plants easily in late winter or spring by cutting a few fleshy stalks from a clump below soil level. Make sure each piece has a root attached to it. It is sometimes easier to remove the plant from its pot and divide it, and then replant the separated pieces. You can also strike a piece bought from a fruiterer. Look for a piece that is fresh, with a good fleshy base. Insert it straight into moist potting mix, then keep the pot in a warm, shady place. Roots will form within two or three weeks.

Eruca vesicaria subspecies *sativa* (rocket)

Rocket resents heat, so sow seeds in spring or early autumn. It likes some shade, regular water and fertiliser. Rocket plants can grow quite tall as they go to seed and will need some protection from wind. Keep the pot near the kitchen door and pick the leaves as you need them.

Laurus nobilis (bay)

Bay trees in the open ground grow into very large trees, but you can grow one in a container for many years. Bay strikes readily from cuttings in late summer and autumn. A fairly slow-growing tree, it can be trimmed to a formal shape or left to develop its own neat style. It is quite tolerant of

Rocket has been a favourite salad herb in Italy since ancient Roman times.

The seeds of coriander are widely used in Indian cooking and are common in spice mixes such as garam masala.

Italian lavender
(*Lavandula stoechas*) is a good companion plant to *Erigeron* and *Ajuga*, as all three flower simultaneously.

Chocolate mint (*Mentha piperita* cv.) makes an unusual garnish for chocolate desserts.

neglect and does not mind if a few annuals or herbs are tucked into its pot. Plant bay in full sun, in a well drained mix, but give it plenty of water in warm weather. Pick the leaves as you need them.

If your bay plant is attacked by scale insects, spray it with white oil, but not on a very hot day.

Lavandula (lavender)
Lavender must have full sun, good drainage and lime added to the mix. Grow it from tip cuttings taken from late spring to autumn. Lavender plants can grow quite large so you will need to repot them as they outgrow the smaller pots. Allow them to dry out between waterings and give little or no fertiliser. Pick the blooms or cut back after flowering.

Mentha (mint)
Mint will grow from any piece of root in semi-shade with moist soil. In fact, it can become quite invasive. (See 'Plant a mint garden' on page 28.) Keep it well watered throughout the growing season, then cut it back hard in winter. Caterpillars like the leaves, and rust can be a problem. If

rust occurs, remove the affected leaves or, if the rust is too advanced, pull the plant out.

Nasturtium officinale (watercress)

Grow watercress from seed or root division in flowing water or in a container half-filled with potting mix, in sun or half sun. As seedlings grow, gradually increase the water in the container. At least once a week, change the water completely. Keep harvesting the stems to maintain growth.

Ocimum basilicum (basil)

Sow basil in spring but not too early as it likes warmth. Space plants 20–25 cm (8–10 in) apart in full sun, and water and fertilise them regularly. Don't allow basil to flower too early or it will stop growing. Pinch out the growing tips often for bushier plants.

Origanum vulgare (oregano)

A perennial herb, oregano needs full sun and lime added to the potting mix. Grow it from seeds sown in spring or from cuttings taken in late spring or summer. The plants need regular cutting back; they become woody after three or four years, and are best started again. Allow the mix to dry out between waterings, and give the plants little or no fertiliser.

Despite its peppery taste, watercress quenches thirst for a short while. Hunters used to carry fresh sprigs for a little refreshment.

Oregano does best in a warm climate; cultivars that have adapted to colder climates have a less intense flavour.

Ocimum sanctum (holy basil) is considered sacred by the Hindus in India, where it is used for medicinal purposes. It is said to drive away mosquitoes.

Petroselinum (parsley)

Sow parsley seeds in spring and again in autumn in warm areas. The seed can be slow to germinate and must be kept damp at all times, though Italian parsley germinates much faster and may take only a few days. Although parsley is a biennial, it is best treated as an annual and replanted each year. It prefers sun, but will tolerate half a day's shade.

Pimpinella anisum (anise)

Sow seeds of this annual herb in spring in a well drained mix with lime added. Anise needs full sun and regular water but should be allowed to dry out between waterings. Harvest it in autumn: hang the stems to dry, remove the dried seeds and store it in an airtight container.

Rosmarinus officinalis (rosemary)

Best grown from cuttings taken from late spring to autumn, rosemary needs perfect drainage and full sun. Add lime to the mix, and allow it to dry out between waterings; don't overwater in winter. Cut sprigs for fragrance or for cooking, and cut the bushes back after flowering in spring to maintain compact growth. Rosemary plants can become large, and will need potting on to larger containers as they grow.

Rumex acetosa (sorrel)

Sow sorrel seeds in spring or divide roots of existing clumps in autumn or late winter. Sorrel prefers full sun but will tolerate half sun. It needs regular water in hot weather and occasional fertiliser. As flower stalks appear in summer

Traditionally,
rosemary was
thought to bring
good fortune
and fertility.

Japanese parsley (*Cryptotaenia japonica*), a perennial which grows to about 1 m (3 ft), tastes like a cross between celery and parsley, and can be used in cooking as a substitute for celery leaves.

Thymus 'Mount Tomah' is a creeping thyme with dark green foliage, which turns golden in winter.

Purple sage (*Salvia officinalis* 'Purpurascens') has attractive foliage and pale mauve flowers.

remove them at the base or the plant will stop growing. Snails and caterpillars can be pests.

Salvia officinalis (sage)

Sage must have full sun and very free-draining potting mix; it will not tolerate wet 'feet' at any stage. Grow plants from seed in spring and from cuttings taken in late spring or autumn. Add lime to the mix. Water regularly until the plants are established, but then only water if the soil is very dry — sage will not survive damp conditions. Pick the leaves as required or pick sprigs of young leaves before flowering and dry them in a dark airy place.

Thymus (thyme)

You can grow thyme from its very small seeds in spring, from cuttings taken in late spring or autumn, or from root divisions. It needs full sun, perfect drainage and lime added to the mix. Water regularly to establish the plant, but when it is growing well, water only occasionally and don't add any fertiliser.

A tenderiser

The Elizabethans used to wrap tough meat in sorrel leaves. This tenderised the meat and gave it a piquant flavour.

seeds and seed pods

The seeds and seed casings from many herbs make wonderful spices. Some are richly textured, some sweet, others fragrant, and of course, all have the added benefit of being longer lasting than fresh and dried foliage herbs. Incorporate seeds and seed pods into dressings and

1 Star anise. 2 Cardamom pods and seeds. 3 Juniper berries. 4 Brown mustard seeds (top) and mustard seeds. 5 White sesame seeds and black sesame seeds. 6 Blue poppy seeds and white poppy seeds. 7 White peppercorns (top), pink peppercorns and green peppercorns.

pickles, curry pastes and stews, or even add them to pot pourris. Alternatively, combine a pod with one other ingredient: add a vanilla pod to a jar of sugar, which will then become infused with the vanilla flavour.

1

1 Nutmeg. 2 Allspice. 3 Cubeb pepper. 4 Pomegranate seeds. 5 Vanilla pod. 6 Aniseed. 7 Celery seeds. 8 Dill seeds. 9 Caraway seeds. 10 Fennel seeds. 11 Cumin seeds. 12 Barberry seeds 'Zareshk'. 13 Coriander seeds. 14 Fenugreek seeds. 15 Nigella seeds.

2   3   4

6

7

8

9

10

11

5

12   13   14   15

Layering

Some herbs, such as mint, send out runners that develop small plants. About six weeks after the runners have taken root, carefully cut them from the parent plant and repot them. You can encourage this by securing runners to the soil with a U-shaped piece of wire.

1 Select a suitable shoot to be layered. At a point at least 30 cm (1 ft) back from the tip of the shoot, use a knife to make an angled cut (about 20 degrees) on the underside of the shoot. The cut should penetrate about one-third of the way through the shoot.

2 Dig a shallow hole in the ground and position the injured section of the shoot in the bottom of the hole.

3 Peg this shoot firmly into place with a wired hoop.

4 Replace the soil in the hole around the shoot and firm the area well.

5 Once the shoot has formed roots, use secateurs to sever the new plant from the parent. Leave it in the same position for another growing season before moving it to a new site.

Secure the layered shoot with a U-shaped wire hoop like this one.

Self-seeding herbs

If you want to encourage a relaxed, cottage feeling in your garden, try to encourage herbs to self-seed. This may mean putting up with some messy plants as you wait for the seed heads to form fully. It also means weeding and disturbing the soil as little as possible, as tiny plants are hard to see and can easily be damaged. Try to keep the garden moist, and wait until spring before mulching so that young seedlings are large enough to be noticed and left undisturbed.

This self-seeding process can often produce chance associations that are far more effective than anything you could design. And often these plants are the ones that remain in old gardens. Johnny-jump-up, or heartsease (*Viola tricolor*) is a self-seeding viola that will keep popping up in unexpected spots.

Division

Divide clumps of perennial herbs — such as chives, valerian and sweet violets — in late autumn or late winter before they start to make fresh growth.

1 Lift the plant from its pot or bed and shake off the excess soil.
2 Gently spread the roots apart and break or cut the clump to separate the young, healthy plants from any dead old wood.
3 Cut off any torn or damaged roots cleanly with secateurs or a sharp knife.
4 Pot each new plant with its own root system in a clean pot.
5 Water it in well and place it in a shady spot for a few days to recover.

Some plants with a fibrous root system, such as thyme and oregano, need not be lifted. Choose a new shoot of young growth with roots already attached and use a sharp knife to cut it from the base of the plant.

Cuttings

A cutting is a small piece of stem taken from a healthy plant that grows roots when it is inserted into a suitable cutting medium. Taking cuttings is an easy and cheap method of propagation and provides you with a plant that is exactly like its parent. It is the best propagation method for woody-stemmed herbs, such as lavender and rosemary.

To strike a herb from cuttings, take the cuttings from a strong healthy plant early in the morning. The cuttings should be about 5–10 cm (2–4 in) long. If you can't plant them straight away, wrap them in damp newspaper and store them in a cool place.

Propagate perennial sweet violets by dividing old clumps in late winter, keeping the crown of the plant clear of the soil. Plant them 15–20 cm (6–8 in) apart in sun or shade. Violets flower in late spring and summer. They need ample summer moisture and a sprinkle of blood and bone for best results.

The roots of this cutting are well established and ready for planting.

Striking cuttings

1 Prepare a small pot with a mix of two-thirds coarse sand and one-third peat moss, and remove the lower leaves from each cutting. If you wish, dip the base of each cutting in hormone rooting powder or liquid.

2 Make a hole in the mix with your finger or a pencil, insert each cutting to about one-third of its length and firm the mix around it. Set the cuttings about 2–3 cm (1 in) apart.

3 Water well, and then cover the pot with a plastic bag to create a mini-greenhouse effect. Don't place the pot in direct sun.

4 Keep the mix damp but not wet. Once roots have formed, plant the herbs out.

Cuttings in water

Some herbs — basil, even rosemary — will send out roots if their stalks are placed in water. Make sure that the leaves do not touch the water. You can make a support by stretching some plastic wrap over a jar and poking cuttings through it into the water. Water roots are more delicate than ordinary roots, so take care when transplanting.

Root cuttings

Although propagating from root cuttings is a simple and quick way of increasing plant numbers, it remains one of the least known propagation techniques. It is the standard method of propagating a few plant species, mainly herbaceous perennials and alpines.

The great advantage of propagating from root cuttings is that you can produce a large number of new plants without disfiguring the plant itself. The roots of suitable plants contain dormant buds that have the capacity to produce new shoots and stems.

The best time to take root cuttings is in late winter and early spring when the plant is dormant. There are two ways of taking root cuttings:

- from plants with thick fleshy roots, such as the horse chestnut (*Aesculus hippocastanum*) and *Echinops*, that are inserted vertically into the propagation mix; or
- from plants with thin wiry roots, such as sea holly or eryngo (*Eryngium maritimum*) and dame's violet or eveweed (*Hesperis matronalis*), that are laid horizontally on top of the propagation mix.

1 Carefully dig around the roots of the plant with a garden fork until they are exposed.

2 Using a pair of secateurs, cut through some of the strongest and healthiest roots, and remove them.

3 Carefully wash the roots and remove as much soil as possible. This will make it easier to see where to cut.

4 With a sharp knife, cut the roots into 5 cm (2 in) long sections. Make the cut on an angle at the bottom end and at right angles at the top: this will make it easier to put the cuttings in the mix the right way up.

5 If the cuttings are thick and fleshy, gently push them into a pot of propagation mix so that the top of each cutting is level with the surface of the mix. If the cuttings are thin, lay them over the surface of the mix.

6 Cover the cuttings with a layer of grit. This will allow air to reach the top of the cuttings without letting them dry out. It also acts as an effective barrier against slugs.

Striking leaf cuttings

1 Insert each stalk, or petiole, in the cutting compost and firm the compost around it.

2 Water in well.

These stems of **black willow** (*Salix nigra*), a traditional medicinal herb, have produced roots after a few weeks in water.

Leaf cuttings

You can propagate new plants from the fleshy leaves of some herbs, including violet. Although you can take leaf cuttings at any time of the year, spring and summer are really the best times.

1 Remove a mature leaf and its stalk, known as the petiole, from the plant.

2 Cut straight across the stalk and dip the end in rooting hormone.

3 Insert the stalk in cutting compost and firm the compost well around it. Several leaves can go into the one pot but make sure they don't touch.

4 Cover the pot with a plastic bag and place it in a well lit spot away from direct sunlight.

5 Keep the compost moist. New leaves will grow from the stalk, feeding off the original leaf until they develop roots.

6 Pot them up and place them on a sunny windowsill. Soon you will have flowering plants.

The range of uses for herbs is extraordinary. It seems such a waste not to harvest and use them all year round, especially when an enormous amount of plant material can be preserved, allowing it to retain much of its fresh glowing colour, form and fragrance.

harvesting and storing

Methods of preserving herbs

The traditional method of harvesting and storing herbs is to air dry them, but more recently, freezing has become popular as a means of storing herbs for use over longer periods when they are out of season. This method is particularly suitable for tender herbs, such as basil and parsley. You can also use a desiccant such as sugar or salt to preserve herbs.

Although the leaves of herbs are typically collected, you can use other parts of the plant too – flowers, stems, roots and seeds. For instance, use herb flowers for both flavour and decoration – add fresh nasturtium flowers to salads, or freeze

The flower heads of *Allium* can be left to dry naturally. The stems emit a slight garlicky smell when they are cut, but immersing them in water dispels the odour.

Harvest nasturtiums for your next salad. The leaves have a peppery flavour and the edible flowers add a decorative touch.

borage flowers in ice cubes and add them to summer drinks. You can also harvest root herbs, such as horseradish, in winter when the plants are dormant, and the seeds of herbs such as angelica, dill and fennel. And for fragrance, lavender (spring) and yarrow (spring and summer) will continue to fill the room with their perfumes in dry form. Silvery foliage is also often aromatic.

When harvesting herbs, cut them with sharp tools: anything that crushes or bruises the stem will make the herbs bleed sap, which will result in loss of flavour and possibly in a mouldy stem. Only cut the freshest, leafiest, upper stems of the plant. Harvest them in the morning on a dry day, when the herbs are full of moisture but the dew has evaporated.

Do not harvest leaves or stems that are brown, wilted, damaged or showing signs of pests and diseases. Store the dry herbs in dark glass jars with screw-top lids.

Air drying

As soon as a flower or leaf is detached from the plant, changes begin to take place within the cells because the supply of moisture has been cut off.

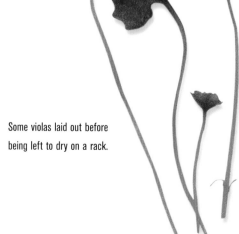

Some violas laid out before being left to dry on a rack.

Most **culinary herbs** can be stored in the fridge. Just place them in plastic bags or lidded containers, and wash them before using. Basil turns black quickly, however. Try storing it as a bouquet in a glass of water or wrapping it in damp paper towels.

An old clothes horse makes a suitable drying rack for flowers and foliage.

The quicker a piece of plant material can be dried, the quicker this process is frozen, trapping the oils within the cells. If the material is dried too quickly, the moisture evaporates too quickly, taking the oils with it. If the material is dried too slowly, the oils are destroyed by decomposition.

The most obvious method of preserving herbs is air drying. Just hang bundles of herbs to air in a dry, dark, well ventilated place. If it is damp or humid, the material will rot, especially where the stems or flowers are touching — for example, at the tying point of a hanging bunch.

Or you can choose other methods that utilise modern technology. Dry herbs in a slow conventional oven, or even in a microwave oven. Wrap the chopped herbs loosely in paper towel and cook them for a minute at a time on high. Always have a cup of water in the microwave, as herbs do not contain much moisture and the oven could be damaged.

Harvesting and drying rosemary

1 Cut the herbs.
2 Make up small bunches of clean, dry stems, varying the number according to their thickness. For instance, bundle rosemary up to 10 stalks at a time, and for bay leaves, dry separate bunches.
3 Hang the bunches upside down in a dry, dark, well ventilated place. The temperature should be between 21° and 32°C (70–90°F) for 5–14 days until they are dry and crisp. When the herbs are totally dry, remove the leaves from the stems by rubbing them through your hands. Place them in dark, airtight glass jars. Label the jars with the name of the herb and the date of harvest, so that they can be used in order of freshness.

Leaves

Harvest leafy herbs when the concentration of aromatic oils reaches its highest point, in mid-summer just before flowering. After flowering starts, the chemical balance within the plant changes and the oils in the leaves are not as potent. They should be mature but not beginning to show signs of ageing. This timing will give you the best flavour or fragrance from plants such as bergamot (*Monarda didyma*), rosemary (*Rosmarinus officinalis*) and sage (*Salvia officinalis*).

With most plants, it is easier to cut whole stems because you can handle them without damaging the individual leaves. Remove all the lower leaves and wipe away any moisture on the stems with some paper towel. Bundle them together in bunches of 5–10 stems, depending on their thickness, and secure them with an elastic band (if you tie them with string, the stems may fall through the loop as they dry and shrink). Hang the bunches upside down in a dark, well ventilated place at a temperature of about 20°C (68°F) until they are dry.

The drying time will vary from days to weeks, depending on the thickness of the stems. Crumble herb leaves that are intended for cooking between your finger and thumb, then store them in a dark and airtight, labelled glass jar. For pot pourri the leaves can be kept whole.

Harvesting and freezing herbs

Chop up leaves and freeze them with water in ice cube moulds, or bundle them into plastic bags and place them directly in the freezer. Suitable herbs are parsley, chives, basil and borage.

1 Collect young tender shoots and keep them out of direct sunlight so they stay cool and fresh.
2 Wash the herbs thoroughly in cold water before cutting them into small sections using a sharp knife or secateurs. Place the chopped herb into the compartments of an ice cube tray and fill each with water. Place the trays in the freezer.

Flowers

Again, only harvest flowers when they are at their peak. Pick flowers in the middle of a dry day just before their prime. Do not collect them when the air is damp or if they are still covered in morning dew, because they will become mouldy and discoloured instead of drying properly. To avoid damaging the petals, remove the whole flower with some of the stalk, then check each flower carefully and discard any damaged ones. Place the flowers in an open container, as in a closed container they may sweat and rot.

When drying flowers, select blooms when they are at their peak.

Once the herbs are **frozen**, decant them into plastic bags and keep them in the freezer, then reuse the ice cube trays.

Wiring flower stems

It is a good idea to wire the flower heads upright before drying so they won't become brittle.

1 All you need is some fine wire and your chosen blooms.
2 Using a piece of fine wire about 50 cm (20 in) long, push one end through the centre of the stem just under the flower.
3 Twist the ends of wire around the stem. For thicker stems, use thicker wire. If wiring for a bouquet or a vase, use green budding tape to disguise the wire.

Dry large flowers by hanging them in bunches in the same way as leaves, in a dark, well ventilated area. Don't be tempted to interfere with the flowers until they have completely dried out or they will droop and disintegrate. Lay small flowers such as borage (*Borago officinalis*) and violets (*Viola* sp.) on sheets of muslin stretched over a wooden frame or metal cooling rack. If you dry the flowers correctly, they should retain almost all their colour. Once dry, the petals or whole flowers should be ready to use. If you're storing flowers for future use, some flowers, such as lavender (*Lavandula* sp.) and chamomile (*Chamaemelum nobile*), can be stored intact; others, such as marigold (*Calendula officinalis*) should be stored with their petals removed.

For best results, cut and dry flowers while they are in peak condition. For instance, lavender (*Lavandula angustifolia* in the step by step sequence opposite) is ready to be cut when the flowers are half to three-quarters open. They will continue to open while they are drying.

A selection of herb vinegars (from left): sage, tarragon and chilli.

Harvesting and drying lavender

1 On a warm, sunny day, when the whole plant is dry, cut the stems with sharp secateurs to avoid bruising the stem or flower stalk. Working on a clean flat surface, sort through the flower stalks, stripping off the leaves and discarding any bruised or broken stems.

2 Grade and sort the stems for size and length, gathering 15–20 stems together at a time. Tie them firmly with an elastic band. Do not use string – as the stems dry and shrink, they will slip through the loop.

3 Hang your bunches from nails or hooks in a dry, dark place with good ventilation. Leave them for 2–4 weeks, depending on the plant and the dryness of the atmosphere. When the stems are completely dry, sort through the bunches again and remove any withered flowers and stems before bunching the lavender into bouquets of about 80–100 stems.

Herb vinegars

Freshly picked herbs make a wonderful addition to a good white wine vinegar or cider vinegar. Use herb vinegars infused with herbs such as basil, chives, dill, fennel, mint and tarragon to add flavour to salad dressings, marinades and sauces.

1 Pick the herbs, wash them and pat them dry.

2 Loosely fill a clean jar with them, pour on enough vinegar to fill the jar, then replace the cap.

3 Store in a warm place for about 3 weeks or until the vinegar is full of flavour. If you desire a stronger flavour, just strain the vinegar and add some fresh herbs.

4 When the vinegar is ready, strain it and pour it into some clean, attractive bottles.

5 Finally, label each bottle.

Drying lavender

1 Cut the stems with sharp secateurs.

2 Sort through the stalks, stripping off the leaves.

3 Grade the stems for both size and length.

preserving herbs

You can add herbs and spices to good quality olive oil and vinegar, or use alcohol in tipples and tinctures for preserving. The best known of these is vanilla essence, but other herbs have also been used in this way — artemisia in absinthe and vermouth, and juniper berries in gin. Why not create your own versions with your favourite herbs and a colourless alcohol such as vodka?

To make vanilla essence, just split 2 vanilla beans and put them in a sterilised glass jar with 1 cup of unflavoured vodka. Cap and store in a dark place, shaking gently every few weeks. It's ready in two months but lasts for ages.

Salt and sugar are also useful preserving agents. Place herb leaves and flowers in containers and surround them completely by sugar or salt, whichever flavour is appropriate, and leave them until they are desiccated. Store the dried herbs in airtight containers for later use. Experiment with your own herb mixes – for example, oregano, marjoram and rosemary for barbecued meat, and the herbs of Provence (these usually include thyme, lavender, savory and rosemary, and sometimes marjoram, basil, sage, fennel or oregano) for southern French cuisine.

Sunflower seeds.

Seeds

Harvest seeds such as juniper berries, vanilla pods, dill seeds, nutmeg and cloves when they are fully ripe, with no visible sign of green. Collect them on a warm, dry day by shaking the seed head into a paper bag, or by cutting whole seed heads and laying them on paper in a seed tray. Put them in a dark, warm, well ventilated location and allow them to dry. Not all seeds turn brown or black when they are dry, so test them for firmness rather than rely on colour alone. Store the dried seeds in packets or envelopes in a dark airtight jar until you need them.

Roots

Harvest the roots and rhizomes of plants such as angelica (*Angelica archangelica*), ginger (*Zingiber officinale*), sweet violet (*Viola odorata*) and valerian (*Valeriana officinalis*) in autumn, when the foliage is dying down and the concentration of oils is at its strongest.

1 Remove the required amount and replant the rest of the plant so that it will survive until the next season.
2 Wash the soil from the roots, handling them very carefully to avoid damaging or bruising them.
3 Lay the roots on baking trays and dry them in an oven at about 50°C (120°F), turning them regularly until they break easily.
4 Cool and store them in an airtight glass or metal container.

Using desiccants

Desiccants draw the moisture out of herbs while supporting them, and can result in a replica that is close in colour, size and texture to the original. A safe drying agent such as sugar or salt can be applied to accelerate the process.

First, ensure all the material is in perfect condition. Pick plants in the afternoon when they are completely dry. Place a layer of salt on the

Ginger.

bottom of an airtight container and gradually pile the salt around the plant material, using a fine brush to ensure that every part of the flower or leaf is fully immersed. Once the plant material is completely covered, replace the lid and seal it with tape. Test the flowers or leaves every couple of days, as they can become too dry and thus very brittle.

Using glycerin

Another way of drying herbs and flowers is to preserve them with glycerin, but make sure you only use this method for decorative purposes. This process depends on replacing the water in the plant with glycerin, which keeps the plant in a stable condition over a long period.

Make up a solution of 60 per cent glycerin and 40 per cent hot water and stir the mixture thoroughly. Cut stems at a sharp angle, and hammer the ends of any woody stems to crush them flat. Place the cut stems in a vase containing about 10 cm (4 in) of the hot solution so that the stems are firmly supported by the sides of the container. Place the vase in a cool, dark place for a minimum of six days so that absorption can fully take effect. At the stage when little beads start to form on the upper part of the plant material, it has absorbed all the glycerin it needs. Remove it from the vase immediately and wash it thoroughly.

The leaves of deciduous and evergreen plants and trees can be preserved in glycerin. This method is particularly good for branches or twigs of beech, eucalyptus, bells of Ireland, ivy, mahonia, choisya, fatsia, pittosporum, aspidistra and holly.

Note that immature plant material cannot be preserved with glycerin, so spring leaves are not suitable for this kind of treatment.

Grouping together plants that complement each other, thus reducing the need for chemical sprays and the overall incidence of insect and disease attack, is called companion planting. Certain combinations of herbs and vegetables actually encourage better growth as well as repel predatory insects. Many herbs, especially those with fragrant foliage, encourage your garden to help itself by attracting beneficial insects.

companion planting

Chamomile, hyssop and mint are good companions for members of the Brassica family, such as this cabbage.

How companion planting works

For thousands of years gardeners have known that certain plants grow well together and complement each other, to the extent that they appear to grow less successfully when they are growing apart. Others seem to be more successful growing on their own; in fact, other plants seem to have difficulty growing close by.

To discourage flies, sprinkle **dried tansy** flowers on pantry shelves.

Scientists have been able to establish that a number of plants actually produce chemicals that seep from their roots, fallen leaves or twigs and that these chemicals have an allelopathic effect on the surrounding soil. In other words, these plants use these chemicals to keep other plants from growing too close to them. This acts to reduce competition from neighbouring plants and helps to ward off pests and diseases or reduce the harm they can do to certain plants. French marigold (*Tagetes minima*), for instance, produces a root exudate that acts as a barrier to perennial weeds such as bindweed and ground elder, as well as deterring nematodes, sometimes called eelworms.

Some companion plants can be used as attractants rather than repellents. Such plants may be used as 'trap plants', to act as bait and draw a particular pest away from a crop onto another plant. In effect, these trap plants will be sacrificed for the good of the main crop. Once the trap plant is completely infested with the pest, remove and destroy the plant and the pests at the same time.

However, the ideal ratio of cropping plants to companion plants is not fully documented yet. If there are too few companion plants present, only a small proportion of the crop will receive protection, but if too many have been planted, crop yield may be disappointing due to the competition between the cropping plants and their companions.

Tansy (*Tanacetum vulgare*)
This pretty and hardy perennial, with its tiny button-like flowers, was once grown in monastery herb gardens to repel pests. When planted near fruit and nut trees, vegetables and berry fruits, it discourages fruit fly, ants, beetles and aphids. Near cabbages, tansy will repel cabbage moth and cabbage white butterfly.

It is also worth remembering that companion planting can disrupt crop rotations, and may actually harbour some pests and diseases, enabling them to survive from one crop to the next.

Organic gardening

You probably dream of a garden spilling over with fragrance and colour, brimming with luscious fruits, health-filled herbs, crisp salad greens and perfect vegetables. This garden is alive with jewelled butterflies and pollen-heavy bees, and filled with the songs of birds.

Plant French marigolds next to tomatoes: they excrete into the soil an enzyme or hormone that deters nematodes from infesting the roots of tomatoes.

The reality never quite matches the dream. Other creatures feast on your Garden of Eden, and nibbled leaves and fruits, webbings and caterpillar droppings mar your visions of perfection. But the balance is easily tipped in favour of your ideal if you use simple organic techniques that will enhance the health of your garden — for example, adding slow-release organic fertilisers and soil improvers such as compost, rotted manures and seaweed supplements; reducing the potential for predators and diseases by using crop rotation and crop sanitation; and using herbs both as companion plants and in environmentally harmless, home-made sprays.

The range of plants in this densely planted herb bed — lavender, mustard, santolina, violas and rue — acts as a natural and attractive way to deter insects from infesting your garden.

Nature in balance

Nature hates any imbalance in the environment, so destroying all insects could leave your plants vulnerable to other problems. A better way is to encourage balance.

- Attract beneficial insects by dotting parsley, dill and Queen Anne's lace about, and by planting perfumed shrubs.
- Birds eat lots of grubs, but will only venture into your garden if there is water to drink and some low-growing bushes for them to perch on in safety. Growing some plants that produce seed and nectar will also encourage birds to stay. And plant some herbs that attract birds – borage, dill, German chamomile, nasturtium, pineapple sage and elder.

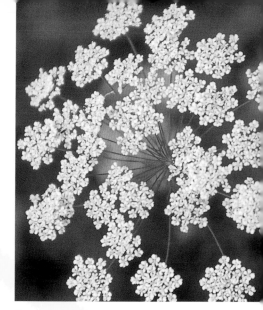

The delicate flowers of Queen Anne's lace (*Daucus carota*) attract beneficial insects such as bees.

Recycle prunings, dead leaves and kitchen scraps in your compost heap.

Herbs and compost

Really good soil can literally be dug with your hands; however, in some gardens a pick axe is more appropriate. Whether your site is very sandy or of heavy clay, the secret to good soil is to add as much organic matter as possible, as often as possible. The compost heap is the heart of any good home garden and fruit wastes, garden clippings and grass cuttings can all go into the heap. Some herbs have long been used to activate compost heaps. Keep a few plants of comfrey (*Symphytum officinale*) in a corner out of the way, and harvest the outer leaves regularly in summer and autumn to add to the heap.

Cooled compost can be forked through the garden or used as a mulch, and it will be full of beneficial earthworms, as well as useful growth-promoting substances and antibiotics. Organic mulches, such as lucerne straw and hay, break down to add organic matter to the soil as well as help to retain soil moisture and reduce soil temperature extremes; later they also add organic matter to the soil. Nutrient-rich comfrey leaves can be added to these mulches. Sawdust mulch, on the other hand, requires nitrogen to break it down so it will temporarily rob the soil of nitrogen, causing crops to yellow: add blood and bone or water with seaweed solution to sawdust mulches. Use grass clippings as mulch, or add them to your compost heap.

Benefits of companion planting

Companion planting is an ancient art that brings together the observations of countless generations of gardeners and farmers: plants are not the totally passive organisms that many imagine. In fact, some species are able to wage biochemical warfare on diseases and predators and can offer this protection to other nearby species. And some species produce chemicals that will stimulate the growth and productivity of another species.

Putting these observations into practical terms, gardeners can place plants together so that one, or even both, partners in the planting benefit. While this seems to be a technique for small-scale gardens, it has also been used by farmers who practise intercropping and barrier planting. Although companion planting has long been regarded as useful, these beneficial interactions have not been well understood until recently. If you could see all the energies weaving through your garden, and all the chemical messages moving backwards and forwards between all the plants and animals, both above and below ground, an incredibly complex and continuously changing picture would emerge.

The foliage of milfoil yarrow (*Achillea millefolium*) can be used to make a tea that will speed up the decomposition rate in the compost heap.

Comfrey (*Symphytum officinale*).

Here small box hedges border a potager bed planted with strawberries, rosemary and varieties of lettuce.

Spatial interaction

Planting a great diversity of plants in a mosaic, rather than in blocks or solid rows of a single variety, will provide your garden with an excellent insurance policy. Instead of providing insects with an endless feast with your conventional planting scheme, you will force insects to hunt for the next target crop plant. This may well be some distance away. And locating that crop may be made even more difficult by the many confusing scent signals emitted by the diverse plants in your garden. These clever tactics are easy to carry out, and remarkably effective in ensuring that you share as little as possible of your garden harvest with the insect world.

The physical effects created by the way plants are arranged in the garden or in a farm crop, including the use of nurse crops, is now known as spatial interaction, and sometimes it can also offer an unexpected form of pest control. The famous traditional 'Three Sisters' garden of the Iroquois Indians, who lived in the north-eastern area of North America, combined corn, squash and beans. We now know that this combination not only offers mutual protection and nitrogen benefits, but also disorients and confuses squash vine borer.

Nurse crops

The simplest beneficial effects offered by plants are purely physical, the result of something as simple as providing shelter from wind, or shading from the sun. Nurse plants in nature, for instance, may have roots that help break up and aerate heavy and compacted soils, or their canopy may offer protection to emerging plants. Farmers have traditionally used nurse crops to protect emerging plants — for instance, planting weed-suppressing annual rye grass or oats to protect and prepare the way for a perennial planting of lucerne; or interplanting raspberry plants with rows of fruit trees, so that the berries are given some protective shading.

Some organically grown squash.

Protect strawberry plants by growing borage (*Borago officinalis*) as a companion.

Nitrogen-fixing plants

Other species can offer beneficial effects to surrounding plants by improving the fertility of the soil, and as a result the health and yield of plants grown with them. Legumes such as peas, beans, lucerne and various clovers are nitrogen fixers — that is, they can take nitrogen directly from the atmosphere and convert it into soil-enriching nitrogen compounds. This nitrogen-fixing ability is due to a bacterium called *Rhizobium* which is found growing symbiotically in the roots of legumes. In Australia, acacias, which are also legumes, are very useful pioneer species on cleared land, providing nitrogen to impoverished soils as well as shade to young plants.

Nitrogen fixers, such as peas and beans, are often planted together with another crop that can benefit from the improved nitrogen fertility — for example, the traditional combination of climbing beans planted with corn.

The Papilionaceae family

Many genera belong to this interesting family. They are roughly divided into three groups:

1 those with fluffy flowers, such as wattles (subfamily Mimosoideae);
2 those with pea-shaped flowers, such as sweet peas (subfamily Faboideae); and
3 those with orchid-like flowers, such as bauhinias (subfamily Caesalpinoideae).

Despite such showy, beautiful blooms, what makes this family so interesting is the roots. All Papilionaceae have roots with nitrogen-fixing nodules which take nitrogen from the soil and convert it into an available form for the plants to use as food.

As a result of this adaptation, many members of the Papilionaceae family are used as green manures or nutritious mulches. Lupins, peanuts, lucerne pea manure and clover all fall into this category.

The annual sweet pea (*Lathyrus odoratus*), shown here, is the most popular member of the sweet pea family, but another one to try is the perennial or everlasting pea (*L. latifolius*), a herbaceous, perennial climber with pink or purple flowers throughout summer and early autumn.

Plants that retrieve nutrients

Other plant species offer benefits to surrounding plants by bringing up nutrients from deep in the ground via their exceptionally long root systems, or by actively accumulating elements useful for plants. Lucerne, also known as alfalfa (*Medicago sativa*), is an excellent example of a plant that retrieves nutrients from deep in the subsoil. It also helps break up compacted soils, while buckwheat (*Fagopyrum esculentum*), with its extensive root system, is a calcium accumulator and a useful breaker of heavy clay soils; it also attracts both hoverflies and butterflies.

Barrier crops

Many companion plants create their beneficial effects on other plants through various kinds of chemical exudates produced by the plants. These exudates can be in the form of volatile oils which form an invisible cloud of oil particles, or in the form of soluble substances released by the roots or shoots.

Chives and purple sage make attractive barrier plants in the vegetable garden.

Nasturtiums readily self-seed, so you need to be vigilant if you don't want them to become a weed.

Plant summer savory with bean crops.

Volatile oils can have a direct effect on various pests and pathogens. For instance, their smell can confuse insects so that they fail to locate their target plants. Other oils act as repellents. Most strong-smelling plants (herbs in particular) have such effects. Try placing strong-smelling herbs such as sage, rosemary, southernwood, thyme, lavender, sweet marjoram, hyssop, nasturtium, tansy (an excellent ant repellent), pennyroyal (also effective against ants) and chives throughout your garden. Plant them also as a barrier and insurance policy around your vegetable patch.

The roots of plants also exude a wide variety of active chemicals. One particularly useful example is that of the strongly scented marigold (*Tagetes* sp.). This genus exudes a chemical called thiopene from the roots which repels nematodes, microscopic worms that burrow into the conducting tissue of the roots of plants such as tomatoes, blocking the tissue and causing wilting and death. African marigold, French marigold and the weedy species *T. minuta* have all been used with considerable success to protect crops. (Calendula, also commonly called marigold, does not have the same effect.) You can mass plant marigold plants to clear your garden of nematodes. Chop the plants back into the soil when they are in full flower, then allow them to rot down before planting a crop.

Garlic is a crop that actively takes up substances in the soil. In California, it is grown organically in huge quantities around the town of Gilroy, not only as a very popular food flavouring exported around the world, but also as an important herbal medicine. To ensure the garlic crop is grown in nematode-free soil, a cover crop of French marigolds is used. Garlic is then planted into the nematode-free soil.

In the home garden, you can plant annual hedges of dwarf French marigold to prevent nematodes migrating into clean soil. If the prolific, brilliantly golden or orange flowers clash with your colour scheme, clip the plants back to a green hedge.

Barrier crops are a very old idea, and were widely used in England from the 16th century on. Companion plants were used to hedge beds of vegetables and were also interplanted between rows. For example, rows of lettuce or peas were separated by rows of chives or garlic to prevent insect attack, and dwarf nasturtiums were planted between rows of broccoli. Several herbs — including sage, hyssop, thyme and rosemary — were used to suppress aphids and cabbage white butterfly, and they were traditionally planted between rows of cabbage.

If you have the time to plan your garden with care, specific companion plants can be grown in conjunction with each crop. Try some of these traditional planting combinations.
• Chives, nasturtiums, basil and parsley with tomatoes
• Nasturtiums with squash and radish
• Summer savory with bean and onion crops
• Horseradish and marigolds (*Tagetes*) with potato crops
• Chamomile, hyssop, sage, rosemary, thyme, marigolds and savory with cabbages, kale, broccoli and Brussels sprouts
• Chives and nasturtiums with celery
• Sage, rosemary and chives with carrots

Trap plants

Another category of companion plants is a group referred to as 'trap plants'. These lure undesirable insects away from vulnerable species — for example, collards protect the closely related cabbage. Other plants act as good neighbours by offering refuge to beneficial insects. Among these useful pest predators are lacewings, hoverflies, predatory mites, ladybirds, various wasp species and mantids. Around the world, researchers are currently designing planting systems that will include habitats capable of sustaining these beneficial insects, to reduce the use of insecticides.

Underplanting tomatoes with basil

1 Clear a space for each basil seedling.
2 Remove the seedlings from the pot. Divide them into bunches of two or three plants.
3 Plant the basil seedlings around your tomato plants and replace the mulch.

pest-repelling herbs

Many herbs contain phenols and other chemicals that repel pests. The most common are naphthalene (the ingredient in mothballs), pyrethrum and citronella; all three are contained in many household sprays. But other herbs deter pests. The *Artemisia* genus — which includes wormwood and southernwood — is known for its moth, intestinal worm and fly-repelling qualities;

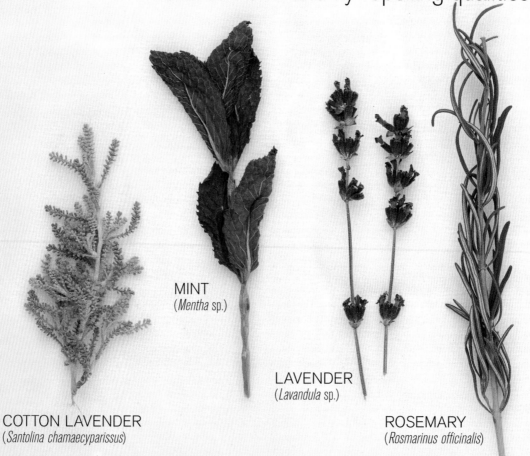

MINT
(*Mentha* sp.)

LAVENDER
(*Lavandula* sp.)

COTTON LAVENDER
(*Santolina chamaecyparissus*)

ROSEMARY
(*Rosmarinus officinalis*)

rue (*Ruta graveolens*) repels cats; and the *Tanacetum* genus — which includes pyrethrum, tansy and feverfew — keeps moths, flies, ants, mice, bedbugs, mosquitoes, cockroaches and mites at bay. Lavender and mint also repel flies and fleas, and look very pretty strewn throughout the house.

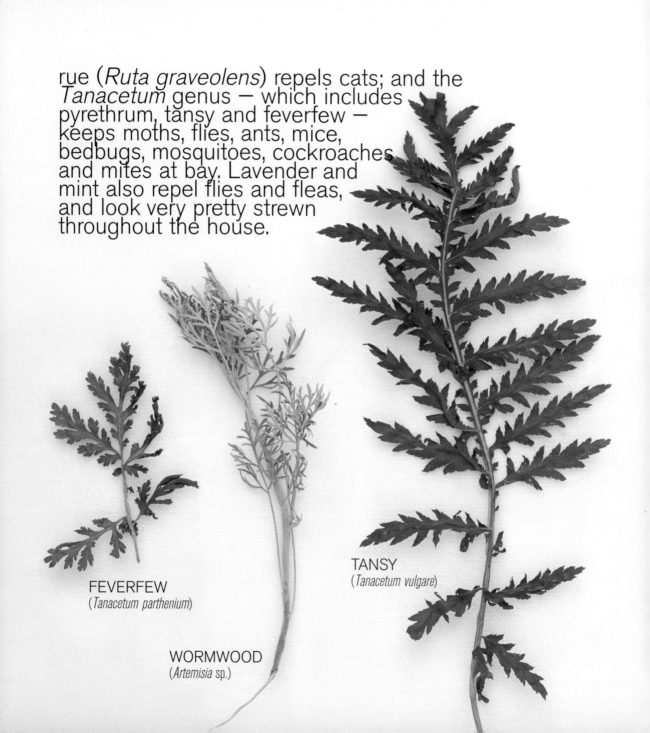

FEVERFEW
(*Tanacetum parthenium*)

WORMWOOD
(*Artemisia* sp.)

TANSY
(*Tanacetum vulgare*)

Some more pest-repelling plants (from left): curry plant, lads love and dogbane.

Crop rotation

Long before science and technology began taking an interest in gardening after World War II, farmers and home gardeners practised a very complex rotation of vegetable crops each season. Phases of the moon were taken into account and the whole method took on almost mystical qualities.

In the garden vegetable patch it is very wise to break the crop relationship cycle. Plant a root crop such as turnip or carrots where you've just had a leaf crop such as lettuce. Plant onions prior to a crop of tomatoes, and peas and beans after cabbages and silver beet. And avoid planting anything in the same family season after season in the same bed — for example, do not plant tomatoes after potatoes, or cabbage after broccoli.

It was Charles 'Turnip' Townsend who introduced the turnip, a root crop, to England from Europe in the early 1700s and advocated its use in crop rotation. The turnip is from a different family to the potato, the most popular root vegetable, so farmers could alternate their root vegetable crops and still practise crop rotation successfully. This basic rotation of crops stops any soil-borne insects and diseases from remaining in the same garden bed year after year, and avoids the depletion of certain soil nutrients that results from planting similar vegetables in the same plot.

Beetroot (*Beta vulgaris*) is a useful root crop for rotation planting.

Unsuccessful combinations

Some planting combinations are negative in effect, however, resulting in reduced growth and productivity. Herbs are not often included in these incompatible combinations, but you should avoid the following:

• hyssop with pumpkins;
• chives with peas;
• dill with carrots; and
• fennel with tomatoes.

Growth suppressors

Soluble exudates from the leaves of some species have been found to create a 'scorched earth' effect, inhibiting the germination of their own seedlings, as well as those of other species, beneath their canopy. Species of walnuts (*Juglans* sp.) and conifers — such as some species of spruce, for instance — are well known for this activity. The black walnut *J. nigra* releases a chemical called juglone which suppresses the growth of many other species, as anyone who has tried to garden below the shade of this species knows. The roots also produce plant toxins.

Various species of the herbal genus *Artemisia*, some of which are known in the United States as sages, can also have this effect. Arid zone species, in particular, use this mechanism to reduce competition for scarce resources such as water and nutrients. Crop scientists are currently investigating this effect to see if it might provide a useful alternative to chemical herbicides. Recently, researchers have found that annual rye crop, cut and left on the ground as a mulch, leaches into the soil chemicals that suppress weed germination, and provides a weed-free environment for many different transplanted commercial vegetable crops, such as broccoli and tomatoes.

Wormwood, an excellent insect repellent, is incompatible with any plant that is planted close by.

Herbs, the good companions

The most common herb companions, together with their effects on companion crops, are listed below.

Herb	Crop	Known effect
Basil	Tomatoes	Repels winged insects
Borage	Strawberries	Improves yield and quality by improving availability of calcium and potassium; provides light shade
Chamomile	Tomatoes Roses Apples Broad beans Brassicas	Known as 'the plant doctor'; repels a number of insects
Chives (including garlic chives)	Roses Apples Carrots Tomatoes Celery Lettuce	Inhibits black spot and scab
Dill	Many	Refuge for hoverflies. Do not plant with carrots
Garlic	Roses	Broad effects
Hyssop	Brassicas	Repels cabbage white butterfly; reputed to improve grape yields. Do not plant with pumpkins or zucchini (courgettes)
Lavender	General	Repels flying insect pests; attracts bees for pollination
Marigold (*Tagetes* sp.)	Tomatoes Garlic Roses	Repels nematodes; repels whitefly
Mint	Brassicas	Repels flies and cabbage caterpillar
Nasturtium	Tomatoes Squash Radish Celery	Repels woolly aphids, whitefly and ants; trap plant for blackfly

Herb	Crop	Known effect
Nettle	General	Repels blackfly
Parsley	Carrots	Deters carrot fly
Pyrethrum daisy	General	Repels a number of pests
Rosemary	Carrots	Repels carrot fly and some flying insects; appears to have general benefits; attracts bees for crop pollination
Sage	Potatoes Carrots Grapes	Repels cabbage white butterfly and a number of other harmful flying insects
Summer savory	Brassicas Beans Onions	Repels some flying insect pests; attracts bees for crop pollination

Beans
underplanted
with coriander.

Herb gardens have special appeal, probably as a result of their long association with humankind, and certainly because of their usefulness, colour, fragrance and texture. They evoke a sense of magic and mystery in the garden, yet team this with a practical element that only useful plants can provide.

herb garden design

Choosing a style

Herbs are suited to all styles of garden. You can grow herbs within your existing garden, without allocating a specific area, dotted among vegetables and flowers, or in pots. Or you can use certain types of herbs as groundcovers and flowering perennials to add decorative appeal to your garden.

A dedicated herb garden can be a feature in its own right. Although historically herbs lend themselves to formal layouts and cottage gardens, there is nothing to stop you using herbs in a modern garden design. The criteria here are the characteristics of the site, the general landscape and the architecture of your house.

Valued for centuries as both a useful herb and an ornamental shrub, lavender is never out of fashion.

Ultimately, your choice comes down to a formal versus an informal herb garden. Formal designs have straight lines, geometric patterns, symmetry and balance. Informal designs are fluid, depending on interesting plant associations for effect and allowing for a softer, free-flow planting scheme. You can also blend styles, using the backdrop of rigid hedges or a strong central axis to anchor less formal plants.

Formal herb gardens

Traditional herb gardens are symmetrical and formal in design. The most common design has two intersecting paths dividing four symmetrical garden beds. These beds are not identical but appear balanced for height, foliage colour and use, with the plants often arranged in rows. Wide walkways are used to separate the beds and give the garden a sense of spaciousness. A centrepiece — such as a large urn, sundial, sculpture or birdbath — is then displayed at the junction of the paths.

The Romans flavoured wedding cakes with anise.

Soapwort (*Saponaria officinalis*) has been used as a herbal remedy for centuries. Growing to about 60 cm (2 ft) high, it likes damp places.

Physic or apothecary's garden

An apothecary's garden supplied the raw materials for the medicines used to heal the sick. Each herb was generally grown in its own pot or bed to make identification and harvest easier: after all, mistakes could be fatal. Before the 16th century, the apothecary was the pharmacist, and apothecaries had their own society.

The most famous physic garden today is the Chelsea Physic Garden in London. It was founded in 1673 as an apothecary garden to train apprentices in identifying plants. Its location near the Thames made the transport of patients and supplies easy, and the milder microclimate allowed many plants to survive the English winter. Over the centuries, this garden expanded, accepting offerings sent from around the world in wardian cases (portable miniature glasshouses), such as tea (*Camellia sinensis*) in 1848 from Robert Fortune. Today it covers 2 hectares (5 acres) and contains 300 different species, all carefully grouped according to their various uses. Grass pathways intersect the garden into square and rectangular beds, and brick and gravel paths form the main pathways. In 1983 the garden became a registered charity.

Large beds of coriander, sage and thyme bookend this modern courtyard design, with four weeping birches underplanted with *Convolvulus*. The sound of water moving along the channels creates an atmosphere of peace and contemplation.

In the 16th century, thyme and santolina were used for hedging, but they quickly became untidy and frequently needed replacing.

Knot gardens

For a more complicated design, there are traditional knot gardens, which were popular in 16th century England from the beginning of Henry VIII's reign. These intricate, geometric designs, contained within a square or rectangle, were usually edged with low-growing hedges of lavender or box, which showed off the subtle characteristics of the herbs. No one is sure of the origins of knot gardens; classical Greek labyrinths or Celtic knots are two possibilities. However, the content of these gardens has been well documented.

Several different types of low-growing shrubbery with contrasting foliage — such as box, santolina and germander — were used to form the outline of an elaborate pattern, designed to be viewed from above. The various species were then planted in such a way as to appear to cross

This potager, designed on the traditional French model, features four intersecting gravel paths. Espaliered fruit trees form a living 'fence', while the pond and statue provide a central focal point.

over and under one another, like threads in a tapestry or embroidery. The spaces between the low hedges were usually left bare; occasionally, coloured gravel was used for added effect. The focus of the true knot is the interweaving pattern of the edging plants themselves.

The ideal knot garden consisted of four squares, each then divided into quarters. Each quarter was of a different pattern, and often told a story or incorporated the owner's initials or emblem. The following combination, *Jardins d'Amour* or Gardens of Love, is one such design. There are box (*Buxus*) borders, in fancy shapes, accentuated by yew trees, the 'infill' planted with flowers.

- *L'Amour Tragique*, Tragic Love, with box planted as blades, swords and daggers, and red flowers representing the blood spilt.
- *L'Amour Adultère*, Adulterous Love, represented by horns and fans, with yellow flowers, the colour of betrayed love.
- *L'Amour Tendre*, Tender Love, with hearts separated by orange flames and masks.
- *L'Amour Passionné*, Passionate Love, again with hearts, but this time the hearts are shattered by passion.

Just part of the famous and elaborate formal gardens of 'Villandry', France, near Tours. A Spaniard, Dr Joachim Carvallo, restored the gardens in the early 20th century, basing the design on 16th century plans.

By the time of Elizabeth I's reign in the latter half of the 16th century, knot gardens were the key element of English gardens. Designs by Thomas Hill, shown in *The Gardeners Labyrinth* (1590), are based on the square, with each square often containing a circle or octagon, a pattern that is thought to represent heaven on earth and opposing life forces. The Elizabethans loved layered meanings, and enjoyed planting these knots with clusters of blossoms like a piece of tapestry.

The French equivalent to the knot garden, the parterre, was designed along similar lines, but featured scrolls and swirls

Hyssop (*Hyssopus officinalis*).

rather than squares and rectangles. Both these complex designs require space and a great deal of maintenance, so be aware of this before you start creating your herb garden.

When choosing plants for a knot garden, select those that are compact, low growing and manageable. Some suggested herbs are thyme, germander, rue, hyssop, rosemary and cotton lavender. Avoid invasive herbs such as the mints. If your planting areas are wide, say, 1 m (3 ft) or more, you can edge them successfully with low hedges. Rosemary (*Rosmarinus officinalis*) is perfect for this, or the box-leafed honeysuckle (*Lonicera nitida*), curry plant (*Santolina chamaecyparissus*) or lavender (*Lavandula angustifolia* 'Munstead').

'Villandry'

In 1532, on the site of an ancient fortress, Jean le Breton built the world famous French potager 'Villandry' in the Loire Valley. Sited on the banks of the river, 7 hectares (17 acres) of gardens of remarkable beauty are terraced on three levels with local stone.

The best known section of the gardens is the ornamental Kitchen Garden at the lowest level. Planted with vegetables and fruit trees, with flowers for ornament, this garden is divided into nine squares, separated by wide *allées*. No two squares are alike in design. The complex cultivation plans are prepared each year, so that each is planted with vegetables in contrasting colours. The result is a giant game board effect.

The origin of a vegetable garden like the one at 'Villandry' goes back to the Middle Ages. Illuminated manuscripts of the period show the abbey monks, using the vegetables at hand, creating patterned gardens. At the corner of each vegetable plot a standard rose was planted to symbolise the monks who tended such gardens.

Making a simple knot garden

You can plant a simple knot garden in any level, sunny, well drained position, preferably sited where it can be viewed from above so that you can appreciate the pattern. An area of about 12 square metres (14 square yards) is large enough for an interesting interwoven pattern.

Experiment first with some sketches, using different coloured pencils to represent a few different plants such as *Teucrium*, *Santolina*, *Lavandula* and *Buxus*. Circles and squares of various sizes, overlaid on each other, will create a geometric pattern of interest.

Once you are happy with your design, draw the plan on graph paper so that 10 cm (4 in) represents 1 m (1 yard), and space the plants onto your design with a tube or cutting plant every 20 cm (8 in) or so.

Using the plan as a guide, transfer it onto the ground with sand, flour or lime dispensed from a bottle or with marking paint. A string line is the best way to create straight lines, arcs and circles (like a large compass from a set point), and a builder's square will result in accurate right angles.

Place your chosen plants on the markings, following the colour-coded plan you have drawn, and double-check the plants at each intersection to ensure that you have achieved the desired interwoven effect.

Select your specimens and plant them with extra care, as the appearance of an established hedge suffers greatly if the odd plant dies. Use water-storing crystals and slow-release fertiliser, and mulch well. Remember to check that the soil level after planting is the same as it was in the pot.

If a **knot garden** sounds too challenging for you, try a simple pattern like these low spirals of box hedges.

A parterre garden, featuring a symmetrical grid of topiarised bay trees encircled by box hedges.

Herbs used for topiary

Topiary has been a popular art form in gardening since the days of ancient Greece. Topiary plants add a touch of formality and punctuation to more casual gardens, and are great architectural features in formal designs, forming living pillars, sentinels and doorstops. Bay and citrus trees were a popular feature in Renaissance and Tudor gardens, but a modern herb garden can expand on this selection by using mintbush (*Prostanthera*), coast rosemary (*Westringia*), rosemary, scented-leaf geraniums (*Pelargonium*), myrtle and lilly pillies. Spirals, mop-heads and pyramids are just a few of the shapes into which you can train plants, and for interesting variations, why not try twisting or plaiting the trunks? For slower growing but longer lived topiary, use *Buxus*, *Taxus* and *Juniperus*.

In this formal **kitchen garden,** passion fruit vine and grapevine smother archways at either end of a gravel path.

Informal herb gardens

This herb garden can take any form, with flowers, trees and shrubs; or you can design a theme garden. Don't limit your use of herbs to specific situations. You can use them to enhance most parts of any garden. Of course, some grow better as groundcovers or as edging plants; others thrive when they are intermingled with different plants in a mixed border. Most, however, are best used where their fragrance and beauty can be appreciated up close.

Paths, and accordingly the garden beds, may also be circular or free form, providing a softer effect. Use informal materials for your paths. A simple patterned

Groundcover herbs and climbers

Dwarf comfrey, prostrate junipers, creeping thymes, pinks, creeping St John's wort and prostrate rosemary are all good carpeters in dry, sunny spots. For damp conditions, try Corsican mint, pennyroyal, peppermint, *Ajuga* and periwinkle.

Add another dimension to your herb garden by providing vertical supports for climbing herbs such as hops, honeysuckle, climbing roses and jasmine.

These tall impressive spires of *Echium wildpretii*, or tower of jewels, grow to about 1.8 m (6 ft) and make a strong architectural statement in a modern herb garden.

brick path is attractive, or you could use a decorative pebble. Terracotta edging tiles or bricks set at an angle give a good edge to both the path and the planting area.

Herbs can work within many other garden styles. For example, tropical 'Bali' gardens and Asian styles can be achieved with underplantings of ginger, cardamom, turmeric and basil. For a modern garden, use herbs of a more sculptural habit, such as lemon grass, artichokes and the clipped shapes of box, yew and germander.

Theme gardens

Some gardeners prefer to select a specific theme for their herb garden and choose the herbs accordingly. Here are some ideas; the possibilities are limited only by your imagination.

- A kitchen garden, planted with herbs such as thyme, sage, basil, tarragon and dill
- An apothecary's garden, including St John's wort, *Myrtus communis*, feverfew, rosemary, sage, garlic and valerian
- A colour garden, such as grey-green (planted with herbs such as horehound, lavender, wormwood and other *Artemisia* species)
- A fragrant garden, with sections for pot pourri plants, aromatherapy herbs and cosmetic plants (including mint, scented geranium, lemon balm, silver thyme and rosemary)
- A garden with different varieties of a specific herb — for example, common sage, 'Tricolor' sage, golden sage, purple sage, clary sage and pineapple sage
- A Shakespearean garden, planted with rosemary, heartsease, roses, woodbine and rue

The grey-greens of **rosemary and cotton lavender** blend beautifully with the vibrant green and yellow of **euphorbia**.

Herbs with interesting leaves
- Silver foliage: southernwood, wormwood, mugwort, pinks, curry plant, lavender, horehound, rue, sage, cotton lavender, *Thymus* 'Silver Posy' and 'Lemon Queen', *Echium*, *Euphorbia marginata*, artichoke
- Gold foliage: golden box, golden lemon balm, ginger mint, gold sage, golden marjoram, *Thymus* 'Doone Valley'
- Variegated leaves: *Ajuga* 'Glacier', variegated apple mint, variegated scented geraniums, *Salvia* 'Tricolor', variegated oregano
- Purple leaves: *Ajuga* 'Purpurea', bronze fennel, Japanese perilla, purple sage, opal basil

Silver and grey foliage plants highlight dull corners, add light to a predominantly dark green garden bed and 'cool down' bright colours. Wormwood and artichoke, shown here, also have striking leaves.

Practicalities
Working on any new garden project is an exciting task, full of possibilities and promise. A herb garden is no different, and also deserves planning and thought. Once you have decided on the type of garden you want, make a rough sketch or drawing on paper. This helps you to visualise what the garden will look like and to calculate the number of plants you'll need. Next, plan your design to scale on a sheet of graph paper, with 1 cm on your paper representing 1 m (or $\frac{1}{2}$ in representing 1 yard) on the ground. Clear and dig over the area and plot out your design by sprinkling flour or lime as an outline.

Some points for consideration include the following.
- Needs. If you're a time-poor chef who still wants some fresh ingredients at hand, seriously consider how many herbs you need. A few pots filled with your favourite culinary herbs may be sufficient. For others, herbs

The purple flowers of *Ajuga reptans* 'Catlin's Giant' and violets, punctuated by a box hedge.

dotted about an existing garden could be a practical option. A totally dedicated space, either small or large, is certainly a delightful and useful area.

• Time. Many people underestimate the time involved in refreshing, replanting and harvesting herbs. While many are tough, hardy perennials, these still need frequent pruning. Annuals and frost-tender herbs need replacing each season or 'bringing in' for the winter. If your herb garden is formal, then you'll need to regularly maintain the desired lines and shapes of your parterre or box hedging.

• Position. Not all herbs thrive in the same growing conditions. Some like it hot, and relish basking in dry, gravelly soils. Others enjoy a cool, sheltered site and rich humus. Site your herbs accordingly, so that you work with nature, not against it. Consider the specific requirements of the herb (sun versus shade, moist versus dry soil).

• Use. If you grow medicinal plants, keep them separate from the kitchen herbs to avoid any accidents.

Using herbs for garden 'pictures'

In the early 20th century, Vita Sackville-West (1892–1962) and Gertrude Jekyll (1842–1932) were renowned for using plants as blocks of colour, creating living pictures in the same way as an artist uses paint. Most famous of all is probably the White Garden at Sissinghurst, created by Vita in about 1946. You can create your own garden art in much the same way by using herbs.

For a white herb garden, try combining yarrow, garlic chives, chamomile, white foxgloves, sweet woodruff, white thyme, white valerian, white roses, lilies and jasmine. Or try herbs with colourful flowers in these combinations.

• Blue/mauve: comfrey, *Ajuga*, borage, hyssop, lavender, rosemary, catmint, some of the salvias

• Yellow: lady's mantle, pot marigold, curry plant, St John's wort, nasturtium, rue

• Red/pink: pinks, bergamot, marjoram, oregano, rose, thyme, valerian, marshmallow

Plants will look better if grouped in clumps of the same species rather than scattered through the garden bed. Edging the herb garden defines the planting area and makes the garden look as if it belongs in the landscape. If the plants are located next to a wall, a side walk or path can provide the boundary. If they are located in a lawn area, a permanent edging of brick or wood can be useful. A defined area looks more 'finished' and is easier to maintain.

Rosa filipes 'Kiftsgate', one of the roses planted in the White Garden at Sissinghurst.

Elements of design

Like any artwork, an interesting garden is made up of several design elements. Line, colour, seasonality, form, texture and grouping are important, as are height (shorter plants in front, taller towards the back) and succession of flowering.

Colour

By choosing a single colour scheme, you can create a garden that gives a sense of space, openness and brightness. Colours can also be used in combination; some colours blend together better than others. For example, a silver-foliaged plant, such as horehound, enhances red or pastel foliage or flowers. Yellow and blue is always a good combination. Orange and blue, yellow and violet, and red and green are all complementary colours and create a strong effect.

Contrast

Another technique to make your garden more interesting is contrast, achieved by placing opposing elements close together to produce an intense or intriguing effect. You can contrast textures, darks, lights, colours, shapes, lines, flower form, flower height – any design element. For example, rounded plant forms look best next to upright ones; a plant with spiky flowers complements a plant with round flowers.

Sissinghurst

Created in the 1930s by the poet and novelist Vita Sackville-West and her husband Harold Nicolson, the historian and diplomat, Sissinghurst lies in the Weald of Kent. It surrounds what remains of an Elizabethan house, built on the ruins of a Saxon castle in the woods. It was falling down by the time the Nicolsons bought it. They restored the castle, and designed and planted the garden.

The Herb Garden at Sissinghurst is enclosed by yews, and contains over 100 varieties of herbs. Accessed via the famous White Garden, it was one of Vita's favourite parts of the garden. It is said that she could identify each herb with her eyes closed, just from the smell of a leaf held under her nose. The garden is designed as four squares, each then divided into quarters with an intersecting central point for each. A main central pathway divides the eastern pair from the western pair. The paths, grass in Vita's day (now stone and brick to cope with the increased foot traffic since it became part of the National Trust in 1967), form a grid. The central feature is a marble bowl on a tripod of lions, bought in Istanbul in 1913.

Herbs have been used in cooking for thousands of years and every cuisine in the world uses USING them, but don't confine your use of herbs to the kitchen. Consider their many other uses — as natural dyes, remedies and medicines, air fresheners and deodorisers. You

HERBS

can also use them to make cosmetics, perfumes, pest repellents and even cleaning products.

For as long as humanity has suffered pain, discomfort and diseases, cures have been sought from the world of plants. There are no records of our earliest experiments with plants, but since herbs have great power to harm as well as heal, the journey to knowledge must have been incredibly risky.

medicinal herbs

Echinacea thrives in full sun and a regularly watered soil. The medicinal plant species are all perennial, and quite beautiful in the garden with their very large daisy flowers of lilac, pink or white. The plants can be raised from seed.

The ancient world

Our earliest records of herbal medicine go back to the ancient worlds of Mesopotamia and Egypt. The Sumerian civilisation in Mesopotamia was extraordinarily advanced in science, mathematics and the arts. The Sumerians were also remarkable agricultural engineers and constructed what must have been inspiring and very productive stepped pyramid or ziggurat gardens (the Hanging Gardens of Babylon, one of the wonders of the ancient world, were in this style). They also constructed vast public parks filled with exotic trees and shrubs brought back by travellers in distant lands. The oldest herbal we have, dating back to 2500 BC, came from Sumer. It includes plants such as bay, caraway, thyme, mandrake, saffron, sesame, poppy and coriander.

The wild poppy (*Papaver rhoeas*) is probably better known to us today as the Flanders poppy, an emblem of those who died in World War I. One of its modern medicinal uses is as a treatment for coughs and insomnia.

Assyria also amassed a remarkable knowledge of medicinal herbs. Tablets that originally came from the library of Ashurbanipal, King of Assyria (668–626 BC), describe more than 250 medicinal plants and 180 mineral-based cures.

The Egyptians too were advanced in their knowledge of agriculture, irrigation and the construction of villa-style gardens for the rich, with water features, grape-shaded walks, and trees such as palms and figs. Included in these gardens were aromatic-leaved herbs and fragrant-flowered plants, their scent trapped by tall protective walls. Egypt also imported from Babylon many dried medicinal herbs, as well as spices and fragrant oils, and specialists called rhizomatists or root gatherers collected herbal plants from the wild. As in Sumer, science and mathematics in Egypt were very advanced. The earliest recorded Egyptian physician of genius was Imhotep, who served the Pharaoh Zoser around 2600 BC. He was also a powerful astrologer and magician, and with time he became more god than man as he entered into the mythology of Egypt. A thousand years later the first surviving Egyptian herbal, the *Papyrus Ebers*, was written.

Greek medicine

The Greek civilisation was built on the foundations of Mesopotamia and Egypt, and it gave rise to several great healers and schools

The fig tree (*Ficus carica*) grows wild throughout the Mediterranean. The milky juice from the leaves will remove warts, and a syrup made from the fruit is a mild laxative.

Egyptian deities

The link between plants and healing was reflected in the realm of the Egyptian gods and goddesses. Osiris, god of vegetation, had a twin sister Isis, who held the power of healing and the renewal of life. Thoth – the god of wisdom, learning and magic – created the prescriptions for cures. He is usually depicted holding in his left hand the staff of life, around which coils a serpent, still the symbol of the medical profession.

of medicine. Asclepius, probably born in Epidaurus about 1250 BC, was famed in his day for what seemed like miraculous cures; after his death, legend enveloped his memory. He was said to have been slain by Zeus, the ruler of the heavens, for daring to rival the god in healing. Asclepius's mythological daughter was Hygieia, the goddess of health.

Perhaps the greatest of all Greek physicians was Hippocrates, often referred to as the 'Father of Medicine', and remembered now for the Hippocratic oath, which has long defined the ethical behaviour of doctors.

Hippocrates was born in 460 BC, and practised for much of his life on the Greek island of Kos, near Rhodes. His surgery was beneath a spreading plane tree in the town square. There were notable physicians before him, but Hippocrates clearly delineated the change to a scientific approach to medicine. He was a man of good sense, and much that he espoused in his approach to healing would be endorsed by modern holistic medical practitioners. He developed a systematic approach to diagnosis, working in a rational, orderly manner, and restoring health not only through the use of herbs but also through changes in a patient's environment, diet and lifestyle. Sadly, he did not leave us a herbal.

However, Theophrastus of Eresus, who was born on the beautiful Greek island of Lesbos in 372 BC, left us two outstanding herbals, *Historia Plantarum* and *De Causis Plantarum*, describing 500 plants. He was a pupil of Aristotle (from whom he inherited his famous garden), and incorporated Aristotle's writings on botany into the herbals.

The most celebrated medical school of its age was the Alexandrian School. Founded in 331 BC in the Egyptian city of Alexandria, the school was famed far beyond the region and attracted leading scholars and physicians. They brought with them healing traditions from many sources, which were integrated within the Alexandrian School, in turn initiating new lines of research.

In the first century AD, Dioscorides, a Greek physician with the Imperial Roman Army, wrote the most influential of the herbals, *De Materia Medica*. This vast work of scholarship attempted to place in one book all the knowledge accumulated by the Alexandrian School, the teachings of Hippocrates, and Dioscorides's own observations and discoveries as a doctor working in Spain, France, Germany and the Near East. He described with precision some 600 medicinal plants. This monumental work remained the standard for the medical profession for the next 1500 years. In the same period the Roman writer Pliny produced

Valerian

Valerian (*Valeriana officinalis*) is an attractive perennial plant with coarse, green fern-like leaves forming rosettes, from which tall stems of large, lacy white heads of tiny flowers emerge. The dried roots were used to make a sedative in World War I to treat shell-shock victims. It is now used as a mild remedy for insomnia, and to relieve stress headaches. Prolonged continuous use is not advised by some authorities. Both dogs and cats find the odd smell of the root irresistible; it is reputed to be the magical attractant carried by the Pied Piper of Hamelin, the nursery rhyme character.

the less scientific but charming 37-volume *Historia Naturalis*, seven volumes of which were devoted to herbal plants.

Physic gardens

The Roman conquest and occupation of much of Europe lasted for 400 years. The Romans were sophisticated in the use of culinary as well as medicinal herbs, and their armies carried with them many herbs for their own use. During the Roman occupation of England, approximately 200 herbs were introduced, many of them naturalising in their new land. Christianity arrived officially in England in the sixth century AD, and Roman herbs became the foundation of the physic gardens created by the great monasteries and nunneries for supplying medicinal plants to the infirmary.

The apothecary's rose (*Rosa gallica officinalis*), grown as a medicinal plant in medieval times, was listed in John Gerard's *Herball* (1597). It is possibly the red rose that was used as the emblem of the House of Lancaster.

Arthritis herb.

Arthritis herb
(*Hydrocotlye asiatica* syn. *Centella asiatica*)
This creeping herb with scallop-edged, fan-like leaves is widespread, from India to Hawaii. It appears to occur in several strains with differing herbal activity. One strain, known as gotu kola or Indian ginseng or pohe kula, is considered to have properties similar to those of true ginseng, and it has been included in the daily diet (two leaves in a salad or similar) in many Asian countries as well as Hawaii for centuries. It is believed to retard ageing, relieve depression and improve energy levels and memory. The strain found in the wild in Australia has developed a reputation for assisting in increasing mobility and decreasing the pain of arthritis, and has become known as arthritis herb.

We can visualise these physic gardens from the plans produced in 820 AD for a great monastery of the period, St Gall in Switzerland. They were intended not only for the reconstruction of the monastery but also to act as an idealised template for the design of Benedictine monasteries throughout the Carolingian Empire. The design incorporated consideration of all the bodily and spiritual needs of the monks according to the strict Rule of St Benedict. The plans included a physician's house opening out onto a garden of herbs, and the herbarius, consisting of geometrically arrayed, raised rectangular beds, each devoted to a single herb such as fennel, pennyroyal, rue, sage and cumin, or to *Gallica* roses and Madonna lilies (both of which were used to decorate the chapels on feast days). The garden was surrounded by borders of rosemary, savory, mint, costmary, lovage, *Iris germanica* and other herbs. Other common plants in such medieval monastic gardens included gilvers (which we now call carnations and clove pinks), peonies, columbines and bugloss (*Anchusa officinalis*).

The garden in a Norman castle often included a flowery mead, a highly contrived grass meadow richly spangled in spring with a mixture of gentle wildflowers and exotic plants from Europe and the Near East.

Echinacea

Echinacea was highly valued as a medicinal herb by Native Americans and by early settlers in America, who used it for healing weeping wounds, boils and abscesses, and to treat snakebite. There are nine species of *Echinacea*, of which three are used medicinally (*Echinacea angustifolia*, *E. purpurea* and *E. pallida*). Today it has a well researched and confirmed reputation for enhancing immune function, and is used as a preventative for influenza and colds. Echinacea is also considered to be useful in the treatment of upper respiratory tract infections. It is not recommended for those who have diabetes mellitis or diseases of the immune system, such as AIDS and MS.

When the Roman Empire crumbled, research in medicine in Europe all but ceased for 600 years. Monasteries and nunneries became the keepers of the flame, protecting the herbal, medical and horticultural knowledge of the past, maintaining libraries and archives and, with the help of skilled calligraphers, copying and distributing treatises between monasteries. They also became the hospitals of their day, treating not only the inmates but also the people of nearby towns, passing pilgrims and travellers.

In health food stores, **echinacea** was the best selling herb of the 1990s.

Medieval England

One of the earliest lists of herbs grown in medieval England was provided in the *Glastonbury Herbal*, written in Anglo-Saxon in the tenth century. It listed both useful native plants and introduced species, and showed evidence of sophisticated horticultural techniques. The *Leechdom*, also written in the tenth century, is a wonderful compilation of medical, herbal and veterinary knowledge. A third important herbal emerged from the Welsh Physicians of Myddffai, a great Welsh school of medicine which rivalled the finest medical schools of medieval Europe.

A decoction is made by boiling, say, the leaves of a herb so that the medicinal properties are extracted.

Nicholas Culpeper's *The Complete Herbal* prescribes a decoction of gooseberry leaves for treating St Anthony's fire. The juice of the gooseberry (*Ribes uva-crispa*) is rich in vitamins A, C and B, and in calcium, sodium and sulphur.

The Norman invasion of England in the 11th century AD saw the art of gardening raised to a new elegance. The massive, highly defended castles were virtually fortified towns. They needed to provide places for leisure, for quiet and contemplation, for sport, and for raising food. Orchards, fish ponds and gardens filled with useful plants were all necessary for withstanding sieges that could last for many months. The ordered, geometrically arrayed pleasure gardens were provided with grass walks and turf seats, and trellised arbours were covered with fragrant climbing roses, convolvulus and honeysuckle to provide privacy and protection. Practice areas for jousting and archery as well as bowling greens provided relief from tedium. The simple, fragrant gardens were filled with herbs and flowers to be used by the lady of the house in producing medicines, toiletries and fragrances in her still room.

English herbals

Greek texts were used virtually unamended and unchallenged for many centuries in England. William Turner's *New Herball*, published in 1551, was the first scientific study to break new ground in England, and it included descriptions of 238 British plants. Two famous herbals, books that were individual and independent in both their ideas and opinions, were to follow.

John Gerard was a physician, and the superintendent of the gardens of Lord Burghley, Secretary of State to Elizabeth I, and an apothecary to James I. His delightful *Herball* was first published in 1597. He based his book on the research of the Flemish physician Dodoens, to which he added his own original voice and scientific discipline. His trials and experiences with the American plants that were now beginning to flood in from the American colonies are part of the *Herball*'s fascination. His

Lenten rose (*Helleborus orientalis*). A tincture of the root is used in homeopathy.

Common sage

Sage (*Salvia officinalis*) is well known as a culinary herb, especially in combination with poultry and pork. *Salvia*'s name comes from the Latin word *salvere*, meaning 'good health'. An old English proverb asked, 'Why should a man die whilst sage grows in his garden?'

Recent research has confirmed many of the traditional medicinal uses of sage. Sage has antioxidant properties; its reputation for prolonging one's life span and improving memory is probably related to this. In the 17th century, the Chinese, who believed firmly in the anti-ageing properties of sage tea, traded with the Dutch as many as seven shiploads of their own *Camellia sinensis* tea leaves for one shipload of European dried sage. The plant also contains natural oestrogen and has been used as a tea to treat symptoms of menopause. Sage is both antibacterial and antifungal in activity, vindicating its traditional use in the treatment of sore gums, and as an effective gargle for sore throats. Sage has also been used as a tonic for the liver and nerves.

A cup of sage tea, taken after a meal, is said to aid digestion. It should not, however, be taken in large quantities.

Foxglove

Foxglove (*Digitalis purpurea*) is known by many delightful folk names, including fairy thimble, in its native lands of western and central Europe, but some names, such as dead men's bells and witch's gloves, hint at its dark side. The leaves are highly poisonous, containing a variety of glycosides, and have been used to strengthen the heart muscle in the treatment of heart disease. The plant is the source of important modern heart-regulating drugs, which are only issued under medical supervision. In the past it was used in the treatment of dropsy, and in cases of pneumonia.

own large garden was also filled with a major collection of European plants, and his fresh, intimate observations remain as valid today as they were in the 16th century.

Nicholas Culpeper was a physician whose herbal was published in 1653. He was a man of decided opinions and of a less scientific bent than Gerard. His herbal included astrology, and subscribed to the old doctrine of signatures in which herbal plants supposedly resembled the disease or part of the body they were intended to cure. The book is a curious mixture, at odds with a time that was so forward looking.

The first herbal written in America appeared in 1569, written by Spanish physician Nicholas Monardes, whose name is honoured by the delightfully aromatic herbal genus *Monarda* (bergamot).

Arab physicians

During the long centuries when science was stifled in Europe, the enquiring spirit of Greece passed to the Arab world. All the major treatises of Greek medicine, including the herbals, were translated by c. 900 AD and had been distributed to the famed libraries of Baghdad, Damascus and Cairo. It was a time of Moslem expansion and conquest across North Africa and as far as Spain. The Arab world drew on the accumulated knowledge of both Europe and the Orient, combining this with their own very advanced medical and herbal knowledge. Among its most brilliant practitioners were Abulcasis, in Spain, whose reputation drew the suffering from all over Europe; the great clinician Rhazes, who was a royal physician in Baghdad; and Avicenna, who wrote the *Canon Medicinae*, which brought together the integrated medical and herbal knowledge of the whole Arab world.

The green tradition

There is a hidden tradition of herbal medicine that too rarely receives mention. Women figure little in the early story of medicinal herbs, yet for the poor they were often the only skilled help available. Herbal knowledge was handed down by verbal tradition or in family recipe books. Women skilled in the healing arts were known as wise women, cunning women or midwives.

Like male physicians for thousands of years before them, these often skilled herbalists frequently included the use of prayer, charms and

Yarrow was once commonly known as kiss-me-quick; the flowers were tucked into wedding bouquets to ensure seven years of love.

White yarrow

Yarrow (*Achillea millefolium*) is native to southern Europe but is also widely naturalised in Australia, New Zealand and North America. It has been used in herbal medicine to improve blood circulation, and as a tea to relieve stomach cramps and treat menstrual problems. One of its earliest recorded uses was to staunch the flow of blood from wounds, especially those caused by metal swords and knives. It was last used in an official military capacity for this purpose in the American Civil War. The pulped leaves have been used for their astringent properties – applied as a poultice to sores, ulcers, piles and acne. (Yarrow should not be used by pregnant women.)

Yarrow makes dense rosettes of fine, feathery, strongly scented foliage, eventually making a neat mat in full to half sun. They bear dense, flat inflorescences of pretty pink, lilac or white flowers. Yarrow is propagated by seed and by division.

incantations to assist their medicine. However, they walked a fine line. If their skills failed, village gratitude for help through childbirth and illnesses could quickly turn to accusations of satanic involvement as fear fed on ignorance.

Charges of witchcraft in England and America reached their height in the 17th century, particularly in Essex around the town of Colchester, where the self-appointed Witchfinder General operated his reign of terror; and at Salem in Massachusetts, where an outbreak of ergot in cereal crops was almost certainly the initial cause. Ergotised grain, caused by infection with the fungus *Claviceps* sp., is well known to cause violent and intense hallucinations as well as the sensation of burning in the extremities. The condition was often called St Anthony's fire in Europe. Such an outbreak, in a population of staunchly evangelical puritans (mainly settlers from 17th century witch-fearing Essex), was an inflammable and fatal mixture.

The word 'witch' is derived from the Old English *wicca*, which means wise. Most modern Wiccans see themselves as seekers of wisdom, attuned to and protective of the natural world, and preservers of ancient

Marshmallow

Marshmallow (*Althaea officinalis*) belongs to the same genus as hollyhock, and it closely resembles a small-flowered perennial hollyhock. The original marshmallow, which was eaten as a sweet, was made from the dried and powdered root of this plant. It contains a mucilage that acts as an excellent thickening agent. This species was introduced early into the American, Australian and New Zealand colonies. Marshmallow tea was used to soothe sore throats, as well as to relieve coughs and diarrhoea. A poultice made from the dried powdered roots was used to soothe inflamed skin, and a decoction of both the leaves and the roots was often included in lotions as a time-honoured remedy for sunburn as well as for chapped hands. The flowers of the true hollyhock, *A. rosea*, were similarly used for their soothing properties, and a poultice of the boiled leaves of the related Australian native hollyhock, *Lavatera plebia*, was traditionally used as a bush medicine to draw boils and soothe irritated skin.

Marshmallow should be grown in moist, well drained soil, in full sun.

knowledge and herbal traditions. Far from being devil worshippers, the Wiccan religion's creed is 'Harm no one', and their worship is of the harmonising male and female power of the cosmos, a belief that echoes the universal yin and yang forces that form the basis of Chinese medicine.

Chinese herbal medicine

The medical knowledge of the Ming dynasty, a period corresponding to the 17th century in Europe, has been estimated to have been 1000 years ahead of that of Europe. But by the turn of the 20th century, the West had made giant strides while China had languished under the Manchu reign. Fortunately, the great herbal and medical traditions of China have survived, and now flourish around the world.

China and Europe approached healing with different philosophies. Chinese medicine was based on the principles of holism and harmony. The legendary Emperor Shen Nong, who lived approximately 5500 years ago, is credited with testing many species of plants for their curative properties, developing a pharmacopoeia, and founding organised medicine. Shen Nong also derived the idea of two opposing and equal principles in nature. Life was seen to be in eternal flux, constantly renewing the delicate balance between these opposing forces.

The great sage Confucius (551–479 BC) created a doctrine of universal order and a complementary code of social ethics. He, too, taught that the two opposing forces of the cosmos, yin and yang, must be balanced to maintain harmony at all levels. A contemporary, Lao Zi, the founder of Taoism, created a philosophy of universal law and order, a world in which harmony is forever being created by the

Elderberry

This herb dates back to ancient Greek times, and is shrouded in mystery and folklore. It is said that Christ's cross was made of elderwood, and that elder would only grow where blood had been spilt. In fact, elderberry (*Sambucus* sp.) grows happily in any temperate climate in sun or shade, and once established, will cope with frosts.

There are a few species, but if you intend to make elderberry wine, sorbet or jelly, be sure to plant the edible *S. nigra* (shown above) rather than the others, which are poisonous.

Selfheal

This ground-hugging herbaceous herb, which is very widely distributed around the world, has very pretty compact spikes of lipped, bright purple flowers in summer. It was recommended by early herbalists for curing tonsillitis and for healing wounds. Selfheal (*Prunella vulgaris*) has astringent properties and it is still widely employed in herbal medicine as a gargle for sore throats, and also for ulcers of the mouth, weeping sores and piles. An infusion of the dried plant is used as a general tonic. A compress of selfheal is also favoured by herbalists for slowly healing wounds.

delicate rebalancing of yin and yang forces. He advocated taking the path of least resistance, allowing this rebalancing to occur without our intervention.

It was against this background that Chinese medicine developed. The body was seen as a part of a greater whole, and health was seen as the result of harmony both within and without. The quick fixes sought by patients of Western medicine were never the true aim of Chinese medicine. Disharmony at deeper levels was considered to constantly re-express itself in one medical problem after another unless a state of balance was reached. Chinese medicine involved the careful holistic evaluation of a patient, and changes in diet, attitude and lifestyle were prescribed together with herbal mixtures.

The great herbal tradition of China, with its vast wealth of materials, remains of the highest value. The Chinese were using narcotic anaesthetics over 700 years ago, ephedra (source of ephedrine) for asthmatics 1800 years ago, iodine for the treatment of enlarged thyroids a millennium ago, and fermentations containing antibiotic substances have long been in use to combat infections. As the quintessential 700 or so herbs employed by Chinese herbalists are tested by Western science, the efficacy and uses of many have already been fully validated.

Selfheal can be grown from seed and by division of the plants.

The New World

In 1747 a small group belonging to a religious sect called The Society of Believers In Christ's Second Coming left Manchester in England for America, where they dreamed of creating 'heaven on earth'. They were led by a woman of indomitable spirit, Ann Lee. The group became known as the Shakers, their name deriving from their trance-like possession during prayer sessions.

In time the Shakers were to found many communities, spreading from Maine to Florida. The Shaker villages became models of self-sufficiency. The communities were committed to providing a simple, virtuous, rewarding and creative life. Even the simplest items were made with an eye to improvement of design, ease of use and harmony of form.

The involvement of the Shakers with the herb industry of North America began modestly, as part of their need to provide the best possible care for their communities. The Shakers were deeply interested in the herbal knowledge of the First Nation (the Native Americans, as they are now known) and gathered many herbs from the wild, growing them in their herb gardens. From the beginning, they took meticulous care in identifying plants, collecting the correct, medicinally active part of the plant, and harvesting plants at the peak of medicinal activity or culinary flavour. At their largest, plantings of herbs in Shaker settlements occupied some 68 hectares (150 acres).

Shaker herb gardens were managed organically. The medical profession welcomed the high quality of their herbs, and the catalogues they issued were amazing in their day. The Canterbury Village catalogue listed over 200 different herbs, and its botanic garden was said to have the largest collection of medicinal plants in New England. In 1831 the New Lebanon Shakers were exporting top quality dried herbs around the world and offering 137 different herbs. The Shakers were the first professional herbalists of America, and thanks to them interest in herbs in the United States never abated.

Apothecary's rose (*Rosa gallica* var. *officinalis* 'Versicolor'), an old herbal rose.

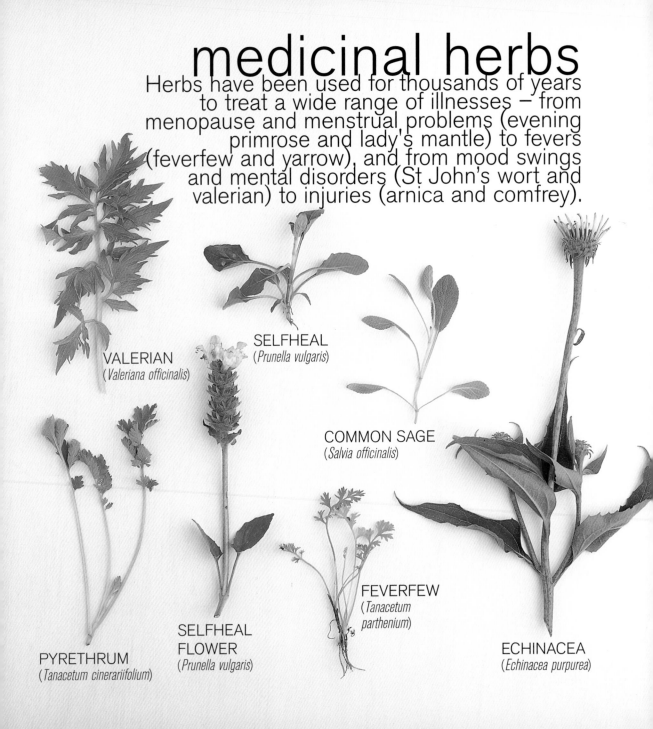

medicinal herbs

Herbs have been used for thousands of years to treat a wide range of illnesses – from menopause and menstrual problems (evening primrose and lady's mantle) to fevers (feverfew and yarrow), and from mood swings and mental disorders (St John's wort and valerian) to injuries (arnica and comfrey).

VALERIAN
(*Valeriana officinalis*)

SELFHEAL
(*Prunella vulgaris*)

COMMON SAGE
(*Salvia officinalis*)

PYRETHRUM
(*Tanacetum cinerariifolium*)

SELFHEAL
FLOWER
(*Prunella vulgaris*)

FEVERFEW
(*Tanacetum parthenium*)

ECHINACEA
(*Echinacea purpurea*)

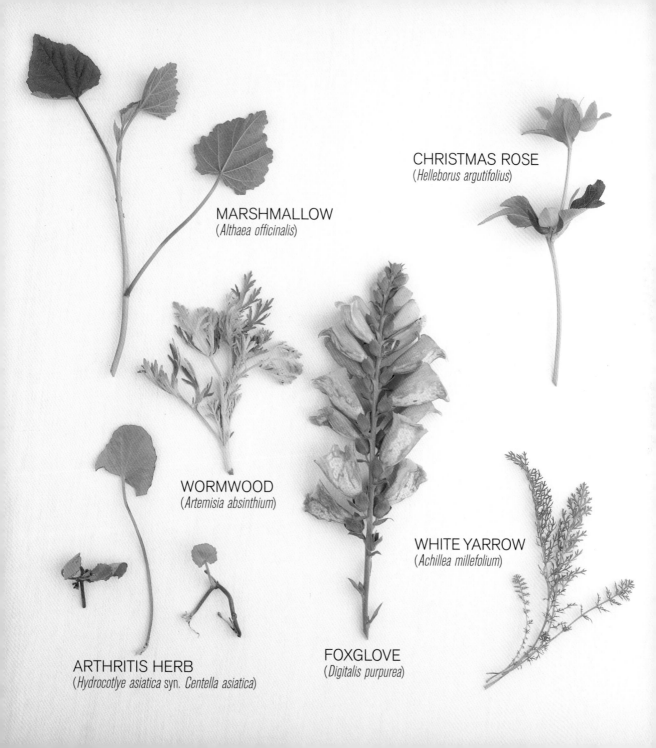

MARSHMALLOW
(*Althaea officinalis*)

CHRISTMAS ROSE
(*Helleborus argutifolius*)

WORMWOOD
(*Artemisia absinthium*)

WHITE YARROW
(*Achillea millefolium*)

ARTHRITIS HERB
(*Hydrocotlye asiatica* syn. *Centella asiatica*)

FOXGLOVE
(*Digitalis purpurea*)

The bark of *Acacia decurrens* is collected from a tree that is at least seven years old. It must then be matured for another year before it can be used for medicinal purposes.

Early Australian settlers

Life was daunting for the early pioneers of Australia; they were thrown almost entirely on their own resources. Free settlers arrived equipped with the seeds and precious potted roots of many valuable medicinal, fragrant and useful herbs. Chinese immigrants following the huge Australian gold strikes of the 19th century brought with them their own armoury of herbal medicine; it is sometimes forgotten that a strong tradition of Chinese medicine has existed in Australia for almost as long as European settlement.

There's a belief that early settlers lived in an encapsulated European world. It is true that many pined for a lost homeland, but early paintings of colonial gardens depicted the inclusion of many native flowers. Desperation or a thirst for knowledge drove some to seek information from the original owners of the land, the Aboriginals.

Dysentery was a major killer in the colonies, but a decoction made from the bark of the green wattle (*Acacia decurrens*) was found to be so effective that it was exported and included in the *British Pharmacopoeia*. Aboriginal herbal medicines employed in the colony included the hardened gum that oozes from wounds in various species of eucalyptus. Known as kino, it was a very effective treatment for diarrhoea, and became a successful export in the 19th century. Aboriginal herbal knowledge was extensive, based on tens of thousands of years of experimentation, and the Australian bush proved to be a fully stocked medicine chest for virtually every ill.

A tea of the leaves of **feverfew** is mildly sedative, and the cooled tea has long been dabbed on the face to fade freckles. The dried leaves can be used in moth-repellent sachet mixes.

Modern herbalism

Interest in modern medical herbalism has been remarkable in the last 20 years. Extensive and exciting research is being carried out on the medicinal herbs of South America, Mexico, North America, Africa and Australia. In response to strong consumer demand, many reputable companies now supply high quality, standardised herbal products to cope with everyday ills.

The term 'aromatherapy' was coined in 1928 by the French chemist Dr René-Maurice Gattefossé, who studied and documented the use of essential oils in maintaining good health. Aromatherapy has ancient roots, and today it is a rapidly growing field of herbal treatment and research, uniting the knowledge of the herbalists with that of the essential oil practitioners. Increasingly it also involves the 'hard sciences', providing evidence of the healing activity of the plants and aromatherapy treatments. The medical profession in France has incorporated essential oil therapy into medical practice and a Chair of Phytotherapy (literally, 'plant therapy') has been established at the University of Paris Nord, where postgraduate studies are undertaken in this field. A major revival is now apparent in the great traditions of herbal medicine.

Feverfew

Feverfew is one of the prettiest and easiest herbs to grow, with dark green, deeply cut foliage and masses of small, golden-eyed, sparkling white daisy flowers. Feverfew (*Tanacetum parthenium* syn. *Chrysanthemum parthenium*) has been used for many centuries to treat severe headaches and migraines. This has been verified by a number of clinical trials, and several valuable medicinal compounds have been isolated from the plant. Many migraine sufferers have reported good results after including a raw leaf in a daily sandwich. The leaves are quite bitter. The success of the herb in the treatment of headaches is attributed in part to the ability of feverfew to relax smooth muscle spasms.

Culinary herbs are so versatile that you can use the leaves, flowers, seeds and stems of this group of plants in a bewildering array of dishes from all over the world. Particular herbs suit different styles of cooking and every cuisine has its favourites.

culinary herbs

Cooking with herbs

Most herbs are best when fresh. Buy them cut or grow them in pots on the windowsill or in the garden. If fresh herbs are unavailable, use dried, but these are often more concentrated in flavour (unless, of course, they are stale) and you only need to use half or less of the quantity specified for fresh herbs. In some cuisines, dried herbs are preferred — for example, the Greeks prefer dried oregano (*rigani*).

Obviously you can use herbs at any time, but the type of recipe they suit often depends on the time of year. Typical summer herbs are basil, dill, mint, oregano and parsley; spring herbs are chives, sorrel and chervil; sage, rosemary and thyme often suit winter dishes.

The leaves, seeds and roots of coriander all have distinct culinary uses.

Storing culinary herbs

- Herbs sold in plastic boxes or cellophane bags keep well in them.
- Put loose herbs in plastic bags and store them in the vegetable crisper of the fridge. Herbs with more robust leaves will keep longer than those with more fragile ones.
- Big bunches of mint, parsley and coriander will keep in a jug of water for a few days. Remember to change the water daily.
- Preserve fresh herbs by setting sprigs into ice cubes.

Cooking tips

When you crush, chop or heat the leaves of a herb, an oil is released, and it is this oil that imparts flavour.

- Chop herbs with scissors, a flat knife or a mezzaluna. Chop large bunches of more robust herbs like parsley in the food processor.
- Fine herbs such as tarragon and chives can be left in large pieces, shredded or snipped.
- Coarse herbs such as rosemary and parsley benefit from fine chopping.
- Flavour vinaigrette or mayonnaise by finely chopping or pounding the herbs in a mortar and pestle, then add the rest of the ingredients.
- Herbs such as basil, coriander and sage discolour if they are chopped too early before use.
- Whole leaves of mint or basil can be steeped in water to make 'tea'. Crush them gently in your hand first to release the aromatic oils.

Scented-leaf geranium.

Agar-agar

Agar-agar is a flavourless vegetarian gelling agent made from seaweed. It is used to set ice cream, Asian desserts and jellies (pictured). Foods set with agar-agar will remain set at room temperature, a useful attribute in hot weather, unlike those containing gelatine. Desserts that have a high acidic content, such as lemon jelly, may need more agar-agar before they will set. Agar-agar flakes, strands, powder or blocks are sold in health food and Asian shops.

Angelica

The angelica variety of most interest to cooks is *Angelica archangelica*, an aromatic herb that resembles a tall parsley plant. It is native to the northern hemisphere and grows well in Scotland, Germany, Scandinavia and Russia, but can be cultivated in warmer climes. In medieval times, it was thought to be an antidote to poison. According to one legend, the Archangel Raphael revealed in a dream that angelica was a cure for the plague.

Today, angelica is regarded more for its culinary qualities: the fresh stems and leaves are used as a flavouring for pastries, confectionery and liqueurs; oil from the seeds and roots is used in the preparation of liqueurs; and the leaves are used fresh in salads. Angelica's most popular use is in cake decoration, where its green stalks are blanched, peeled and boiled, then candied in sugar to produce a vivid green colour.

Cupcakes decorated with strips of candied angelica.

Annatto

Annatto is a bright orange food colouring, which is extracted from the dark red, triangular seeds of a small tree (*Bixa orellana*), native to South America. Although the seed is edible, it has little flavour and its culinary value lies more in its colouring properties. Also known as achuete and anchiote, annatto is used as a colouring agent in Filipino, South American, Southeast Asian and Caribbean cooking. Usually the seeds are fried in oil or lard and then discarded, and the remaining yellow fat is used to fry vegetables or meat to give them a golden yellow colour.

When ground into a powder or paste, annatto is used to colour butter, margarine and smoked fish. Washed-rind cheeses, such as Livarot, are sometimes dipped in annatto colouring to deepen the colour of their rind, while the colouring of some cheeses, such as Red Leicester, is also enhanced with annatto.

Arrowroot

A starch powder obtained from the root of a tropical plant (*Maranta arundinacea*), arrowroot is used as a thickening agent. It is tasteless and the fine powder becomes clear when cooked, making it useful for thickening clear sauces. Arrowroot must be slaked (mixed with a small amount of water to form a smooth paste) before it is mixed with a hot liquid for use in sauces, puddings or pie fillings. Heat the sauce only until thick and remove it immediately, as overcooking will cause it to thin again.

Bay leaf

The glossy green leaves of an evergreen tree (*Laurus nobilis*), bay leaves are used to add a strong, slightly peppery flavour to many dishes. The bay leaf was probably introduced into Europe by the Romans, who held the bay in high esteem: they used it to make

Bay leaves go with fish, lamb, marinades, pork, potato, soup and tomato.

laurel wreaths to crown their poets as well as their athletic and military victors. The berries of the bay tree and the leaves of other laurels (such as the bay rum berry) are poisonous.

Bay leaves can be used fresh or dried, and are usually removed before the dish is served. Add one or two to enhance stews or stuffings; add to a bouquet garni; insert a leaf under chicken skin; use to flavour rice; or add to the milk infusions used in baked custards or béchamel sauce.

Fresh bay leaves have a stronger flavour than dried. Wash fresh leaves well and store them in the fridge for up to three days. Dried bay leaves will keep in an airtight container for up to six months.

Bouquet garni

Used for flavouring sauces, stews, soups or stocks, a bouquet garni is a bundle of herbs tied together with string. It should be removed at the end of cooking so, to make this easier, tie the end of the string to the handle of the saucepan. If you are using dried herbs or peppercorns, wrap them in muslin and tie off with string.

Cardoon

A popular vegetable in southern Europe, the cardoon (*Cynara cardunculus*) is an edible thistle related to the artichoke. Cardoons are cultivated for their fleshy, ribbed stalks, similar in flavour to a combination of celery and artichoke. Like celery, cardoon is blanched (that is, covered while growing to exclude light) as this makes the stalks more tender.

When cooking cardoons, peel off any tough outer ribs before using them. They brown very quickly, so cut them into pieces with a stainless steel knife and put immediately into water with a squeeze of lemon juice. Cardoons can be braised or baked, but are usually boiled slowly, then baked with butter. They can be topped with Parmesan, béchamel sauce or anchovy butter. In Italy, tender young cardoons are traditionally eaten raw with bagna cauda — a dip made with olive oil, butter, chopped anchovies and garlic — or deep-fried in batter and served as antipasto. They can also be used to top bruschetta or be mixed with cheese as a filling for ravioli or tortellini.

Making a bouquet garni

Wrap the green part of a leek around a bay leaf, a sprig of thyme, a sprig of parsley and celery leaves. Tie the bundle with string, leaving it long at one end for easy removal. Vary the herbs to suit the dish.

LEMON GRASS
(*Cymbogon citratus*)

THAI BASIL
(*Ocimum basilicum* 'Anise')

PERENNIAL CORIANDER
(*Eryngium foetidum*)

VIETNAMESE MINT
(*Polygonum odoratum*)

CURRY LEAF PLANT
(*Murraya koenigii*)

LEMON BASIL
'SWEET DANI'
(*Ocimum* sp.)

asian herbs

Asian herbs have experienced a surge
in popularity with gardeners, just as
various Asian cuisines have in
restaurants. It is now easy to buy Thai
basil, coriander, Vietnamese mint and
perilla to use as fresh foliage; chillies,
kaffir lime, lemon grass, curry leaf plant,

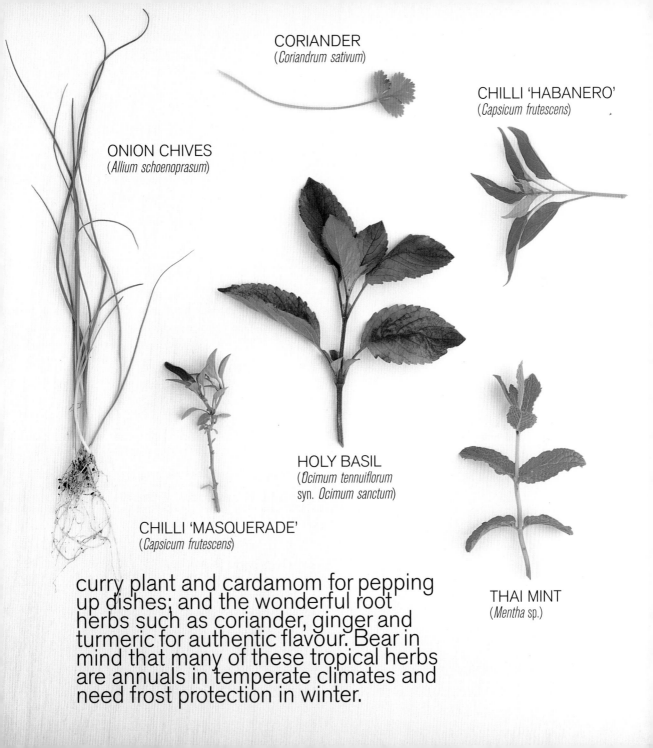

CORIANDER
(*Coriandrum sativum*)

CHILLI 'HABANERO'
(*Capsicum frutescens*)

ONION CHIVES
(*Allium schoenoprasum*)

HOLY BASIL
(*Ocimum tennuiflorum*
syn. *Ocimum sanctum*)

CHILLI 'MASQUERADE'
(*Capsicum frutescens*)

THAI MINT
(*Mentha* sp.)

curry plant and cardamom for pepping up dishes; and the wonderful root herbs such as coriander, ginger and turmeric for authentic flavour. Bear in mind that many of these tropical herbs are annuals in temperate climates and need frost protection in winter.

Celery

Celery (*Apium* sp.) is grown for its stalks, roots and seeds. The ancient Greeks, Egyptians and Romans used wild celery for its medicinal properties and crowned their victorious athletes with the leaves. In the 16th century, the first cultivated form of celery was developed; it was usually eaten cooked.

Celery grows as a cluster of long ridged stalks, which vary in colour from white to green. Celery stems are often grown under cover to prevent them from becoming too dark and too strong in flavour. Stems are eaten raw in salads; as crudités; cooked and served as a vegetable; braised in tomato or cream; or used to add flavour to stocks, soups and sauces. The tender inner leaves can be used in salads or eaten with the stalk. Buy celery that is not too big, with crisp, fresh stems. Celery has a high water content so it should be stored in the crisper drawer of the fridge, wrapped in plastic. To revive wilted celery, sprinkle it with water and put it in the fridge until it becomes crisp again.

Chrysanthemum greens

The young leaves are used in salads and stir-fries and the edible flowers are used in Chinese cooking. Chrysanthemum greens are also known as chop suey greens and garland chrysanthemum.

Dandelion

The dandelion usually seen in supermarkets and used as a salad green is a cultivated version of the wild variety. The younger, tender leaves of wild dandelion (*Taraxacum officinale*) are edible too, but only if you're sure they haven't been treated with pesticides. Cook the leaves like spinach or use them raw in salads, dressed with a strong-flavoured oil such as hazelnut or olive oil. The word 'dandelion' is derived from the French *dents de lion*, 'lion's teeth', referring to its jagged leaves. In France, it's called *pissenlit* or 'wet-the-bed', on account of the plant's diuretic qualities.

Salade lyonnaise

1 Tear 2 handfuls dandelion leaves into pieces and place them in a large bowl.
2 Fry 4 rashers streaky bacon, cut into pieces, and add to the leaves.
3 Cut 2 slices bread into cubes and fry in the bacon pan to make croutons, then add to the salad.
4 Make a vinaigrette dressing and add 1 teaspoon mustard, then toss through the salad.
5 Poach 4 eggs and serve on top.
Serves 4.

Elderberry

The elderberry is the tart red, purple or black fruit of the elder tree (*Sambucus nigra*). Elderberries can be eaten raw but their slight sourness makes them better suited to being cooked in jams, pies or in wine. The creamy white, honey-scented flowers are also edible and can be used to flavour cordials or sorbets; infused in tea; used as decoration in salads; or dipped in batter and deep-fried.

Fennel

Native to the Mediterranean but now widely grown, fennel (*Foeniculum vulgare*) is cultivated for its aromatic leaves and seeds, similar in flavour to aniseed. The fine feathery leaves can be snipped like dill and used to flavour fish dishes, dressings or sauces. Florence fennel (*Foeniculum vulgare* var. *azoricum*), known as *finocchio* in Italy, is cultivated for its thick stems and bulbous base, both of which may be eaten raw like celery; the base may also be braised, sautéed or added to soups.

Braised fennel

1 Cut 4 baby fennel bulbs into quarters and blanch them in boiling water for 5 minutes.
2 Drain well.
3 Fry the fennel in butter until browned, then add 1 teaspoon brown sugar and caramelise.
4 Add 1 tablespoon white wine vinegar and 150 ml (5 fl oz) chicken stock. Cover and simmer until the bulbs are tender.
5 Boil until the liquid is reduced, then stir in 2 tablespoons double cream.
Serves 4.

Fiddlehead fern

The young fronds or croziers of the oyster or ostrich fern (*Osmunda cinnamomea*), which grows wild in Europe and America, have a flavour that is similar to asparagus. The young shoots are usually boiled and served with a sauce, added to stir-fries or eaten raw in salads. Fiddlehead ferns are sold fresh or tinned.

From left: dried elderflower, and elderflower jelly and cordial.

Elderflower cordial

1 Make a sugar syrup by boiling 2 L (3½ pints) water with 1 kg (2 lb 4 oz) sugar until the sugar dissolves and the syrup thickens slightly (the syrup will feel greasy when you rub your finger and thumb together).
2 Pour the syrup onto 6 elderflower heads in a glass container and leave to steep overnight.
3 Strain and add lemon juice to taste, and keep bottled in the fridge for a few days. Dilute with water, if necessary.

flowers

The use of edible flowers in cooking is a tradition that dates back several centuries in Europe. Flowers can be added to food merely as decoration, or to give it texture, flavour and colour. Always confirm the identity of the flower and check it is edible before use. Take care that any flower used as food — wild or cultivated — has not been sprayed with poisonous chemicals.

Some flowers used in cooking are roses, violets, marjoram, lavender, mint, oregano, fennel, marigold and nasturtium. Add marigold and nasturtium to salads, but toss them in after you have added the vinegar dressing or they will turn brown. Use rose petals in jellies, jams or cordials, and use lavender to flavour custards and biscuits. Saffron stamens are used to colour and flavour dishes. Frosted flowers make excellent decorations. Make them by dipping blooms in beaten egg white, then in caster sugar.

Edible flowers
- Essential oils are stronger in flavour than floral waters.
- Fresh petals impart more subtle flavours than dried.

Jamaica flower or rosella

Not to be confused with the ornamental hibiscus plant that grows in tropical areas worldwide, Jamaica flower (*Hibiscus sabdariffa*) is a tropical and subtropical plant grown for its enlarged, fleshy, deep red sepals. The sepals are edible, slightly tart in flavour and may be bought fresh, dried or frozen. When dried, they may be infused in teas; used fresh, they may be cooked into jams or a sauce similar to cranberry. In the West Indies and the Caribbean, the flower is used to make wine. It also adds colour and flavour when mixed with rum and spices to make drinks. In Mexico, the Jamaica flower is used to make a drink (pictured at left) by infusing the flower in boiling water, then adding sugar.

Lavender

Apart from being universally recognised as an ornamental shrub, with its silver foliage and unmistakable perfume, lavender can also be used to great effect in the kitchen. The flowers of lavender can be used fresh or dried to impart their scent to sugar or ice cream. Crystallised flowers can also be used as wonderful embellishments on cakes.

Lavender ice cream

1 In a saucepan put 8 washed and dried stems of English lavender with 600 ml (1 pint) thick cream and 1 small piece lemon rind. Heat until almost boiling, then stir in 160 g (6 oz) sugar.
2 Strain through a sieve. Gradually pour onto 4 egg yolks, lightly whisked in a bowl.
3 Return to the pan. Stir over low heat until thick enough to coat the back of a spoon. Do not boil.
4 Pour into a chilled metal tray to cool. Freeze until frozen around the edge, but not in the centre.
5 In a food processor or bowl, beat until smooth. Freeze again and repeat this process twice more.
6 Cover with greaseproof paper and freeze. Serves 6–8.

Rose

Rose petals can be boiled in water or sugar syrup and used to flavour food, or crystallised and used for decoration. All rose petals are edible as long as they haven't been sprayed with any chemicals. Rose-water, made from a distillation of petals, is used in the Middle East and India to flavour dishes such as Turkish delight, baklava and lassi. It gives a sweet fragrance to curries and rice dishes. The thicker, sticky sugar syrup is used in Middle Eastern sweets and pastries.

Rose sugar syrup

1 Put 500 g (1 lb 2 oz) caster sugar in a heavy-based saucepan.
2 Add 250 ml (9 fl oz) water and 2 teaspoons lemon juice. Bring the mixture to the boil, stirring frequently.
3 When the sugar has all dissolved, reduce the heat and simmer for about 10 minutes, or until the mixture is syrupy. Do not stir while the liquid is simmering.
4 Stir in 1 tablespoon rose-water, then remove from the heat and cool.
Makes 500 ml (17 fl oz).

Saffron

Saffron is the orange-red stigma of one species of the crocus plant (*Crocus sativus*), and the most expensive spice in the world. Each flower consists of three stigmas, which are hand-picked, then dried — a labour-intensive process. Its flavour is pungent and aromatic, and its colour intense, so only a little is used. It gives flavour and colour to such dishes as bouillabaisse, paella, risotto and pilaf, as well as saffron cake and buns. Saffron is sold in both powdered and thread form (the whole stigma). But beware — there is no such thing as cheap saffron. The best comes from Spain, Iran and Kashmir.

Cooking saffron

Saffron threads are usually soaked in warm water, stock or milk for a few minutes to infuse. The mixture is then either strained or added, with the threads, to the dish. The threads can also be added at the end of cooking.

Galangal

A spicy root, similar to ginger in appearance and preparation, galangal (*Alpinia galanga*) is used in Southeast Asian cooking, especially in Thailand, Indonesia and Malaysia. There are two types. The most widely known is greater galangal from Indonesia, a knobbly root with creamy white flesh and a delicate peppery ginger flavour. Lesser galangal, from south China, is smaller, with an orange-red flesh and a pungent and more peppery flavour.

Galangal has a tougher, woodier texture than ginger and needs to be chopped finely before use. Cut it into thin slices and add it to soup, and use it in curry pastes or in recipes that call for ginger. Buy galangal with pinker stems as these are fresher than the browner ones. Galangal is also available dried, ground or in brine — in which form it is easier to use.

Galangal lasts for months in the fridge.

Garlic

A strongly flavoured bulbous herb from the same family as the onion and the leek, garlic's folkloric powers are legendary. Each head is made up of a cluster of 10–16 cloves, and both the head and individual bulbs are covered with a paper-like skin. There are many varieties of garlic (*Allium sativum*), each differing in size, pungency and colour, but the most common are the white-skinned American or Creole garlic; the pink or purple Mexican or Italian garlic; and the larger Tahitian garlic.

In dishes such as aïoli, tapenade and pesto, garlic is indispensable, and it adds flavour to a variety of sauces, stews and meats. Don't be tempted to use more than the specified amount, as garlic will overpower the other flavours in the dish.

Garlic is freshest in summer when the bulbs are firm and the cloves harder to peel. Later in the season, the garlic begins to dry out — it is easier to peel but the flavour is quite intense. Choose fresh, plump-looking garlic with a white skin and fat neck as these have a more delicate flavour; discoloured garlic or bulbs that are sprouting will have a rancid flavour. The green shoots of garlic are also available in some areas. They can be used like chives and snipped onto salads and stir-fries. Garlic can also be eaten as a vegetable, barbecued or roasted whole or as cloves.

Cooking garlic

- Raw garlic is more potent than cooked. When garlic is cooked, some of the starch converts to sugar, making the garlic less pungent.
- Be careful not to overbrown or burn garlic as it can become very bitter.
- Chopping or crushing garlic releases the flavours.
- Crush a whole garlic clove by putting it under the flat blade of a knife and banging the knife with your fist.
- If the clove has sprouted, cut out the green sprout from the centre.
- Flavour oil with garlic by frying slices in oil, then discard the slices.
- Brush whole garlic bulbs with olive oil and barbecue until soft.

Aïoli

A classic of Provençal cuisine, aïoli is a strongly flavoured garlic mayonnaise made with egg yolks, garlic and olive oil. The name is formed from the Provençal *ail*, meaning 'garlic', and *oli*, meaning 'oil'. Serve aïoli with salads, egg dishes, fish soup, cold poached fish or with hot or cold vegetables.

Aïoli

1 Put 6 peeled garlic cloves, 2 egg yolks and a pinch of salt into a blender and blend the ingredients until a thick paste forms.
2 With the motor running, add about 250 ml (9 fl oz) of olive oil, drop by drop, until the aïoli is thick and creamy; however, if it gets too thick, add a little lemon juice.
3 Season to taste.
This recipe can also be made using a mortar and pestle. Serves 6.

Skordalia

A traditional Greek garlic sauce, skordalia is served cold with grilled or fried vegetables (especially eggplant/aubergine), meat, poultry and fish, such as salt cod fritters with boiled eggs and in soups. It is also used as a dip for raw vegetables and bread. Today skordalia may be thickened with either puréed or mashed potatoes, as well as the original breadcrumbs, or almonds, pine nuts or walnuts. Classically made in a mortar and pestle, the oil is added drop by drop until a thick mayonnaise-like consistency is achieved.

Skordalia

1 Mix 250 g (9 oz) mashed potato with 2–3 crushed garlic cloves and 1 slice day-old bread, which has been first soaked in cold water and squeezed dry.
2 Using electric beaters or a mortar and pestle, beat in 185 ml (6 fl oz) olive oil, allowing the oil to slowly drizzle into the mashed potato, then add 2 tablespoons white wine vinegar and 1 tablespoon lemon juice and season well.
Serves 8.

Ginger

Ginger is the knobbly, beige-coloured rhizome of a tropical plant (*Zingiber officinale*). Ginger is indigenous to Southeast Asia, but is now grown all over the world in tropical climates. It was originally used in Europe in powdered, dried, crystallised or preserved form, but as Chinese, Indian, Middle Eastern and Caribbean cooking spread, ginger became increasingly available and can now be bought fresh year-round.

Store fresh ginger in the fridge tightly wrapped in plastic film. Unless it is very fresh, ginger is usually first peeled, then grated or sliced. If it's fibrous, it may be easier to grate it, preferably with a bamboo or ceramic grater.

Ginger goes with coconut milk, coriander, garlic, lemon, lime juice, pear, rhubarb, soy sauce and spring onion.

Types of ginger

Fresh At its best when young and juicy — the root is covered in a tender skin and has a sweet, peppery flavour. As it gets older, the flavour strengthens but the flesh becomes more fibrous. Add to curries or Asian dishes.

Ground (powdered) Mainly used in baked goods such as gingerbread, ginger cake and biscuits.

Preserved and crystallised Pieces of ginger that have been boiled in sugar syrup to preserve them. Crystallised ginger is then removed from the syrup. Use in baking, or drizzle the syrup on ice cream or fruit.

Pickled Thin slices of young ginger, pickled and often dyed pink. Eaten as a palate cleanser between pieces of sushi.

Mioga A close relative of ginger that is noted for its fragrant buds and stems, mioga is sliced thinly and used to garnish or give flavour to soups, tempura and sashimi.

Ginseng

Ginseng (*Panax ginseng*) is an aromatic root found in Asia and North America. In the past, it was thought that its human-like shape was a sign that it was a remedy for ailments afflicting all parts of the body. Ginseng is still widely recognised for its health-giving properties. The Chinese consider it to be 'the root of life' and add it to soups. In Korea it is infused for tea.

Gingerbread men

1 Mix 340 g (12 oz) plain flour with 2 teaspoons ground ginger and 1 teaspoon bicarbonate of soda.
2 Rub in 110 g (4 oz) butter and add 150 g (5½ oz) dark brown sugar, 1 beaten egg and 4 tablespoons golden syrup.
3 Mix to a dough.
4 Cover and chill for 30 minutes.
5 Roll out the dough to 6 mm (¼ in) thick, then cut out the men with a cutter.
6 Push currants in the dough for the eyes.
7 Bake at 220°C (425°F) for 8–10 minutes.
8 Cool and decorate with glacé icing.
This recipe makes about 20 men.

Clockwise from bottom left: ginseng root, ginseng tea, tea granules and ginseng drink.

Horseradish

A plant cultivated for its pungent, spicy root, horseradish (*Armoracia rusticana*) is generally grated — the greatest concentration of flavour is just under the skin — and used as a condiment or in sauces. Folded into cream, horseradish makes a good accompaniment to roast beef, but also goes well with smoked fish and other meats. The young leaves can be used in salads. When not available fresh, it can be bought bottled or dried. Once peeled, it can be stored for a few days in vinegar.

Jerusalem artichoke

Neither from Jerusalem nor an artichoke, this winter root (*Helianthus tuberosus*) is a native of Peru and a relative of the sunflower (in Spanish, *girasol*, mispronounced in English as 'Jerusalem'). They have a mildly sweet, smoky flavour. Finely slice artichokes and add them raw to salads; boil or roast them like potatoes; or use them to make wonderful velvety soups and mashes. After you have cut them, drop the pieces into water with a squeeze of lemon juice to stop them going brown.

Roasted Jerusalem artichokes

1 Scrub 750 g (1 lb 10 oz) Jerusalem artichokes, then toss them in 2 tablespoons olive oil with plenty of seasoning.
2 Put them on a baking tray and roast at 200°C (400°F) for about 40 minutes, or until tender in the centre, then drizzle with a little hazelnut or walnut oil.
3 Serve as a vegetable or, for a salad, toss with rocket leaves and fried cubes of bacon. Serves 4.

Horseradish cream

1 Lightly whisk 150 ml (5 fl oz) double cream.
2 Fold in 2 tablespoons grated fresh or bottled horseradish, 2 teaspoons lemon juice, a pinch of salt and sugar.
3 Don't overwhisk the cream as the acid from the lemon juice and horseradish will act as a thickener — if the cream is heavily whisked from the start, it may separate.
Makes about 185 ml (6 fl oz).

kitchen herbs

Basil

There are several types of basil (*Ocimum* sp.), all of which have a different flavour. Genoa or sweet basil is the best known. It has a spicy flavour and is used extensively in Italian cooking. Opal basil has purple leaves, Greek basil has smaller leaves and a pungent flavour, and Thai or holy basil complements Thai and Southeast Asian dishes. Basil should be torn, not chopped, and added to hot food at the last moment to preserve the flavour. It doesn't dry well.

Chervil

Chervil (*Anthriscus cerefolium*) has delicate, lacy, pale green leaves that deteriorate quickly, so they should be added to hot dishes just before serving. One of the classic *fines herbes*, it has a subtle parsley flavour with a hint of aniseed. Use it with fish, in salads or with creamy dishes.

Comfrey

Comfrey (*Symphytum* sp.) belongs to the same family as borage. Its smaller leaves, dipped in batter and fried, can be eaten as a vegetable. The bell-shaped flowers can be used for decoration in salads.

Coriander

The roots of coriander (*Coriandrum sativum*) are used in curry pastes, the stems are used when a strong coriander flavour is needed, and the leaves are added at the end of cooking, both as a flavouring and as a garnish. Coriander is used extensively in Asian, South American, Mexican, Middle Eastern and Mediterranean cuisines. It goes very well with chilli, lime juice and meat dishes. Coriander freezes well.

Marjoram and oregano

Traditionally used to flavour tomato sauces in Italian and Greek cooking, marjoram and oregano (*Origanum* sp.) are usually used dried. They can be

Pesto

1 Put 2 crushed garlic cloves in a mortar and pestle, add a pinch of salt and 50 g (1¾ oz) pine nuts. Pound to a paste.

2 Gradually add 50 g (1¾ oz) basil leaves and pound the leaves against the side of the bowl.

3 Stir in 75 g (2½ oz) grated Parmesan, then gradually add 150 ml (5 fl oz) olive oil. Use immediately or store covered in the fridge for one week. If storing, cover the pesto surface with a thin layer of olive oil.

Serve with pasta or barbecued meat. Makes 250 ml (9 fl oz).

added to sausages and stuffings. Both herbs have a strong flavour and should be used sparingly.

Mint

Traditionally used in British cooking to go with lamb, mint also goes well in salads and with steamed fish. There are several types of mint (*Mentha* sp.), including apple mint, peppermint and spearmint.

Parsley

Available as flat-leaf (Italian) or curly-leaf, parsley (*Petroselinum* sp.) can be used as an ingredient as well as a garnish. Flat-leaf parsley tends to be stronger in flavour but the two can be used interchangeably.

Rosemary

Rosemary is a strong-flavoured herb: either chop it very finely or use small sprigs and remove them before serving. Rosemary (*Rosmarinus officinalis*) goes well with roast lamb and pork, and in breads.

Sage

Sage leaves are traditionally used with onion to stuff goose and in Italian cuisine to flavour butter served with pasta, as well as in pork, veal and liver dishes. Use sage (*Salvia officinalis*) sparingly as the flavour can be strong.

Tarragon

Tarragon (*Artemisia dracunculus*) has a hint of aniseed to its flavour and is used in many classic French dishes. It is important to use French tarragon and not Russian, which has a coarser flavour.

Thyme

There are many varieties of thyme (*Thymus* sp.) and all have the same small leaves that can be used as a flavouring in casseroles and soups. Thyme gives a rich, aromatic flavour to slow-cooked food and roasts.

Rack of lamb in herb crust

1 Mix together 1 teaspoon mustard, 1 tablespoon fine breadcrumbs, 2 tablespoons chopped fresh herbs (such as mint, parsley and thyme) and 2 teaspoons butter to form a paste.

2 Season to taste.

3 Press onto the skinned side of a trimmed rack of lamb and roast skin side up at 200°C (400°F) for 25 minutes.

Serves 2.

Kuzu

Both the stem and leaves of the kuzu plant (*Pueraria lobota*) are edible, but the vine is mainly grown for its tubers, which are ground to make a grey starch powder called kuzu. Similar in texture and function to cornflour, kuzu is used mainly in Chinese and Japanese cuisine as a thickener in soups, sauces and glazes, and for dusting food before it is fried.

Lemon grass

With a subtle lemon flavour and fragrance, lemon grass (*Cymbopogon citratus*) adds a refreshing taste to many Thai and other Southeast Asian dishes. Strip off tough outer layers and use whole in soups by lightly bruising the stems (remove before serving); finely chop and use in curry pastes; thinly slice the paler lower part of the stem and add it to salads; or use whole as skewers for cooking meat, prawns and chicken.

Store lemon grass by wrapping it in plastic and storing it in the fridge for up to two weeks. Lemon grass can also be bought dried in sticks or in powdered form, when it is called sereh powder. If lemon grass is unavailable, use grated lemon zest instead. Lemon grass goes with chicken, chilli, coconut, ginger, pork and seafood.

Lotus

The lotus is a member of the waterlily family (*Nymphaea* sp.), with beautiful white and pink flowers. In cooking, it is the root that is most commonly used. When sliced horizontally, it displays a floral-like pattern of holes. This decorativeness, along with its crisp, delicately flavoured flesh, is much appreciated in Chinese and Japanese cuisine.

First peel the root, then slice it before eating it raw or cooked. Add it to salads or stir-fries, or cut it into chunks, stuff it, or serve it as a vegetable. Store in water with a squeeze of lemon juice to prevent it from turning brown. The seeds are also edible, eaten out of the hand or used in Chinese desserts and soups, and the leaves are used to wrap food such as whole fish for cooking. Lotus root can be bought fresh, dried, frozen and canned.

The thick, bulbous base of the **lemon grass stem** can be used instead of lemon zest to flavour desserts.

Lotus root and vegetable stir-fry

1 Thinly slice 1 peeled lotus root and 2 zucchini (courgettes).
2 Heat a small amount oil in a frying pan, then briefly fry 2 crushed garlic cloves and 1 tablespoon
   grated ginger.
3 Add the lotus root and zucchini (courgettes), and stir-fry for 2 minutes, then add 1 chopped
   carrot, 1 chopped red capsicum (pepper) and 12 snowpeas (mangetout), cut in half, and fry for a
   further 2 minutes.
4 Add 2 tablespoons oyster sauce, 1 tablespoon soy sauce, 1 teaspoon sesame oil and toss together.
5 Add some snowpea sprouts and toss everything together until the sprouts are wilted. Serve the
   vegetables with noodles or rice.
Serves 4.

Mastic

Mastic is a resin collected from *Pistacia lentiscus* bushes on the Greek
island of Chios. Related to the pistachio, it has an earthy, aromatic flavour
and is used for flavouring Turkish delight and ice cream. It is also used in a
Greek liqueur called *mastika*, and in Egyptian and Moroccan cuisine. It was
probably the original chewing gum, and the
source of the verb 'masticate'.

Mesclun

Originally a mixture of the leaves and shoots of
young plants, served as a salad, today mesclun
is a Provençal mixture of salad leaves and
herbs. A typical one may include rocket and
dandelion leaves, curly endive and chervil. It is
seasoned with a vinaigrette of olive oil, *fines
herbes* and garlic. A mesclun salad provides a
contrast of both flavour and textures by
combining mild and bitter tastes and soft and
crunchy textures. Only young leaves should be
used. In Provence, mesclun is served with
baked goat's milk cheeses, pieces of bacon,
croutons, or chicken livers fried in butter.

The word 'mesclun' is derived from the Nice dialect *mesclumo*, meaning 'mixture'. A similar mixture in Rome is called *mescladisse*.

Millet

Millet is a grass seed which is used as a cereal in many African and Asian countries as it can grow in areas of extreme aridity and heat. Millet (*Panicum miliaceum*) can be boiled in water, milk or stock, is a good accompaniment to spicy casseroles and is used to thicken soups. The flour is used for flat breads and griddle cakes, but as it lacks gluten it is not suited to many types of baking. Millet can also be fermented and made into a crude beer, or malted and made into a more sophisticated brew.

Mustard

Made from the ground seeds of the mustard plant (*Brassica* sp.), mustard is a condiment. There are many species, but it is usually the black (the hottest and most pungent), brown and white (sometimes called yellow) seeds that are commonly used. Prepared mustard is made by macerating the seeds in liquid — such as water, vinegar or wine — then grinding them to a fine paste. Some mustards are flavoured with other ingredients such as herbs, honey, chilli or garlic. The pungency, colour, flavour and texture of the mustard will depend on the type of seeds used and the style of mustard.

Whole mustard seeds are used to flavour marinades and sauces, and in a host of Asian recipes. They are widely used in pickling. In Indian cooking they are fried in oil until they pop. Mustard oil (extracted from the seeds) is also popular. Mustard powder is simply ground mustard seeds and can be added to salad dressings, mayonnaise and sauces. It helps the emulsification of sauces such as mayonnaise and vinaigrette. The powder can be mixed with water and used in the same way as prepared mustard,

Clockwise from bottom left to centre: smooth mustard, mustard oil, mustard powder, yellow and brown mustard seeds, and wholegrain mustard.

Dijon

American

German wholegrain

Hot English

which should be stored in the fridge as it loses its flavour at room temperature. Store mustard seeds and powder in a cool, dry place.

Types of mustard

French These most famous mustards include Dijon, Bordeaux and Meaux. Dijon is a strong, smooth, pale yellow to light brown mustard. The seeds are blended with white wine or verjuice (the juice of unripe vine grapes). Meaux is a milder mustard of unmilled crushed seeds.

American A mild mustard, sometimes flavoured with sugar, vinegar or white wine, served with hot dogs and hamburgers.

German Typically dark, medium to hot, usually eaten with German sausages or cold meats.

English Made from brown and white seeds, smooth and very hot. Use with roast beef and ham, with hard cheeses such as Cheddar, or as a condiment with sausages, herring or mackerel. Often prepared from mustard powder.

Serving suggestions

- Rub a little of your favourite mustard onto ham before baking it, or onto a chicken before roasting.
- Add some to a white sauce or soup for extra flavour.
- Combine some mustard with a little oil, chilli and soy sauce for a quick meat marinade.
- Mix mustard with softened butter, add some chopped fresh herbs and use on top of beef or pork steaks.
- Cook some cocktail sausages, then add 1 tablespoon wholegrain mustard and 1 tablespoon honey and toss everything together.

Nettle

Despite its reputation as a stinging weed, the nettle (*Urtica* sp.) is edible. The stings are caused by little hairs on the leaves, which lose their irritating properties when cooked. Nettles are rarely available commercially, so if picking them from the wild, ensure they aren't from areas that have been sprayed with pesticides. Wear gloves and choose plants with small leaves and soft stems. Prepare nettle in the same way as you would spinach and use it in soups, braise it with onions or use it to stuff ravioli.

Okra

Okra (*Abelmoschus esculentus*) is a slender, five-sided pod that contains numerous white seeds. When young, okra is eaten as a vegetable; the older pods are usually dried, then powdered and used as a flavouring. When

cooked, okra releases a sticky, gelatinous substance, which serves to thicken stews and soups such as the Cajun and Creole dish, gumbo. Okra is also used extensively in India, the Caribbean, Southeast Asia and the Middle East. It can be eaten raw in salads or blanched, then dressed in a vinaigrette.

Buy pods that are tender and healthy green in colour. They should snap rather than bend and should be no more than 10 cm (4 in) long. If too ripe, the pod will feel very sticky. To prepare, gently scrub okra with paper towel or a vegetable brush. Rinse and drain, then slice off the top and tail. If using as a thickener, blanch okra whole first, then slice and add it to the dish about 10 minutes before the end of cooking. In some recipes, the pod is used whole, thus preventing the release of the sticky substances within. Okra goes with eggplant (aubergine), onion, capsicum (pepper) and tomato.

Young, fresh **okra pods** are eaten as a vegetable.

Onion

Onions (*Allium cepa*) are used in just about every nation's cuisine, adding a depth of flavour to dishes, although they are a delicious vegetable in their own right. Onions grow as single bulbs (globe) or in clumps (aggregate), although most onions sold in the West are single bulbs. They are sold as either dry onions or green onions. Dry onions are left to mature in the ground where they develop a papery skin; green (spring or salad) onions are pulled out while young and the bulb is still small. Onions are also sold dried, as flakes, in a powder-like onion salt or as fried flakes.

Types of onions

Brown The most common, and available year-round. Varieties include a sweet onion called vidalia, Spanish onions, pickling onions and cipolline, small flat onions.

White Generally mild and slightly sweet. Can be used for cooking or salads. Pearl onions are small white onions, which are ideal for pickling but can also be added whole to stews and casseroles.

Red Delicious in salads, adding both flavour and colour. Good for barbecues and grilling. When cooked, red onions have less flavour than other varieties, although they can be slightly sweeter.

Storing onions

Store onions in a cool, dark place, but not in the fridge as their strong odour will permeate other foods. If stored correctly, they will keep for up to two months. The exceptions are red and spring onions.

Cooking onions

- Slicing onions causes the cell walls to rupture, releasing the sulphurous contents. When mixed with air, these turn into allyl sulphate, which irritates the eyes.
- If frying onions, don't chop them in the food processor as they release too much liquid and will steam rather than fry. To bring out their sweet flavour, sweat them gently over low heat without letting them brown.

Pandanus

Long, flat, emerald green pandanus leaves (*Pandanus* sp.) are used for their colour and fragrance and as a food container — which also imparts flavour — in Southeast Asian cooking, particularly in Indonesia and Malaysia. The leaves are crushed and added to dishes such as rice or curries during cooking or tied in a knot so they fit easily into the pot, then removed before the dish is served. For colouring (in Malaysian and Indonesian sweets, for example), the leaves are boiled and the colour extracted.

Pandanus leaves are sold in bundles and are available both dried and frozen. Dried ones lack the intensity of flavour and the frozen leaf is much less fragrant.

Pandanus leaf essence, called *bai toey* in Indonesia, is a brilliantly coloured fragrant flavouring used in cakes and sweet dishes. In sweet dishes, vanilla extract is an acceptable substitute.

Pandanus leaves impart their flavour and aroma to fish or meat during grilling, baking or barbecuing.

Green peppercorns

Black peppercorns

White peppercorns

Peppercorn

True pepper (vine pepper) is black, green or white. The three varieties come from the same plant (*Piper nigrum*) but are picked at various stages of ripeness (see 'Types of pepper' below). Red pepper, Sichuan pepper, cayenne pepper and other peppers are not true peppers but were so called because pepper was an expensive commodity. Pepper contains piperine, which is an alkaloid, and it is this that gives pepper its distinctive flavour. Pepper is sold whole, cracked, and coarsely or finely ground. Freezing makes the flavour of pepper more pronounced.

Storing pepper

Freshly ground black pepper is more pungent than pre-ground, which loses its flavour quickly and should not be stored longer than four months. Whole peppercorns will last about one year in a cool, dark place.

Types of pepper

Green pepper Picked when unripe and usually preserved by artificial drying or by bottling in brine, vinegar or water. Poivre rose are green peppercorns that have just begun to turn reddish.

Black pepper From berries that are red, but not completely ripe. When left to dry, they shrivel and take on a dark colour. This is the most pungent and flavourful of peppers.

White pepper From ripe, red berries that are soaked in salt water until soft, then the white seed is removed and dried. White pepper is less aromatic than black but hotter and sharper, so use it sparingly. Useful for seasoning white sauces.

Sago

Sago is a starch extracted from various Southeast Asian palms (*Cycas* sp.), processed into a flour or granulated into little balls called pearl sago. Pearl sago is commonly made into milky baked or steamed puddings in the West. In Southeast Asia, sago is used both as a flour and in pearl form to make desserts such as the Malay dessert, *gula melaka*, a mixture of sago, palm sugar and coconut milk.

Sago pudding

1 Put 125 ml (4 fl oz) golden syrup, 75 g (2½ oz) sago, 400 ml (14 fl oz) milk and 350 ml (12 fl oz) cream in a saucepan and bring to the boil, stirring.
2 Simmer for 10 minutes, then allow to cool.
3 Stir in 2 eggs, 1 teaspoon vanilla essence, 1 teaspoon grated lemon rind and 2 teaspoons lemon juice.
4 Transfer mixture to an ovenproof dish and bake at 170°C (325°F) for 1 hour.
Serves 6.

Contrasts of colour, flavour and texture make a lively salad.

Salad leaves

A wide variety of lettuces and herbs with different coloured and flavoured leaves are the main constituents of salad. Leaves can be used for looks, flavour, or both. For example, red leaves have a bitter flavour, and like peppery green rocket, need to be offset by more delicate flavours. To make a mixed salad, you need a good combination of textures and flavours. Lamb's lettuce (corn salad or mache), is slightly nutty in flavour. Purslane has a slightly sour, peppery taste. Young beet leaves (buy them attached to the root) have a good green colour and earthy flavour, and mizuna has dark green, feathery and glossy leaves. Mustard leaves are pungent, and crisp lettuce leaves like cos add crunch. Both the flower and the peppery leaf of the nasturtium can be used in salad, as well as herbs such as mint, chervil and basil.

Sassafras

Sassafras is a North American native tree (*Sassafras albidum*) whose virtues were much lauded by the Indians and early Spanish colonists. Sassafras leaves are dried and used to make sassafras tea and filé powder, a flavouring and thickening agent in the Creole stew of gumbo. The fragrant lemon-scented oil extracted from the bark of the root is used in the cosmetic industry for its perfume; to flavour soft drinks, root beer, ice cream and confectionery; and in the health food industry.

Clockwise from top left: toasted sesame seeds, roasted sesame oil, gomasio (made from sea salt and lightly toasted sesame seeds), white and black sesame seeds, and sesame seed biscuits.

Sesame seed

Sesame seeds come from a tropical or subtropical plant (*Sesamum orientale*) that produces seed pods which, when dried, burst open. They are then shaken to encourage the release of hundreds of tiny seeds. Sesame seeds are usually cream in colour, but may also be yellow, reddish or black, depending on the variety. The seeds can be used raw, but when toasted, take on a nutty, slightly sweet flavour. Sesame seeds are used in cooking throughout the world — scattered over burger buns, on bread, and as garnishes for salads. In the Middle East, they are used in halvah, are crushed to make tahini or ground with chickpeas to produce hummus. In Japan, sesame seeds form the basis of seasonings such as gomasio.

Because of their high oil content, the seeds become rancid quickly. Purchase them in small amounts or store them in the fridge for up to three months. Sesame seeds may also be frozen.

With its tart, lemony flavour, **sorrel** makes a delicious addition to mayonnaise. Serve it with crustaceans.

Sorrel

Sorrel is a leafy green plant that grows wild in northern Asia and Europe. There are many species, including common sorrel and round-leafed (French) sorrel, the mildest in flavour. Sorrel (*Rumex acetosa*) has large, spinach-like leaves that have a lemony, acidic, slightly bitter taste, due to the presence of oxalic acid. Sorrel can be used in a mixed green salad; cooked like spinach; made into soups, purées and sauces; or used as a flavouring herb in omelettes.

Sumac

A reddish purple berry used extensively as a spice in Lebanese and Turkish cooking, sumac has a fruity but mildly astringent lemony flavour. The seeds are dried, then crushed or powdered. Sumac (*Rhus eoriaria*) is used in many dishes to add flavour and colour to meat, fish, pilafs and vegetables. (See the recipe for sardines, at right; sumac is an ingredient of ras el hanout.)

Tamarind

The tropical tamarind tree (*Tamarindus indica*) is prized for its pods, each containing a sticky, fleshy sweet-sour pulp wrapped around small hard seeds. The pulp is used in Indian curries and chutneys, or in sauces such as Worcestershire sauce. It may be sweetened into syrups and sweetmeats. Tamarind is sold in ready-made concentrated paste in jars, or in blocks or cakes that still contain the seeds.

Cut off a little, mix it with hot water and press it through a sieve to extract the pulp. Store the paste in the fridge, where it will last up to a year.

Vanilla

True vanilla comes from the pod of a climbing orchid vine (*Vanilla planifolia*) native to Central America. The pods are picked when green, when they have no flavour, then they are left to sweat and dry in the sun. This process causes them to shrivel, turn deep brown and acquire a light coating of small, white vanillin crystals. True vanilla is expensive, partly because of the labour-intensive methods of obtaining it and also because the flowers are hand-pollinated on the one day of the year that they open.

Good quality vanilla pods have a warm, caramel vanilla aroma and flavour, and should be soft, not hard and dry. Bury a pod in a jar of sugar and let the flavour infuse the sugar, or soak the whole pod in hot milk and use it for custards and ice cream. For extra flavour, use the tip of a knife to slice down the pod to allow some of the tiny, potently flavoured seeds to escape.

Vanilla is sold as pods or distilled into pure vanilla extract (or essence). In these forms, vanilla is quite expensive. Synthetic or imitation vanilla flavouring – which must be labelled as such – is cheaper, but the flavour is inferior.

Marinated sardines

1 Mix 1 crushed garlic clove with 1/2 teaspoon salt and 2 teaspoons ras el hanout.
2 Add enough oil to make a paste and rub into 18 sardine fillets.
3 Fry in oil until browned; remove from pan.
4 Cook 1 chopped onion with 3 chopped tomatoes, 2 teaspoons sumac and 1 chopped chilli for 5 minutes.
5 Add 185 ml (6 fl oz) water and cook a further 5 minutes. Add 4 tablespoons lemon juice and season. Pour over the sardines and cool to room temperature.

Serves 6.

After use, wash the **vanilla pod**, dry it thoroughly and store it wrapped in plastic in a cool, dry place. The pod can be used up to four times.

The use of herbs in essential oils, perfumes and cosmetics dates back to ancient civilisations. There are many simple herbal preparations that you can use to tone, clean, moisturise or simply refresh your skin. Hair rinses and bath preparations, too, can be quickly made from herbs.

cosmetic herbs

In the 16th century, an Italian perfume – called 'Frangipani' after its Italian creator, the Marquis Frangipani – was used to scent gloves. When the frangipani flower was discovered in the Caribbean, its perfume was considered reminiscent of the scented gloves, so the flower was called frangipani. However, the genus name, *Plumeria*, commemorates Charles Plumier, a 17th century French botanist. *Plumeria rubra* is shown here.

Cosmetics through the ages

Herbs have been used in perfumes and cosmetics for thousands of years. The ancient Egyptians held their preparations in high regard and were entombed with them so they could continue to adorn themselves in the afterlife. They treated wrinkles with a mixture of frankincense, wax, moruga oil, cyperus grass and fermented plant juice, and chewed herbs for bad breath. A cure for baldness required placing chopped lettuce on the bald patch, while grey hair was treated with an ointment – juniper berries and two other plants were kneaded into a paste with oil, then heated before being applied to the hair.

The Greeks used fragrant oils to ward off illness, sprinkled furnishings with scented waters and placed garlands of flowers around the necks of their guests. The Greek philosopher and scientist Theophrastus (c. 370– c. 287 BC) wrote an early study of perfumes, *Concerning Odours*, in which he described how a poultice on the leg could sweeten the breath — the essences permeated the skin and then entered the circulatory system.

The Romans adapted many of the Greek uses of perfumes. Both the Greeks and the Romans used the powdered root of *Acorus calamus* (sweet flag) as talcum powder, and it was also widely used in Elizabethan times.

The musk rose (*Rosa moschata*) inspired great English poets such as Keats and Shakespeare.

Roses, hyacinth, myrtle and jonquil were popular in seventh century Eastern civilisations; the wealthy surrounded themselves with plants that were either aromatic or produced strongly fragrant flowers. Musk was the most popular fragrance, and when building their places of worship, followers of Mohammed mixed it with mortar for a lasting fragrance. Since the days of the Prophet, Muslims have used miswak, a natural brush and toothpaste from *Salvadora persica*, a tree that is native to southern Egypt and the Sudan.

In medieval Europe, herbs were commonly used for cosmetics, perfumes and washing. Chamomile was used in water for handwashing; lavender was used in personal baths and scent; and nutmeg was set in silver and used as scented jewellery. Rosemary

Grasse

The first perfume laboratory in Grasse was set up by the Italian Catherine de'Medici in the 16th century. She had come to France to marry Henry II. As there was also an established tanning industry in Grasse at the time, the two industries joined forces to produce perfumed gloves, which aristocrats held to their noses to screen out the often overwhelmingly unpleasant smells of urban living. In the 18th century the leather industry declined, and the craftsmen turned their attention to manufacturing perfume.

leaves were boiled in white wine and used as a face wash, while thyme was used as an astringent.

Perfumes came into general use around the time of the reign of Elizabeth I of England, when exotic new fragrances were brought back from the New World by Spanish and English explorers.

Scented flowers and aromatic gardening fell into decline during the 18th century when landscape gardening, with its emphasis on dramatic vistas rather than floral displays, became popular. The Victorians remedied this to some extent with their love of flower beds, although they tended to concentrate on colour rather than fragrance.

By the turn of the 20th century, however, the aromatic garden had become popular again and in more recent times there has been a revival of interest in both aromatherapy — the use of aromatic plant extracts and essential oils for healing and cosmetic purposes — and gardening.

Commercially, the interest in aromatic plants has never been more intense. Today perfume is a huge industry. The town of Grasse in southern France is one of the largest centres in the world for the production and development of fragrances, and it heavily invests in plant-breeding programs designed to produce varieties with greater concentrations of sought after oils.

Rosemary (*Rosmarinus officinalis*).

Lavandula angustifolia.

Essential oils

Essential oils are the concentrated natural chemicals within the plant that contain fragrance. Although they are often used simply as perfume as well as in the manufacture of cosmetics, some also have therapeutic value. When applied by massage or in baths, the oils penetrate the skin and quickly enter the bloodstream and lymphatic system. Inhaling the aroma is also believed to affect your emotions and mood.

Types of oils

Essential oils may be held within various parts of the plant, including the flower, leaf, bark, roots and rind. In flowers, the oil is stored in cells on both surfaces of the petals, although the concentration is usually greater on the upper surface. In leaves, the oil is stored in one of three ways:

- deep within the leaf or in capsules that require some pressure to release the oil;
- in cells on or near the surface, to be released when the temperature rises; or
- in glandular hairs on the underside of the leaf.

Obtaining essential oils

Removing essential oils from the plant without losing the fragrance is at the heart of perfume production. Commercially, this may be done by several methods, including extraction, distillation and expression. If you wish to make your own essential oils, you can use a simple home enfleurage process.

I know a bank whereon the wild thyme blows,
Where oxlips and the nodding violet grows
Quite over-canopied with luscious woodbine,
With sweet musk-roses, and with eglantine

A Midsummer Night's Dream, William Shakespeare

Hyacinths.

Each **essential oil** has its own property and can be matched to a purpose. Try clary sage and basil for tiredness; peppermint and ginger for nausea and digestive problems; and sweet marjoram and rose for insomnia.

Buying and storing oils

If you buy essential oils rather than make your own, always read the label beforehand to check where the company sources its ingredients and whether it runs checks for purity. If the oil is labelled as 'aromatherapy oil', it has probably been mixed with a carrier oil such as grapeseed oil. Although this is necessary if you wish to apply the oil to the skin through massage, for example, you should remember that it reduces the life of the oil from years to months.

All essential oils oxidise over time, so look for oils sold in dark-tinted glass bottles and avoid any that have been on display in a hot window, since heat and sunlight accelerate the deterioration process. Keep the bottles firmly sealed, and store them in the fridge.

When blending your own oils, use a glass eye dropper to measure the quantities, and always shake the bottle well before use. Label the bottle, too, and add the date of purchase.

Home enfleurage

To produce small quantities of your own essential oil, follow these steps.

1 Gather the fresh flowers of the plant you wish to use, remove the stalks and place the flowers in a glass jar half-filled with good quality grapeseed or jojoba oil.
2 After 24 hours, remove the flowers, squeeze them (allowing the liquid to run back into the jar), and then discard the flowers.
3 Add some fresh flowers to the jar.
4 Repeat this process until the oil is saturated with perfume.
5 Finally, add an equal quantity of pure (ethyl) alcohol, tightly screw a lid onto the jar and shake daily for 2 weeks.
6 Pour the fragrant alcohol off the olive oil and use it as required.

Clary sage
(*Salvia sclarea*).

Using essential oils

You can use essential oils in many ways around your home. Depending on which fragrance you select, the effect can be stimulating or relaxing.

Massage

Essential oils are highly concentrated and when used on the skin should be diluted in a carrier oil, such as grapeseed or jojoba. Olive oil aids itchy skin but its smell will overwhelm that of the essential oil. For use on the body, for every 50 ml (2 oz) of carrier oil, add 20 drops of essential oil; 10 drops for use on the face; and 5–10 drops for use on children.

Perfume

To preserve the scent of essential oils as perfume, you need to mix them with alcohol in a ratio of about 1:5. A simpler method is to add a few drops to a tissue tucked discreetly into your clothing — it will last for several hours. You can also create a unique fragrance by mixing oils together. Try our recipe for eau de cologne, opposite.

Chamomile flowers and rosemary and sage leaves are useful in hair rinses. Perfumes are also well known for their use of herbs. In Victorian times vanilla pods were rubbed all over the body, and from the 19th century lavender fields in Provence have been harvested for this industry. Rose, boronia and jasmine oils are three other well known plant extracts in the perfume industry.

Lavender, mint, rosemary and marigold are relaxing, while sage and lovage (shown here) are said to stimulate.

Vaporisation

Ceramic burners usually consist of a shallow saucer over a night-light candle. The heat from the candle causes drops of oil (either used alone or in a small quantity of water) to evaporate and scent the air. Or you can place a few drops of oil in a dish of water on a radiator or a sunny windowsill. Try some of these.

- Eucalyptus for its refreshing scent
- Basil for concentration
- Rose for improving your mood
- Lavender for relaxation
- Peppermint for staying alert

According to Dioscorides, the Greeks and Romans used the rhizomes of *Iris germanica* in perfumery.

Eau de cologne

Ingredients

150 ml (6 oz) vodka

60 drops orange essential oil

30 drops bergamot essential oil

30 drops lemon essential oil

6 drops neroli essential oil

6 drops rosemary essential oil

50 ml (2 oz) distilled or boiled water

Method

1 Combine the vodka and oils in a bottle and leave for
a week. Shake daily.

2 Add the water, shake and set aside for 4–6 weeks.

3 Strain through a filter and funnel into a second
sterilised bottle.

Warning

Do not apply undiluted essential oils to the skin. If you have
sensitive skin, use a small amount of oil to check for a reaction.
Never massage areas of the body that have broken skin, rashes,
swollen joints or varicose veins. Anyone with a heart condition
should avoid massage. Pregnant women and people with high
blood pressure or epilepsy should consult a qualified
aromatherapist before using essential oils.

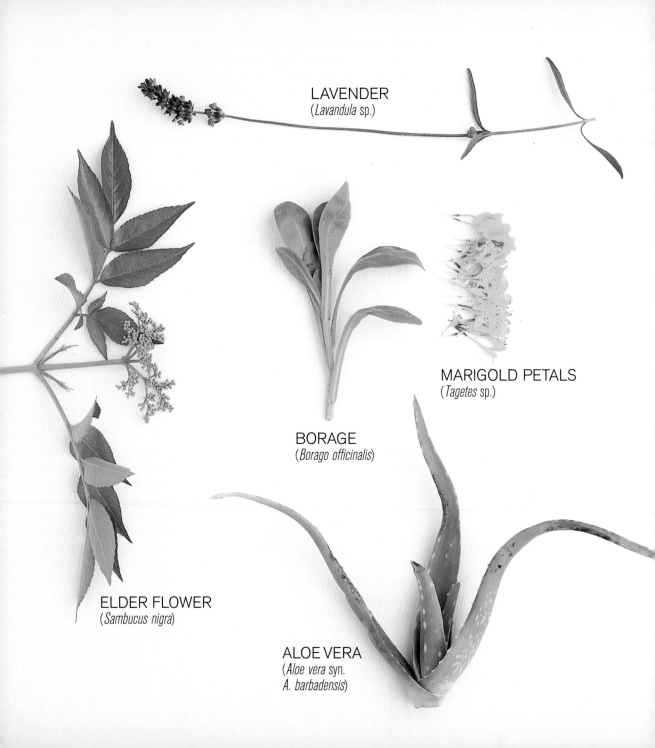

LAVENDER
(*Lavandula* sp.)

MARIGOLD PETALS
(*Tagetes* sp.)

BORAGE
(*Borago officinalis*)

ELDER FLOWER
(*Sambucus nigra*)

ALOE VERA
(*Aloe vera* syn.
A. barbadensis)

LICORICE
PLANT
(*Helichrysum petiolare*)

GOLDEN
FEVERFEW
(*Tanacetum parthenium*
'Aureum')

CHAMOMILE
(*Chamaemelum nobile*
syn. *Anthemis nobilis*)

WILD
STRAWBERRY
(*Fragaria vesca*)

herbs for
cosmetics
Herbs can be used to beautify
our bodies. Some, such as aloe and
wild strawberry fruit, are known for
softening and whitening the skin. Others,
such as borage, are key ingredients in
facials, while fennel seed, feverfew
leaves and calendula flowers make
natural face cleansers.

To refresh sore feet, add 5 drops of peppermint oil to a bowl of cold water. Bathe the feet for 10 minutes.

The flower heads of lavender.

Cosmetic recipes

Ready-made toiletries and cosmetics are welcome conveniences of 21st century life, but home-made ones are luxurious and making them can be fun. If you are sensitive to the ingredients in such preparations, making your own helps you to avoid any known irritants and allergens.

The earliest cosmetics were made at home and housekeeping manuals traditionally included recipes for head to toe care. Some of them contain ingredients we'd have difficulty finding today, but many, including those given, use simple ingredients that are still appealing.

Bath oil

Legend has it that Cleopatra enjoyed bathing in asses' milk. This would be rather difficult to arrange today, and possibly distasteful as well. A simple bathing indulgence, more attuned to our modern senses and circumstances, involves adding drops of essential oil to a hot bath.

After a busy or stressful day, add 5–10 drops of your favourite essential oil to a filled bath, then lie back and relax. Make sure the water is not too hot or the fragrance will be quickly lost.

To relax, try:
- chamomile (*Chamaemelum nobile*)
- jasmine (*Jasminum officinale*)
- valerian (*Valeriana* sp.)
- lavender (*Lavandula angustifolia*)

The fruit-scented, creamy yellow flowers of the lime tree (*Tilia* sp.), shown at left, are the perfect ingredient for a relaxing herbal bath.

Children's bubble bath

The children can help make this as long as a supervising adult deals with the boiling water.

Ingredients

4 tbsp flower petals or heads (eg. rose or lavender)

300 ml (11 fl oz) boiling water

300 ml (11 fl oz) bottle of baby shampoo

12 drops essential oil (eg. lavender)

Method

1 Place the petals in a bowl, cover them with boiling water and leave for 15 minutes.

2 Strain the flower water into a second bowl.

3 Add shampoo and the drops of essential oil.

4 Pour the mixture into plastic bottles.

5 Shake each bottle for several minutes. Store any extra bottles that are not in use in a cool, dark place.

Aromatherapy oils in the bath

Essential oils and aromatherapy oils are sold in an extremely concentrated form. They are ideal bath mates when added drop by drop to running water. But their soothing qualities can turn toxic if too much is used. Never use more than 10 drops of oil in a bath.

For stimulation, use:
- basil (*Ocimum basilicum*)
- bay (*Laurus nobilis*)
- lemon balm (*Melissa officinalis*)
- lemon verbena (*Aloysia triphylla*)
- mint (*Mentha* sp.)
- rosemary (*Rosmarinus officinalis*)
- sage (*Salvia officinalis*)
- thyme (*Thymus vulgaris*)

Bath bags

An aromatic herbal bath can be both pleasurable and therapeutic, especially after a busy day in the garden. Gather a square of muslin into a little bag shape, fill it with flower petals, tie the bag and hang it under the running water as you fill the bath. For example, try a mix of oatmeal and petals of rose, lavender and chamomile. The oatmeal is a gentle cleansing agent. Or experiment with fresh herbs. You can either mix them together or use each one individually.

Chamomile face mask

A very simple face mask can be made from chamomile flowers, honey and bran. It softens the skin and leaves it feeling beautifully smooth and refreshed.

Ingredients
1 tbsp dried chamomile flowers or 3 tbsp fresh ones

1 cup boiling water

1 tsp honey

2 tbsp bran

Method
1 Make an infusion, using dried or fresh chamomile flowers and boiling water. Allow the infusion to stand for about half an hour and then strain.

2 Warm the honey in a pan and mix it with about ⅓ cup of the chamomile water and the bran.

3 Spread it on your face, leave it for about 10 minutes and then wash it off.

Dried chamomile flowers.

When used in a herbal bath, **fennel** (*Foeniculum vulgare*) has a stimulating effect.

Fennel face cleanser

This fresh mixture made from fennel seed, buttermilk and honey is a lovely way to cleanse your face naturally.

Ingredients

1 tbsp fennel seed
1 cup boiling water
2 tbsp buttermilk
1 tsp honey

Method

1 Crush or roughly chop the fennel seed and then pour boiling water over it. Let it stand for about half an hour before straining it into a small bowl.

2 Add the buttermilk and honey to the fennel seed water and mix it all together.

3 Pour the mixture into a completely clean container and refrigerate it until it is cool. Store it in the fridge and use it as needed.

Feverfew moisturiser

This complexion milk acts as a moisturiser and will help to discourage blackheads and fade skin blemishes.

Ingredients

½ cup fresh feverfew leaves
1 cup milk

Method

1 Place the fresh feverfew leaves and milk in a saucepan. Simmer for about 20 minutes and leave it to stand.

2 Strain the liquid into a clean container and refrigerate.

3 Apply it to the skin with cotton balls and let it dry.

4 Rinse off with lukewarm water.

Scented cream

Once open, this cream must be kept refrigerated as it does not contain any preservative.

Ingredients

50 ml (2 oz) unscented base cream (available from chemists)

8 drops essential oil (eg. lavender, chamomile, or a combination)

Method

1 Add the drops of an essential oil to the base cream.

2 Stir well.

Rose water and glycerine hand lotion

Ingredients

150 ml (5 fl oz) rose water

100 ml (3½ fl oz) glycerine

1 drop pink or yellow food colouring

Method

1 Add the rose water and colouring to the glycerine little by little.

2 Mix together with a hand whisk.

Tansy-leaf skin freshener

This easy-to-make skin freshener has a strong tansy fragrance. Splash it onto your skin straight from the fridge.

Ingredients

1 cup fresh tansy leaves

1 cup water

1 cup milk

Method

1 Place all ingredients in a small saucepan and bring to the boil.

2 Simmer for 15 minutes, then leave the mixture to cool.

3 Strain the liquid from the saucepan into a clean container and then refrigerate it.

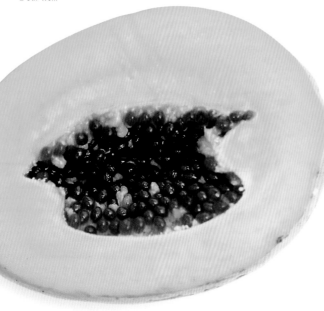

Half a ripe paw paw (*Carica papaya*).

Paw paw mask for oily skin

To use the mask, smooth it over your face and leave it for 15 minutes until it is almost dry. Break the mask up by rubbing your hands all over your face, then rinse with warm water. Finish off with a cold splash.

Ingredients

Half a ripe paw paw (papaya)

1 tbsp fuller's earth

1 tbsp natural yoghurt

1 tbsp orange blossom water

Method

1 Using a wooden spoon, rub the paw paw flesh through a sieve, then add the fuller's earth and yoghurt.

2 Mix thoroughly, before adding the orange blossom water.

Sterilising glass jars

To sterilise a glass jar, place it in a saucepan with enough water to cover. Bring it to the boil, then boil for five minutes. Use tongs to remove the jar. Dry it in a warm oven.

Hair rinse

There are a number of herbs you can use to make fragrant hair rinses. Shampoo your hair first. Chamomile rinses brighten fair hair, rosemary rinses help control greasy hair and also add shine to any hair, and sage rinses darken grey hair. Always use an old towel to dry your hair after using a herb rinse — sage, in particular, will stain the towel.

Ingredients

5 cups water
1 cup chamomile flowers, fresh rosemary tips or sage leaves

Method

1 Place the water and chamomile flowers, fresh rosemary tips or sage leaves in a saucepan and bring the mixture to the boil.
2 Simmer it for 15 minutes and let it cool. The sage rinse should stand for several hours.
3 Strain and bottle it, ready for use.

Some home-made cosmetics (left to right): feverfew cleanser, rosemary hair rinse and some chamomile leaves.

Scents are extraordinarily evocative and can bring to mind memories of childhood, places or people long gone. Their power should never be underestimated. The one element all fragrant plants require is shelter: the more sheltered the position, the stronger the scent will be.

scented herbs

How plants use scent

Everything in nature evolves for a reason and the fragrance in plants is no exception. Scent performs two main functions: it attracts pollinating insects and protects the plant from pests. But why do some plants have a strong fragrance while others have none at all? And why are there so many different fragrances? You can discover the answers to these questions by looking at the life cycle of the plants themselves and also the environment they inhabit — for example, bees are attracted to the colour blue, so some plants that grow in areas colonised by bees produce blue flowers and therefore have no need of scent.

Lemon savory (*Satureja biflora*) is a lemon-scented groundcover that flowers in spring and summer.

Lavandula stoechas.

Protection

Plants can use the essential oils in their leaves and stems to deter attack by pests and browsing animals. For example, ants appear to intensely dislike the scent of mint (*Mentha*) and will avoid it at all costs. Try deterring ants by growing mint near the entrances to your home.

Many highly aromatic plants — herbs, for example — originate in hot, arid areas. In these conditions they protect themselves from drying out by releasing oils that remain in a vapour around the surface of the leaf. The effect is then further enhanced if the leaf is covered with hairs that can trap the vapour.

Pollination

All plants rely on pollination to ensure the continuation of the species, and the majority rely on insects. This allows cross-pollination between individual plants so that genetic

Leaf perfumes

Leaf perfume is subtle compared to that of flowers; however, while a flower's perfume reduces when dried, leaf fragrance is persistent and can increase as the water evaporates, concentrating the essential oils. Some of the same oils are found in both leaves and flowers, so some leaf fragrances conform to flower scent groupings. Apple mint (*Mentha suaveolens*) smells of apples and falls into the fruit-scented group, as does clary sage (*Salvia sclarea*), a hardy biennial with leaves that smell of fresh grapefruit when bruised.

These are the main types of leaf perfume.
• Turpentine group. These plants have a resinous aroma — for example, that of rosemary.
• Camphor and eucalyptus group. Plants in this group — such as sage (*S. officinalis*), chamomile and thyme — have a medicinal scent which clears the nasal passages.
• Mint group. A tangy, fresh scent such as that found in mint.
• Sulphur group. A heavy cloying smell, as in onions and garlic.

Spearmint (*Mentha spicata*).

material is constantly mixed and the plants that result are strong and healthy.

Scent is an important way of attracting insects. The more sheltered the location, the more the plant relies on fragrance to attract insects, since they are less likely to be conveyed on the wind. The most fragrant plants are those that grow in shaded places or flower during the night. Most night-flowering blooms open for a single night and die after fertilisation. The lower temperatures and higher humidity levels of evening and night-time trigger the release of fragrance. The heaviest fragrance occurs in white flowers and those with thick, waxy and velvety petals: thinner petals cannot retain essential oils, so the fragrance is quickly lost. The more pigment or chlorophyll present in the petal, the less oil is produced, so those flowers with little or no colour contain the most oil.

Insects and birds are involved in the pollination process, and each is attracted by a different means. The competition to attract them is fierce and some plants have developed very specific relationships with their pollinating agent. A mutual dependence can evolve so that the life cycles of both the insect or bird and plant are closely connected.

- Bees are primarily attracted by certain colours, particularly blue, and by markings that direct the insect to the centre of the flower. Blue flowers often have very little scent because the colour is sufficient to attract bees.
- Flies are attracted by disgusting smells with no appeal to other insects. Some malodorous herbs that attract flies are stinking Benjamin (*Trillium erectum*), lords-and-ladies (*Arum maculatum*) and bugbane (*Cimicifuga*).
- Many birds appear to be blue/green colour-blind; the flower colours that attract them are crimson and gold. Fragrance has no part to play.
- The few flowers that rely on beetles to pollinate them usually emit a fruity scent, such as lemon balm (*Melissa officinalis*).

Butterflies are especially attracted to shrubs with a sweet scent such as lavender (*Lavandula*), lilac (*Syringa*) and butterfly bush (*Buddleia*), and to herbaceous perennials such as pinks (*Dianthus* sp.). Here, a monarch butterfly (*Danaus plexippus*) is pollinating a *Buddleia*.

Potted kumquats, underplanted with lobelia, punctuate alternating clumps of lavender and violas along this path.

Bergamot (*Monarda* sp.)

Native to North America, bergamot replaced Indian tea in many American households following the Boston Tea Party of 1773. The common name, bergamot, comes from an Italian word because the crushed leaf resembles the small bitter Italian orange that is used in aromatherapy, perfumes and cosmetics. Native Americans used bergamot for colds.

Making the most of fragrance

With some careful planning, you can enjoy scented herbs both day and night in key areas of your garden. Here are some ideas.

Paths

Whether they lead to utility areas, such as the compost bin or the garden shed, or are designed to meander through different areas of planting so you can enjoy your garden to the full, paths are an essential part of the garden. Even the dullest looking path can be enlivened with careful planting. Use an edging of fragrant, low-growing plants that can be clipped back if they start to encroach too much on the path itself. Some aromatic herbs suitable for spilling out onto paths are thyme (*Thymus*), chamomile (*Chamaemelum*), lavender, marjoram (*Origanum majorana*) and lemon balm. These herbs release fragrance when they are bruised.

Outdoor entertaining area

If you regularly cook outdoors on a barbecue, plant a range of fragrant and delicious herbs nearby. In the heat of the day these herbs will smell wonderful as they release their essential oils into the air, and they will always be ready for you to use. If you plant a herb like mint, which repels ants, then you'll have a dual-purpose herb garden.

Typical summer herbs are dill, basil, mint, oregano and parsley; spring herbs are chives, sorrel and chervil; and typical winter herbs are sage, rosemary and thyme.

Scent at night

Some plants are scented only in the evening so that they can attract night-flying insects, such as moths. For instance, evening primrose (*Oenothera*), mignonette (*Reseda*) and sweet rocket (*Hesperis*) all smell delightful in the evening. Plant them near open windows and doors, and near an outdoor sitting area.

Special features

If you have a special feature or focal point in your garden, such as a statue or water feature, you could experiment with planting fragrant plants in order to build up the intensity of the aroma or fragrance as you approach the feature. Try not to overdo it, though: an overpowering fragrance can make it unpleasant to linger in one spot; the idea is to enhance, not compromise, your garden feature.

Choose plants whose fragrance you most enjoy, but ensure that they are suitable for the situation. For instance, try some strikingly beautiful waterlilies (*Nymphaea* sp.) — see pages 29–31 for more information — or the pretty cinnamon-scented sweet flag (*Acorus calamus*) around a water feature.

A fragrant lawn

Low-growing, matting plants such as thyme release their fragrance when crushed underfoot, and provide an unusual cover for many situations. Here are some ideas.

- A path of pennyroyal
- Carpeting patches of thyme between stepping stones
- Corsican mint as a groundcover in a fernery
- A herbal carpet in an area too small for a lawnmower

In China, **waterlilies** are traditionally grown in large glazed pots, raised on plinths in the middle of a courtyard, allowing them to be admired without any distractions.

Planting a herb carpet

1 Position your chosen herbs until you are happy with the result, then dig a hole for each herb and plant it. Backfill.

2 Finish with pebble mulch and water in.

3 Granite setts provide an attractive foil for the carpeting herbs.

- A spectacular carpet of thyme on a sunny bank (there are many types to choose from: creeping thyme comes in pink, crimson and white-flowered varieties, and there are also golden, orange-peel scented and variegated leaf types)
- A fragrant chamomile footrest beneath the garden seat

Choose herbs that grow from stolons or runners so that they can cover any bare patch that may develop. The mint family will grow in areas with poor drainage or dappled shade, otherwise most herbs like good drainage and plenty of sun.

The carpeting thymes were favourites of Edna Walling, the garden designer. *Thymus carnosus* has tiny aromatic leaves. It is slow growing and very compact, with pure white flowers in summer. 'Pink Chintz' was another of Walling's favourites. *Thymus* x *citriodorus* 'Silver Queen' has silver-white foliage and 'Aureus' has tiny golden yellow leaves. All carpeting thymes are deliciously fragrant when crushed.

Consider growing a lawn of thyme — imagine stretching out on a herb lawn, with the crushed leaves releasing their subtle perfume as you relax. Or try one of these:

- *Chamaemelum nobile*
- *Chamaemelum nobile* 'Treneague'
- *Mentha arvensis*
- *Mentha pulegium*
- *Mentha requienii*
- *Thymus praecox*
- *Thymus pseudolanuginosus*
- *Vinca minor*

Fragrant hedges

A garden hedge is more than just a boundary to a property, keeping out unwanted animals and people, and providing privacy. A hedge can also be used as the 'skeleton' of your landscape, helping to create garden rooms for you to decorate, conceal utility areas and unsightly views, and act as a windbreak.

Whether you are planting a low hedge for edging a path or a tall one to act as a privacy screen and property boundary, you can add another dimension to your living fence by choosing fragrant plants. Lavender, for instance, has a bushy habit that makes it ideal for growing as a fragrant hedge in an informal garden. However, it doesn't respond well to excessive pruning, making it unsuitable for a formal hedge. Some alternatives to lavender are rosemary, cotton lavender and salvia, which also make good low, informal hedges.

Pruning a hedge

If you are growing a hedge for its aromatic leaves, you can prune it regularly to maintain the shape without affecting the production of fragrance. If you have selected a particular hedging plant because of its flowers, however, the timing is critical: the buds and flowers should not be removed before their best display.

This low-growing hedge surrounding a small lawn combines rosemary and cotton lavender.

The flower of the bog sage (*Salvia uliginosa*).

The Lamiaceae family

Also called Labiatae, this family of mainly annual or perennial herbs and the odd shrub is characterised by aromatic foliage, square stems and flowers with a tongue-like appearance; the 'tongue' acts as an insect landing pad. It comprises about 200 genera (including *Salvia*, *Thymus* and *Lavandula*) and 3200 species. It is an economically important family, as many of these plants contain essential oils for cooking, perfumery and medicines. The mint family can be found worldwide: mint in Europe and Africa; basil in Asia, the Pacific Islands and the Middle East; and *Westringia* sp. in Australia.

Success with a herb lawn

1 To prepare a herb lawn, first remove all weeds from the site, then use a product containing glyphosate to poison any that have bulbs so they won't reappear.
2 Plant your herb lawn in a well drained soil that is rich in humus, or dig in plenty of compost or manure.
3 Rake the soil to a level finish and plant herbs 20 cm (8 in) apart.
4 Water well and refrain from walking on the lawn for about one month or until the plants are established.
5 Weed regularly and plant any bare patches with rooted pieces from well grown plants.

Hedges require regular trimming to keep them looking good. Start trimming from the bottom so that the clippings fall clear. A hedge should be wider at the base than at the top. This allows vital light to reach all parts. Hedge trimmers and shears give more control, especially if you want a particular shape. Don't use a mechanical pruner on large-leafed plants as it damages the leaves.

If your hedge has grown out of control, check that your particular type of shrub will reshoot after pruning. Start by cutting the top of the hedge first, then one side. Wait until that side has greened up before you prune the other side.

Remember to feed your hedge and mulch it to keep it looking good for years to come.

Lavender hedges were once used as clotheslines: laundered items were placed on the bushes to dry, and in the process they became impregnated with lavender oil.

How to plant a hedge

1 For a really straight hedge, mark out the run with a string line. Dig a trench at least 60 cm (2 ft) wide and 45 cm (18 in) deep.
2 Incorporate lots of well rotted manure or compost. Fill in the trench. This will create a small mound.
3 Using a measuring stick, space out all the plants. Dig a hole for each plant, add some slow-release fertiliser and water crystals, and plant, ensuring that the soil is not built up around the trunks.
4 Tip prune all new shoots to encourage branching. Do this for the first few seasons so that you develop a well branched hedge that is thick to the base.
5 Trim to shape. Secateurs allow precise cutting and are suitable for pruning all informal hedges. They are ideal for the initial shaping of young plants. For larger plants in an informal hedge, use shears: they produce the best shape and leave the foliage unmarked. They can also be used on formal hedges for a perfect, but time-consuming cut, or you can use electric hedge trimmers in slow, even cuts.

Geum sp.

Fragrant roots

Several herbs have fragrant roots, although the scent is not detectable unless you dig up the plant. Blessed herb (*Geum urbanum*) is a herbaceous perennial with short, thick rhizomatous roots that smell of cloves when dried. Chocolate root (*Geum rivale*) is moisture loving with thick, rhizomatous roots smelling of chocolate. Sweet flag (*Acorus calamus*) produces a camphor-like smell and was once used as a strewing herb for floors.

To get the best effect from a **fragrant hedge,** grow it in a formal design, keeping it quite closely clipped to the desired height and outline. Trim the plants at least once a year, or more often for the more vigorous herb varieties.

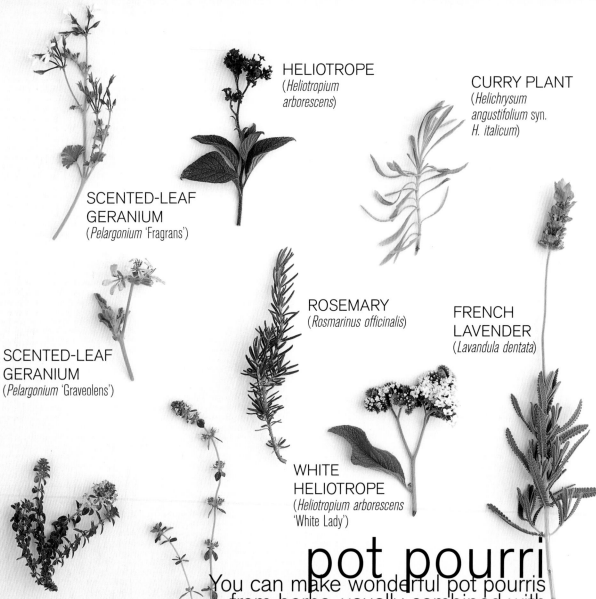

HELIOTROPE
(*Heliotropium arborescens*)

CURRY PLANT
(*Helichrysum angustifolium* syn. *H. italicum*)

SCENTED-LEAF
GERANIUM
(*Pelargonium* 'Fragrans')

ROSEMARY
(*Rosmarinus officinalis*)

FRENCH
LAVENDER
(*Lavandula dentata*)

SCENTED-LEAF
GERANIUM
(*Pelargonium* 'Graveolens')

WHITE
HELIOTROPE
(*Heliotropium arborescens* 'White Lady')

PINK CREEPING
THYME
(*Thymus serpyllum* 'Pink Chintz')

PINK
THYME
(*Thymus x citriodorus*)

pot pourri

You can make wonderful pot pourris from herbs, usually combined with rose petals or geranium leaves. With so many herbs to choose from, you can customise a pot pourri for any part of your home. For example,

FLORAL AND HERB
POT POURRI

CITRUS-SCENTED
POT POURRI

LAVENDER
AND HERB
POT POURRI

you could have a
warm mixture in the
hallway or a sweeter bedroom bouquet.
Herbs such as lavender, violet, rosemary,
basil, mint, sage, thyme, cinnamon, clove,
juniper and star anise are all favourites.

Pot pourri recipes

Here are some recipes to get you started. Once you've mastered the basic principles, try out different combinations, depending on what you grow in your own garden.

Dry pot pourri

Use dried flowers, leaves, berries, spices, peel or bark to make dry pot pourri mixtures. You'll need a fixative to preserve the blend. Fixatives are available as powders and are often perfumed, which you should take into account when choosing your ingredients. The most common fixative is orris root, which has a violet scent. Use it in a ratio of about 15 ml (1 tbsp) of orris root to every 250 ml (1 cup) of plant material. Essential oils are ideal for refreshing pot pourri but add only a few drops at a time or the fragrance will be overpowering. You can purchase fixatives and essential oils from health food shops, some Asian supermarkets and some craft shops.

Herb and lavender pot pourri

Ingredients

1 cup lavender flowers (*Lavandula angustifolia*)

½ cup dried spearmint (*Mentha spicata*)

½ cup dried marjoram (*Origanum majorana*)

½ cup dried oregano flowers (*Origanum vulgare*)

2 tbsp powdered orris root

2 tsp lavender essential oil

Method

1 Mix the ingredients together well, then place the mixture in a plastic bag for 2 weeks to mature.

2 Shake it regularly.

3 Transfer it to an ornamental bowl.

Experiment with different materials. If you don't like sweet fragrances, a citrus pot pourri may appeal to you.

Floral and herb pot pourri

Ingredients

½ cup rose petals

¼ cup violets

½ cup marigold flowers

½ cup lavender

¼ cup cornflowers

¼ cup sweet mixed herbs

1 tbsp orris root powder

2 tsp cinnamon powder

5 drops rose oil

3 drops lavender oil

2 drops lemon oil

Method

1 Place the dried flowers and herbs in a bowl and gently mix them together with a wooden spoon, being careful not to break the flower petals.

2 Place the orris root and cinnamon in another bowl and, using an eyedropper, add the essential oils. Mix everything together thoroughly.

3 Add the orris root and cinnamon mixture to the dried materials and stir with a wooden spoon.

4 Place in a brown paper bag, fold over the top and fasten with a clothes peg. Store in a cool, dark place for 2–4 weeks, shaking the bag gently every few days to blend the ingredients. It should then be ready for use.

Lemon-scented pot pourri

This recipe uses oakmoss as the fixative.

Ingredients

4 cups lemon verbena leaves

1 cup lemon-scented geranium leaves

½ cup basil

½ cup lemon thyme

½ cup dried lemon peel (freshly ground)

½ cup dried orange peel (freshly ground)

½ cup caraway seed

1 cup oakmoss

2 drops lemon verbena oil

2 drops bergamot oil

Method

Mix the leaves together. Mix the peel with the caraway seed. Tear oakmoss into small pieces, place in a bowl and add essential oils. Rub the oil through the oakmoss, then mix thoroughly with the leaves, peel and seeds. Place in an airtight container for about a month, stirring occasionally. It will then be ready for use.

For thousands of years, herbs have been used in households as fabric dyes, insect repellents and air fresheners, even furniture polishes and general cleaners. Try out some of these safe, non-toxic recipes using herbs from your own garden.

herbs for household use

Dogbane (*Plectranthus ornatus* syn. *Coleus cannis*) has succulent leaves with a rather unpleasant smell, which is said to repel dogs.

Fabric dyes

Before synthetic dyes were developed in the 19th century, dyes were made from plants, animals, insects and minerals. For instance, red fabrics from Tutankhamen's tomb that have been chemically analysed show the presence of alizarin, a pigment extracted from madder (*Rubia tinctorum*). The plants were dug up, and the roots were washed and dried before being ground into a powder. By the 19th century the most widely available fabrics were dyed madder, known as 'turkey red'. Madder was used until the late 19th century when synthetic dyes were developed.

Dandelion (*Taraxacum officinale*).

By the fourth century AD, other plant dyes — such as woad, weld and indigo — were in use. Purple dye was once extracted from a Mediterranean mollusc called a purple fish (*Murex*), found near Tyre in Phoenicia in the Mediterranean. This dye was so expensive only royalty could afford it, hence the association of purple robes with kings and queens.

Until the Middle Ages, woad (*Isatis tinctoria*) was used in Europe to dye fabric blue. The leaves were dried and ground, then mixed with water to make a paste. By the 1630s, woad was replaced by indigo; the leaves were fermented and the sediment purified. The material remaining was made into chunks or 'cakes'. Indigo was a popular dye because it was colour fast to both washing and light, and being a substantive dye, it did not need a mordant to fix the colour. The manufacture of indigo lasted until the early 1900s: in 1905 the scientist who developed aspirin, Adolf von Baeyer, won the Nobel prize for developing a process which produced indigo synthetically.

If you want to experiment with dyes using herbs from your own garden, try some of these ideas.

- Pink: strawberries, raspberries, cherries
- Green: spinach leaves, grass
- Red: dandelion root, beets, rose hips, red onion skins, madder
- Blue/purple: red cabbage, elderberries, blueberries, cherry roots
- Yellow: onion skins, marigold blossoms, celery leaves
- Brown: sumac leaves, walnut hulls, tea, juniper berries, coffee grinds

The Romans prized saffron highly and used it in cooking, dyeing and in oils. Saffron is the dried stigma of the autumn crocus (*Crocus sativus*), which flowers only in hot, dry weather. It is expensive, as more than 70 000 blooms are needed to produce just 500 g (1 lb) of saffron. The Romans liked to show off their wealth by strewing saffron on the floors of their villas.

The autumn crocus (*Crocus sativus*). Each flower has three red stigmas.

Air fresheners

These days flowers and aromatic herbs are popular in pot pourris and linen sachets, but they were once used as 'strewing' herbs. The Koran mentions that the floor of the Garden of Paradise is covered with wheaten flour mixed with musk and saffron. In medieval Europe, the packed earth floors and small windows of the times meant that buildings and churches smelled musty, so fragrant seasonal flowers, herbs and sweet-smelling grasses and rushes were strewn on the pews and floors. Herbs were particularly useful for strewing as they released a fragrance when someone walked on them. Thyme repelled unpleasant odours, and wormwood deterred fleas. So important was this aspect of domestic life that royal households had an official 'Strewer of Herbs'.

The scented rush (*Acorus calamus*) had many uses in addition to strewing: it also yielded a volatile oil from the leaves, and the root could be used to flavour beer and wine, or could be dried and powdered for use as talcum powder.

Other plants were used only for their repellent qualities. Dried tansy flowers were sprinkled on pantry shelves to deter flies. Green rushes strewn on the floors could attract fleas and other insects so it was customary to burn repellents such as fleabane to avoid infestation.

Boil 8 cloves in 2 cups of water for a few minutes to rid the kitchen of an offensive cooking smell.

dyeing herbs

Using natural plant dyes is an art. The delight of harvesting berries and leaves, and mashing, chopping and boiling like an alchemist can only be understood once you've experienced it,

SORREL
(*Rumex scutatus*)

ELDERBERRY
(*Sambucus nigra*)

JUNIPER
BERRIES
(*Juniperus* sp.)

COMFREY
(*Symphytum officinale*)

and the satisfaction of watching these concoctions turn fabric into colour swatches is well worth the time.

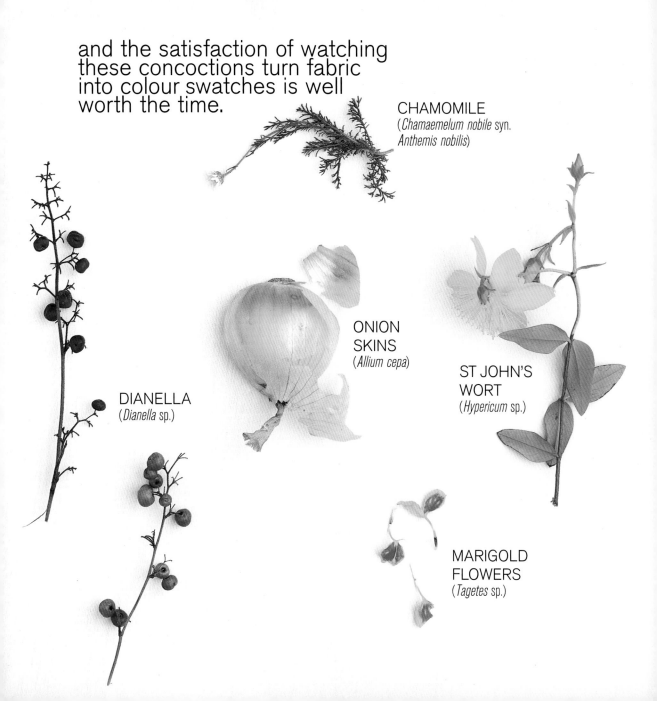

CHAMOMILE
(*Chamaemelum nobile* syn. *Anthemis nobilis*)

ONION SKINS
(*Allium cepa*)

ST JOHN'S WORT
(*Hypericum* sp.)

DIANELLA
(*Dianella* sp.)

MARIGOLD FLOWERS
(*Tagetes* sp.)

Pomanders were another popular device for warding off disease, and Elizabethan pomanders consisted of an apple, orange or lemon stuck with cloves and then dried, or a container with a sponge soaked in scented vinegar. Later, silver pomanders were made, based on the orange, with filigree segments hinged at the base and held by a clasp at the top, each of which could hold a separate perfume.

Scented sachets

Fragrant sachets in drawers and wardrobes not only make your clothes smell fresh, but they also help deter moths and silverfish. Here are some suggestions that are quick and easy to make.

- To add a fresh smell to your wardrobe or chest of drawers, take a couple of teaspoons of pot pourri or dried lavender, place it in a piece of lightweight fabric, such as muslin or cheesecloth, and tie it with a ribbon.
- Or fill light sachets with mixtures of ground cloves, nutmeg, mace, caraway seeds, cinnamon (30 g or 1 oz each) and orris root powder (90 g or 3¼ oz).

Pomander

Ingredients
Firm-skinned orange
Fresh cloves
1 tsp orris root powder
1 tsp ground cinnamon

Method
1 Wash and dry a firm-skinned orange and stud it evenly all over with fresh cloves.
2 Place the orris root powder and the cinnamon in a brown paper bag with the orange, and shake the bag to coat the orange.
3 Store the bag in a dark place for a month, then remove the orange and brush it free of powder.
4 Tie a ribbon around the orange and finish with a loop at the top.

A pomander could also be used to disguise unpleasant smells, from overpowering body odours to streets with open sewage drains.

Other herbal moth deterrents include sachets of cedar chips, dried rosemary or southernwood (*Artemisia abrotanum*), shown here. Place these among your clothes. If these cause irritation you may need to store vulnerable clothing in sealed plastic bags.

Lavender bag

The essential oil of lavender kills germs and provides fragrance. Put lavender sachets or bags in a drawer to prevent the contents from becoming musty. This lavender bag will retain its scent longer if you keep the stalks on.

Ingredients

Lavender in full bloom

Newspaper

Muslin or fine cotton

Ribbon

Method

1 Cut the lavender and spread the stems out to dry on newspaper, either in the sun or in another warm place.

2 Cut fabric, such as muslin or fine cotton, to the size and shape required for a bag.

3 When the lavender is dry, insert a bunch into the bag so that the stems stick out of the opening.

4 Close the opening with hand stitching or a length of ribbon.

5 Trim stalks to a length of 4 cm (1½ in).

Moth sachet

A sachet filled with this mixture will repel moths for up to a year. Make several and tuck them among your woollen clothes and stored blankets.

Ingredients

1 cup rosemary

1 cup tansy

1 cup thyme

1 cup mint

1 cup southernwood

½ cup cloves (freshly ground)

½ cup dried lemon peel (freshly ground)

Method

Crumble all the herbs together and mix with the cloves and lemon peel. Spoon the mixture into sachets and tie with a ribbon.

Rue

A sturdy evergreen herb with blue metallic, feathery leaves, rue is useful as a disinfectant and as an insecticide. In medieval Europe, rue (*Ruta graveolens*) was used in the sickroom to drive away disease-carrying insects. Plant it by doors and windows to repel mosquitoes, flies and other insects, and rub it over pets to help reduce fleas.

Herb pillow

Some herbs are thought to promote peaceful sleep and sweet dreams, and so a pillow filled with sleep-inducing herbs can be a practical addition to your bedroom. Place the mixture in a muslin sachet and tuck it into the pillowcase with your usual pillow.

Ingredients

1 cup dried rosemary

1 cup dried lavender

1 cup dried lemon verbena

1 cup dried lemon thyme

3 cups dried scented geranium leaves

Method

Mix the materials together in a large bowl. If you like, add a preservative such as orris root and a drop or two of essential oil (follow the recipes for pot pourri on pages 180–1).

Rose-scented geranium leaves add a sweet perfume to a pot pourri mixture.

Herbal insecticides

Use herbs to make environmentally friendly insecticides.

Pyrethrum

Many insecticides are now synthesised forms of pyrethrum. To make your own spray, follow these steps. Use the mixture as needed as a contact spray for aphids and other sapsuckers. Other foul-tasting concoctions can be made from chilli, garlic, wormwood and quassia chips.

1 Finely chop the flowers and leaves of the pyrethrum daisy.
2 Immerse them in water overnight.
3 Strain the water through a muslin cloth and store it in a
  container. Spray it on plants as required.

All-purpose insecticide

You can make an all-purpose insecticide for spraying any plants plagued by caterpillars, aphids or flea beetles.

1 Combine equal quantities of mint,
  chopped onion, garlic, and lavender tops
  and stems in enough water to cover.
2 Leave the mixture for 24 hours, then
  strain it.

Place fly-repellent plants at doorways and on verandahs. These include lavender, sweet woodruff, lemon verbena, mint, thyme, rosemary, bay, chamomile and basil.

Chilli and soap spray

1 Gather the ingredients and materials you'll need: chillies, soap, grater, sharp knife and chopping board. You'll also need a spray bottle and some water.

2 Grate some soap (or use pure soap flakes instead). Add soap flakes to a spray bottle that is nearly full of water.

3 Chop about 8 chillies. Add the chillies to the bottle and screw the lid back on. Shake the contents vigorously and spray your home-made insecticide onto any plant.

Chive tea

Make your own chive 'tea' for treating mildew on plants.

1 Harvest a generous amount of chives from your vegetable garden, or buy some. Roughly chop the chives.

2 Add the chives to a watering can. Cover with boiling water and steep for at least 1 hour before using.

Warning: wash your hands thoroughly after handling chillies.

Chilli tea

For a spicy insecticide or as a deterrent to rabbits and other animals, use a food blender to purée 20 or so chillies to form a paste. Mix the paste with water, then leave it to stand so the pulp can settle. Use the strained 'tea' as a spray on a still day so that it won't blow into your eyes.

Garlic spray

Use this garlic spray for aphids, mites and small caterpillars. Garlic also provides some fungicide protection.

Ingredients

12–15 chopped garlic bulbs

2 tbsp mineral oil

7 g (¼ oz) soap

600 ml (21 fl oz) water

Method

1 Soak the chopped garlic in mineral oil for 24 hours.

2 Dissolve the soap in the water and slowly add it to the garlic mixture.

3 Strain the mixture through fine gauze, before storing it in a china or glass container.

4 Dilute it before using – 1 part soap and garlic mixture to 50 parts water.

To remove the smell of **onions** from your hands, rub them well with celery or parsley.

To deter flies from colonising your garbage bin, wipe around the top of each bin with citronella or tea tree oil. Alternatively, soak strips of old sheet in a repellent solution made from 10 drops of citronella oil and 3 drops of peppermint oil mixed in 4 cups of water. Hang the strips inside the bin.

Cleaning preparations

Essential oils are used in cleaning preparations for both their fragrance and their disinfecting qualities.

Basic household soap cleaner

Use this versatile cleaner in the following ways.

- Laundry detergent. Suitable for machine washing or hand washing, for front loaders and top loaders. Use about 2 cups per load.
- Prewash. Soak heavily soiled items in a solution before washing.
- Washing up liquid. Make up a solution of 1 teaspoon to 5 L (9 pints) of water.
- Dishwasher detergent. Use 1 cup per load. (*Note:* It doesn't remove tea and coffee stains.)
- Carpet or upholstery stain-removing foam. Add 1 cup of hot water. When cool, beat to a light foam and spoon over the stain. Leave it for ten minutes then wipe with a sponge dipped in white vinegar.

Ingredients

100 g (3½ oz) pure soap

1 cup washing soda crystals

1 cup white vinegar

3 tsp eucalyptus oil or tea tree oil

Few drops lemon or lavender pure essential oil for fragrance

10 L (18 pt) cold water

9 L (16 pt) hot water

Method

Grate the soap into a large saucepan and cover with 2 L (3½ pt) of cold water. Bring to the boil, add washing soda and stir until completely dissolved. Stir in eucalyptus oil, vinegar and essential oil. Pour into a bucket, add the hot water then stir in the cold water. When cool, transfer to smaller containers and label.

Diluted **tea tree oil** keeps the toilet brush and bowl germ-free.

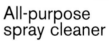

All-purpose spray cleaner

This all-purpose cleaner is suitable for the kitchen and bathroom.

Ingredients

4 L (7 pt) hot water

2 tbsp cloudy ammonia

½ cup white vinegar

2 tbsp baking soda

2 drops lavender or lemon oil

2 tbsp basic household soap cleaner

Method

In a bucket, mix all the ingredients into the water. Cool, then fill spray bottles.

Grow your own herbs and use them fresh or dried — in cooking, pot pourris, cosmetics, HERB perfumes and home remedies. They are a joy to grow: generally, they love sunshine and don't need much watering; indeed the flavour is richest if they aren't encouraged

DIRECTORY

to grow too lushly. Give them good, well drained soil' and some fertiliser occasionally.

Achillea millefolium
YARROW
ASTERACEAE/COMPOSITAE

CONDITIONS
Climate. Best grown in cool climates where winters are always frosty but grows reasonably well in warmer areas. It is not suitable for the tropics.

Aspect. Full sun is essential. This vigorous grower is well suited to growing in rockeries or on banks.

Soil. Well drained, not-too-rich soil is ideal. Plants will rot if the soil stays wet for long periods after rain or watering.

FEATURES
Yarrow is a low, mat-forming perennial that has dense, dark green, fern-like foliage. Flat heads of small flowers appear on top of tall, mostly leafless stems during the later summer months and in autumn. They may be white, pink or yellow.

GROWING METHOD
Planting. Propagate by dividing the roots of mature plants in early spring or autumn, or by sowing seed in spring in trays or punnets of moist seed-raising mix. Barely cover the seed and place the containers in a warm, bright but shaded spot until germination is complete. Gradually expose containers to more and more sun, then transplant seedlings into their final site when they are big enough to handle.

Watering. Water deeply but occasionally; yarrow has deep roots that will find water at lower levels in the soil.

Fertilising. No fertilising is necessary.

Problems. No particular problems.

Pruning. Cut plants to the ground in middle to late autumn or after frosts have started. New growth will appear in spring.

HARVESTING
Picking. Harvest leafy stems and flowers on a dry morning when plants are in the early stages of full bloom. Tie them together and hang upside down in a dry, dim, airy place. If they are intended for dried arrangements, hang each flower separately.

Storage. When the stems are dry, remove the flowers and leaves from their stems, crumble the leaves and break up all the stems into small pieces. Mix stems, leaves and flowers together and store the mixture in airtight jars.

Freezing. Not suitable for freezing.

USES
Culinary. Young, small leaves have a slight, pleasantly bitter flavour. Add a few chopped young leaves to salads or sandwiches.

Medicinal. Herbal tea made from the dried stems, leaves and flowers is a good general pick-me-up, blood cleanser, tonic for the kidneys and, reputedly, a slimming aid.

Gardening. Yarrow is a good choice for informal or meadow-style plantings, or for planting on dry, infertile banks where other flowers are difficult to grow. It has the slightly unkempt look of a wildflower.

FEATURES

Garlic grows from a bulb that consists of several segments, the strongly aromatic cloves that have led to its widespread culinary use. This perennial plant also has a long list of medicinal uses. Its erect, grey-green leaves stand about 60 cm (2 ft) tall. Nondescript white flowers appear in summer, then the plant dies back for its winter dormancy.

GROWING METHOD

Planting. In mid-autumn or early spring, break cloves from a fresh head of garlic. Push into soil that is well dug over and crumbly so that the pointy end is 1–2 cm (less than 1 in) below the surface. Space cloves about 20 cm (8 in) apart, cover with soil and water in well. Mulch lightly with compost, rotted manure or rotted grass clippings.

Watering. Newly planted garlic needs moisture for its developing roots but does not want to be sodden during autumn and winter. If rain does not fall, water deeply once a week. Gradually reduce watering as the weather warms up in spring as garlic needs a hot, dry summer to mature the bulbs.

Fertilising. Apply complete plant food at planting time.

Problems. Aphids may cluster on leaves and flower buds but are easily rubbed off by hand. Bad drainage or overwatering causes bulbs to rot.

HARVESTING

Picking. Harvest garlic in autumn or summer if the leaves have yellowed. Don't cut the dead leaves off – use them to plait the bulbs together for storage. After harvest, wash the bulbs clean and then leave them in the sun for a few days to dry.

Storage. Dried bulbs may be strung together and hung in a dry, airy place for use as needed.

Freezing. Not suitable for freezing.

USES

Culinary. Garlic has hundreds of uses in virtually every type of cuisine. It is an essential ingredient in many European and Asian dishes, and it is used in vinegars and herb butters. The chopped leaves can be lightly stir-fried.

Medicinal. Garlic has antibiotic and antiseptic properties; it is useful in lowering blood pressure and cholesterol, and is said to have beneficial effects on the immune system. Regular intake of garlic reduces susceptibility to colds and improves the digestive system. A sliced clove rubbed over a cut will clean and sterilise the wound.

Gardening. Garlic is often planted under roses to help deter aphids and other rose pests.

Allium sativum
GARLIC
LILIACEAE

CONDITIONS

Climate. Grows well in a wide range of climates, but dislikes the high summer heat, humidity and rainfall of the tropics, where it can be grown in deep pots of sandy potting mix if sheltered from constant rain.

Aspect. Full sun is essential.

Soil. Good drainage is also essential but garlic grows in any crumbly, reasonably fertile soil. Dark, sandy loam with rotted organic matter and 1 cup of lime per square metre (square yard) is ideal.

Allium schoenoprasum, A. tuberosum
CHIVES
LILIACEAE

CONDITIONS

Climate. Chives are very adaptable and can withstand extremes of high and low temperatures. They are frost hardy.

Aspect. Grow best in full sun but tolerate partial shade. In very hot, dry climates they may require a little shade and humidity.

Soil. Prepare beds well with organic matter such as compost and blood and bone fertiliser. Good drainage is essential. If growing chives indoors, use potting mix and fertiliser.

FEATURES

Chives are perennial herbs that make an attractive edging for a herb garden or bed of mixed annuals and perennials. They grow in clumps from very small bulbs that send up 30 cm (12 in) tall grass-like, hollow, tubular, green leaves, tapering to a point at the top. The flowers of the common chive (*A. schoenoprasum*) take the form of a dense, globular head of pinkish to pale purple blossoms. Chinese or garlic chives (*A. tuberosum*) have a flower head composed of star-like, white flowers and flat, narrow, light to dark green leaves.

GROWING METHOD

Planting. Sow seeds directly into the garden during spring. Prepare drill holes and plant about ten seeds together as a clump, 1 cm (½ in) deep. Firm the soil over and water. Keep the soil moist throughout the germination period of 2–3 weeks. Thin out so that the clumps are about 20 cm (8 in) apart. Alternatively, young plants can be raised in seed beds and transplanted into the garden when one month old, again in clumps of ten, 20 cm (8 in) apart. If planting clumps in rows, space the rows 30–60 cm (1–2 ft) apart to allow inter-row cultivation. Bulbs can also be lifted and divided in autumn or spring every two years once the plant is established.

Watering. Water well, especially during hot months.

Fertilising. At planting time, dig in complete plant food. Apply liquid or soluble fertiliser every four weeks.

Problems. Generally free of diseases but watch for aphids in hot weather. Treat with the appropriate spray.

HARVESTING

Picking. Chives are ready to crop when they reach about 15 cm (6 in) high during summer and autumn (autumn to spring in tropical areas). Do not snip off just the tips or the chive will become tough and fibrous. Clip the leaves or blades close to the ground, leaving about 5 cm (2 in) still intact. Harvest chives regularly to keep the crop growing.

Storage. Chives do not store very well.

Freezing. Chives can be frozen for about six months. Chop them, wrap them in small packages with plastic wrap, and then freeze them for use when needed.

USES

Culinary. Leaves of the chive *A. schoenoprasum* have a delicate onion flavour. Add them to soups or casseroles during the last moments of cooking. Use the chopped leaves in salads, as a garnish and in the French *fines herbes*. The flowers can be eaten fresh in salads or made into delicious herb vinegars or butters. All parts of the Chinese chive (*A. tuberosum*) have a mild garlic flavour and the unopened flower bud has a special place in Asian cuisines.

Gardening. Recommended companions for roses, carrots, grapes, tomatoes and fruit trees.

FEATURES

A bitter-juiced, succulent perennial, aloe vera grows to about 60 cm (2 ft) high and wide in the open garden but is much smaller in containers where growth is restricted. A strong, fibrous rooting system supports a single, sturdy stem. The fleshy, pale green leaves with paler blotches have spiny, toothed edges. The bell-shaped flowers are borne on long branches in summer, while the capsule-like fruit are triangular and contain many seeds.

GROWING METHOD

Planting. Can be grown from seed or by division of the parent plant. New shoots must be 'pruned' or leaves will turn bright green and grow horizontally rather than vertically. When new shoots are 10 cm (4 in) tall, break them off from the parent and repot in soil made up from equal parts of coarse river sand, garden loam and decayed garden compost or cow manure. Water well, then leave for three weeks to form a network of water-seeking roots.

Watering. Allow the plant to become fairly dry in between waterings; water only very lightly during winter, more often during the growing period when the leaves begin to thicken.

Fertilising. Excessive fertilising may slow growth.

Problems. Almost non-existent, but watch out for root rot in wet soils.

Pruning. Aloe vera grows from the centre. Cut older, outside leaves to keep the plant in balance and in shape. These leaves do not grow back once cut.

HARVESTING

Picking. Harvest leaves as required but always cut larger, lower leaves first as they have more juice. This also promotes new growth from the centre. Trim the thorny edges of the leaves and split the leaf across its width to extract the gooey gel. As the gel ceases to flow, scratch the exposed leaf and continue to do so until only the green leaf skin is left.

Storage. Wrap whole or partially used leaves in foil and store them in the fridge for several days, or bottle the extracted juice.

Freezing. Can be frozen for six months.

USES

Cosmetic. The juice of the leaves is applied directly to the skin as a softening agent and for minor wounds (insect bites, scratches or cuts) and sunburn. Astringent and drying, it is often combined with lanolin and vitamins A and E to intensify its soothing qualities.

Aloe barbadensis syn. *A. vera*
ALOE VERA
ALOEACEAE/LILIACEAE

CONDITIONS

Climate. Aloe vera is best grown in tropical and warm zones.

Aspect. Full sunlight and good drainage. Grow indoors in direct light. Protect from heavy frosts.

Soil. Should drain rapidly and be reasonably open; roots will rot if exposed to long periods of wet soil. If soil and water are too alkaline, growth may be slow.

Aloysia triphylla
LEMON VERBENA
VERBENACEAE

CONDITIONS
Climate. Prefers moist, warm climates. High summer humidity in the tropics may cause it to be short lived. Plants are sensitive to cold weather and are best grown in containers in cooler regions.

Aspect. Prefers a sheltered, sunny position with protection in winter.

Soil. Likes rich soils. Needs mulching against frosts.

FEATURES
A large, bushy deciduous shrub that can grow to 1 m (3 ft) or more in height, lemon verbena has long, lemon-scented, narrow leaves. Spikes or sprays of small white to mauve flowers appear in the axils of the leaves in summer. Its fragrance is released when you brush against the leaves in the garden. Grow lemon verbena in containers, and in cooler climates indoors, although container plants do not reach the same height as specimens grown in the garden.

GROWING METHOD
Planting. Grow from softwood cuttings in summer or hardwood cuttings in autumn. Trim a 12 cm (5 in) piece from the parent bush, and remove a third of the upper leaves and a few of the lower leaves. Place in a mix of two-thirds coarse sand and one-third peat moss. Moisten the soil and cover the pot with a plastic bag to create a mini-greenhouse. Pot on into good quality potting mix when the cutting has taken root and shows renewed leaf growth. Plant out in the garden when the plant is growing strongly.

Watering. The plant is reasonably tolerant of dry conditions and normal garden watering is sufficient.

Fertilising. Use complete plant food every six weeks or apply controlled-release granules as directed on the packet.

Problems. Spider mite and whitefly weaken the plant by sucking plant juices from the leaves and stems. Hose leaves frequently, or use organic soap and pyrethrum or recommended chemical sprays for these pests. Watch out for powdery mildew, which causes foliage to wilt, on the upper surfaces of the leaves. Spray or remove diseased plants.

Pruning. Prune each season to contain its straggly growth habit. This is an ideal plant to train into a formal shape as a standard or topiary.

HARVESTING
Picking. Sprigs of leaves can be harvested all year long. If leaves are required for drying, cut the bush back during summer and early winter. Hang the branches in a cool, airy place and strip off the leaves when they are dry.

Storage. Store dried leaves in airtight jars. The fragrance is retained for some years.

Freezing. Wrap in plastic wrap and then freeze for up to six months.

USES
Culinary. Dried leaves can be used for herbal tea or in cooking where a lemon flavour is required, as with fish, poultry, marinades, salad dressings and puddings.

Craft. The strong fragrance makes dried leaves a popular component of herb pot pourris and sachet fillings.

Gardening. Lemon verbena is an attractive border plant.

FEATURES

A member of the ginger family, this perennial forms a clump of leafy stems up to 2 m (6–7 ft) tall. Leaves are glossy and light green, about 50 cm (20 in) long and lanceolate in shape. Unremarkable flowers appear in summer and autumn and are followed by spherical, red fruits. The plant is native to tropical Southeast Asia. It can be grown in large containers.

GROWING METHOD

Planting. Plant sections of fresh rhizome bought in spring from an Asian grocery store or good fruit market. Cut the rhizome into sections about 8 cm (3 in) long, each with an obvious green growing tip. Allow the cut ends to dry for a few days and then plant horizontally 8–10 cm (3–4 in) below the surface and water in. Alternatively, lift an existing plant in late winter and replant some of the rhizomes as above. Growing from seed takes much more time. Sow the seeds into punnets or trays of seed-raising mix. Cover lightly, moisten and place on a heated seed-germinating pad in a bright, warm place. Keep moist, and when seedlings are big enough to handle, prick out into individual containers. Plant out when at least 15 cm (6 in) tall.

Watering. Keep plants well watered from the time growth appears in spring until autumn when the top growth begins to die back. These plants are from rainy, tropical areas and expect a lot of rain in summer. Plants in pots may need watering every day during the hotter periods of summer.

Fertilising. Apply a complete plant food at planting time or when growth begins, and then feed the plant each month with liquid or soluble plant food. Mulch around the plants with rotted manure. Potted galangal should be fed fortnightly with liquid or soluble fertiliser and it is a good idea to mix a tablespoon of controlled-release fertiliser into the potting mix at planting time.

Problems. No particular problems.

HARVESTING

Picking. Galangal is usually lifted in autumn when the leaves begin to deteriorate. Detach the rhizomes for culinary use and save one or two for replanting next year's crop.

Storage. Cleaned rhizomes may be stored in the crisper bin of the fridge for a few weeks. They can also be pickled for long-term storage and they keep reasonably well in a cool, dark, well ventilated cupboard.

Freezing. Not suitable for freezing.

USES

Culinary. Reminiscent of ginger but with a distinctly different flavour, galangal (also known as Laos powder) is a popular addition to many dishes of Indonesian, Thai and Malaysian origin.

Alpinia galanga
GALANGAL
ZINGIBERACEAE

CONDITIONS

Climate. Best in tropical areas but grows satisfactorily, if a little slowly, anywhere frost-free. Where winters are cold but summers long and hot, try planting after the last frost in winter or spring and lifting after the first frost of autumn.

Aspect. Takes bright dappled sun or part shade in the tropics, but needs full sun and a warm, sheltered position elsewhere.

Soil. Best in deep, fertile, free-draining soil with plenty of rotted organic matter. Roots rot in wet soil. Use top quality potting mix for pots.

Anethum graveolens
DILL
APIACEAE/UMBELLIFERAE

CONDITIONS

Climate. Needs a warmish, dry summer but can be grown with some success in cooler regions that are frost-free.

Aspect. Prefers full sun; may need support and protection from winds.

Soil. Dig plenty of organic matter into the garden beds to improve water retention, as these plants mature through the drier months of spring and summer.

FEATURES

An annual herb growing to 1 m (3 ft), dill looks very like fennel, with its thread-like, feathery, blue-green leaves. It has a single, thin tap root rising above the ground to form a long, hollow stalk. This stalk branches at the top to support a 15 cm (6 in) wide mass of small yellow flowers, appearing in clusters in summer. Flat oval seeds, brown in colour, are produced quickly and in great quantities.

GROWING METHOD

Planting. Plant dill by seed any time except during winter. Dill will quite often self-sow, so choose a permanent position for the initial plantings. Successive planting every fortnight is recommended to ensure that there is continuous cropping. Sow the seeds in shallow furrows, with at least 60 cm (2 ft) between the rows, and then thin the seedlings out to 30 cm (1 ft) apart when they have reached approximately 5 cm (2 in) in height.

Watering. Keep the plants well watered, especially during hot weather.

Fertilising. Mulch well throughout spring and summer with rotted organic matter such as compost or old manure.

Problems. No particular damaging pests or diseases affect this plant.

HARVESTING

Picking. Dill leaves can be picked within two months of planting. Clip close to the stem in the cooler parts of the day. Several weeks after the plant blossoms, pick the flower heads and place them in a paper bag. Store the bag in a cool, dry place until the seeds ripen, then cut the stems and hang them upside down until the seeds ripen and fall.

Storage. Leaves and stems can be frozen and pieces cut off as required. They do not keep for more than a couple of days in the fridge before drooping and losing flavour. Dry leaves by spreading them thinly over a firm, non-metallic surface in a warm, dark place. After drying, place them in an airtight container. Seeds are dried in a similar manner.

Freezing. Leaves can be frozen for up to six months.

USES

Culinary. Dill has a pronounced tang. Use fresh leaves in salads and as a garnish. Use the seeds ground or whole in cooked dishes, as well as in the making of vinegars, pickles and herb butters. Add the dried leaves to soups or sauces. It is a great favourite in fish dishes. Tea can be made from the seeds.

Gardening. Dill is considered an ideal companion plant for lettuce, cabbage and onions.

FEATURES

Growing up to 2 m (6–7 ft) tall with a spread of around 1.5 m (5 ft), angelica is a majestic, stout-stemmed, perennial herb with big toothed leaves made up of several leaflets. The tiny honey-scented, greenish yellow flowers are produced in clusters in spring; winged seeds follow later in the summer. All parts of angelica are subtly, sweetly aromatic.

GROWING METHOD

Planting. Grow from seed as soon as it is ripe. Sprinkle seeds onto a tray of moist seed-raising mix and barely cover. Keep evenly moist. Expect germination in 3–4 weeks but germination is not always reliable. For a few plants, lift two-year-old plants in early spring and divide roots into smaller sections. Replant immediately into loose, friable, fertile soil.

Watering. Keep soil moist. The plant is native to cool rainy areas.

Fertilising. Apply complete plant food once in early spring when new growth begins and again in early summer. Mulch around plants with compost or rotted manure.

Problems. Angelica is short lived, usually dying after two years, but if it doesn't flower it grows for up to four years: snip off flower stems as they form.

Pruning. No pruning is necessary. In cold climates it dies back to the ground each winter.

HARVESTING

Picking. Collect the seeds by harvesting the whole flower head just as it ripens. Place in a paper bag in a warm, dry place until the seeds fall from the head. Separate the seeds from the dross before storing. For the best flavour, cut stems after they bloom. Pick leaves at any time. Dig roots just as flowers are forming and wash clean immediately.

Storage. Store seeds in an airtight jar. Crystallise stems before storage; dry and grind leaves before storing them in airtight containers. Store clean roots in a cool, dry, dark and airy place until needed.

Freezing. Not suitable for freezing.

USES

Culinary. Eat crystallised stems and leaves as sweets or use them to decorate cakes. Use leaves to make a herbal tea.

Medicinal. Tea made from any part of the plant can be taken to soothe nervous conditions and to ward off colds. Avoid frequent or heavy consumption of any part of the angelica plant as it is known to exacerbate certain medical conditions. Diabetics should avoid the plant altogether.

Craft. Use dried stems, leaves and roots in making pot pourris.

Gardening. Angelica is a handsome plant that makes an attractive addition to a planting of perennial flowers in cool climates.

Angelica archangelica
ANGELICA
APIACEAE/UMBELLIFERAE

CONDITIONS

Climate. Cool climates are best as the plant needs to rest over winter. In frost-free areas angelica is soon exhausted by continuous growth.

Aspect. In cold climates where summers tend to be mild, grow in full sun. Where summers are hot, part shade is essential. Shelter from wind.

Soil. Needs well drained but moisture-retentive and fertile soil.

Anthriscus cerefolium
CHERVIL
APIACEAE/UMBELLIFERAE

CONDITIONS
Climate. Grows best in a cool climate but tolerates humid tropical areas.

Aspect. Prefers filtered shade during summer and survives over winter if kept in the sun. Ideal for indoors if grown in a sunny position.

Soil. Rich in compost and well drained. Add lime to strongly acid soils. Mulch plants against extremes of temperature.

FEATURES
Chervil is a small, hardy annual herb that has a long cropping period. Looking rather like parsley, it grows to about 30 cm (12 in), the small light green leaves turning pinkish in hot sunny weather. Only the lower leaves have stalks. The leaves are usually curly but there is a variety with plain ones. Very small, white flowers are borne in clusters (called compound umbels) during summer. The herb has a very subtle flavour, somewhere between anise and parsley.

GROWING METHOD
Planting. Successive plantings every two weeks until the weather becomes too hot ensure a long cropping period. In the garden, plant under or near larger plants that provide shade and protection. Chervil does not transplant well, so sow seeds into their final position. Cover only lightly, even exposing the seeds to the sun a little, but keep the seeds moist. Germination occurs within 10 days. Thin seedlings to 25 cm (10 in) apart when they are 5 cm (2 in) high.

Watering. Water well as moisture is essential at all times.

Fertilising. Side dress chervil occasionally with a soluble and nitrogen-rich fertiliser to promote leaf growth.

Problems. No specific diseases but aphids can be a pest. Treat with appropriate sprays as vigorous hosing does not seem to work.

HARVESTING
Picking. Chervil leaves are ready to cut from about 6–8 weeks after planting.

Storage. The leaves can be made into a herb butter. The leaves are not really suitable for drying: they can be dried rapidly in an oven but they do tend to lose their flavour.

Freezing. Wrap herb butters in plastic wrap and store them in the freezer.

USES
Culinary. Both stems and leaves can be used as a flavouring in foods. Use fresh whole sprigs in salads or as an attractive garnish. If you are using chervil in cooking, be sure to add it at the end of the cooking process, because long periods of heating will give it a bitter flavour. Chervil is one of the main ingredients of *fines herbes* used in French cooking. It can also be used effectively in herb butters.

FEATURES

This popular vegetable grows to 25 cm (10 in) tall with erect, succulent semicircular stems and bright green aromatic leaves. If it is not cropped, the plant will produce flowers and then seeds. All parts of the plant are edible and can be used in a wide range of herbal remedies.

GROWING METHOD

Planting. In all areas sow seeds in spring. In warm and tropical regions sow through the summer. Sow seeds 6 mm (1/4 in) deep into trays or punnets of fine seed-raising mix. Water with a fine mist spray and keep evenly moist. When seedlings reach about 2 cm (1 in) tall, gently prick them out and pot them into small, individual containers of quality potting mix. Grow on in these for around two months, and then plant out into a prepared bed.

Watering. Always keep plants evenly moist. If the shallow roots are allowed to dry out, the stems become bitter and stringy.

Fertilising. Ensure the bed contains plenty of rotted organic matter. Feed the plants fortnightly with liquid or soluble fertiliser that contains a high proportion of nitrogen.

Problems. Inspect plants frequently for signs of damage by snails, slugs, aphids and caterpillars; pick pests off by hand. If chemical control is necessary, use a product with the lowest toxicity available (for example, pyrethrum, garlic or fatty acid based sprays).

HARVESTING

Picking. Pick outside stems individually or harvest the whole plant when mature. Pick small quantities of leaves at any time but do not continually strip the leaves. If you want seeds, let a few plants go to seed; the stems may be too stringy to eat.

Storage. Store seeds and dried leaves in airtight containers. Stems are best used fresh, but they can be frozen. Store cleaned roots in the crisper bin of the fridge for a month or more.

Freezing. Stems cut into sections and blanched in boiling water can be frozen for several months.

USES

Culinary. Use stems in salads, soups and stews; crumble dried leaves and use them as flavouring.

Medicinal. Seeds, chewed whole or made into tea, are a diuretic and help eliminate toxins that aggravate gout and arthritis. Stems and leaf stems share this attribute and are more palatable. A tincture made from celery root has a history of use as a remedy for kidney and arthritic disorders. Juice, made from the whole plant, is said to be good for bladder infections.

Apium graveolens
CELERY
UMBELLIFERAE

CONDITIONS

Climate. Tropical to cool climates but does best in cooler areas.

Aspect. Full sun is essential.

Soil. As celery should be grown fast, plant into well dug, very fertile soil. Dig in well rotted manure to improve the soil fertility and condition.

Armoracia rusticana
HORSERADISH
BRASSICACEAE/CRUCIFERAE

CONDITIONS
Climate. Cool and warm climates are most suitable.

Aspect. Full sun is essential.

Soil. Grow in deep soil that has been dug over deeply – a vegetable patch is ideal. This plant enjoys good conditions and thrives in well drained soils that are rich in rotted manure.

FEATURES
Although it is a perennial plant, horseradish is often grown as an annual. It is a rather weedy looking plant, consisting as it does of a clump of big, soft, spinach-like leaves, and it is best grown tucked away in the vegetable patch. In spring a stem of unremarkable, off-white flowers rises from the centre of the clump.

GROWING METHOD
Planting. Dig up the root system in late autumn and replant in spring to control the plant's ability to spread rapidly. Add new plants to the garden as root cuttings. In mild areas plant them in autumn but where winters are severe, spring planting is better. Allow about 30 cm (1 ft) between plants. The following autumn, take 20–25 cm (8–10 in) cuttings of the straight, thin side roots. These may be replanted immediately in mild areas, but in cold places they are best kept over winter in just damp sphagnum moss, soil or sand. Replant in spring.

Watering. Keep horseradish moist during spring and summer. If you are growing it in the vegetable patch, give it the same watering as other vegetables.

Fertilising. Mix a ration of low-nitrogen fertiliser into the planting hole and drench two or three times during the growing season with a low-nitrogen liquid or soluble plant food – one designed to promote flowering is ideal. Too much nitrogen makes excess leaves and poor quality roots.

Problems. Snails, slugs and caterpillars are all drawn to the fleshy leaves and will strip young plants quickly if not controlled. Lay bait for snails and slugs, and either pick off and squash caterpillars or spray plants with preparations containing *Bacillus thuringiensis*, a biological control that kills only caterpillars.

HARVESTING
Picking. The main harvest is in autumn although side roots can be snipped off in summer for immediate use. Scrape soil away from the main root, replacing it when the desired roots have been cut. For the main harvest, lift the plant, ensuring that all roots are removed (or the plant will regrow). Use selected side roots for regeneration, the rest for processing.

Storage. Fresh whole roots can be stored in the fridge for about two weeks while the grated roots can be made into horseradish sauce or pickled in vinegar.

Freezing. Whole roots can be wrapped in foil and frozen for up to six months.

USES
Culinary. Horseradish sauce is a popular condiment with beef but it also goes well with other meats and fish. Add it sparingly to sauces and salad dressings.

Medicinal. Horseradish is an instant remedy for blocked noses but is not an easy medicine to take. It has antiseptic properties and is said to ward off colds if small amounts are eaten regularly. Highly nutritious, it contains high levels of vitamin C and many essential minerals.

FEATURES

The two culinary varieties grown are French tarragon (*A. dracunculus*) and Russian or 'false' tarragon (*A. dracunculus* var. *dracunculoides*). French tarragon is a perennial herb that spreads by rhizomes or underground stems, sending up erect stems to a height of 40–50 cm (15–20 in) or more. The leaves are olive green and have an anise flavour. It dies down over winter and regenerates in spring. It must be propagated by division. The tarragon seed offered by some nurseries is Russian tarragon. This keeps some of its foliage and is more vigorous but has a much more bitter flavour. Tarragon needs to be replanted every few years as plants lose their vigour over time. White or greenish flowers appear in late summer.

GROWING METHOD

Planting. Propagate by root division. Lift the plant during spring, divide it and replant the pieces in pots or in the garden, spaced 60 cm (2 ft) apart.

Watering. Keep well watered but ease off over winter. Soils should be damp but not soggy.

Fertilising. Apply complete plant food once in early spring. Mulch French tarragon over winter when it has died down.

Problems. No specific pests but it does suffer from downy and powdery mildew. Fungal growths may appear on the leaves, which wilt and die. Remove affected plants and burn them. Root rot may also be a problem.

Pruning. Pick out flower stems to promote leaf growth.

HARVESTING

Picking. Pick leaves during summer but take care not to bruise them.

Storage. Leaves can be dried although much of the flavour and some of the colour will be lost in the process. Place them on racks or hang stems in bunches in a warm, dry place, and then store them in airtight jars. Leaves can be preserved in vinegar.

Freezing. Wrap leaves in plastic wrap and freeze for up to six months.

USES

Culinary. Tarragon is one of the classic French *fines herbes* used to enhance the flavours of various foods, from fish, meat and dairy foods to herbed vinegars, butters, sauces, vegetables and soups. Leaves of Russian tarragon lack the aromatic oils of the French variety.

Artemisia dracunculus
TARRAGON
ASTERACEAE/COMPOSITAE

CONDITIONS

Climate. Cool and warm climates provide the best conditions but grows well in hot, arid areas if watered regularly. If winters are not cool enough to cause the plant to go dormant, it will be short lived.

Aspect. Prefers full sun or partial shade.

Soil. Needs well drained, sandy soils that do not hold moisture for too long, especially over winter when the rhizomes may rot. Dig in some organic matter.

Borago officinalis
BORAGE
BORAGINACEAE

CONDITIONS

Climate. Grows in all climates except extreme cold.

Aspect. Prefers a sunny spot but grows in most positions, including partial shade; needs plenty of space. Grows quite well indoors if placed in a sunny corner.

Soil. Grows well in most soils that are aerated, moist and mulched to keep competitive weeds down. Indoors, grow borage in a deep pot, with a moist and fertile potting mix.

Support. The brittle stems may need staking to prevent wind damage.

FEATURES

A fast-growing annual or biennial growing to 1 m (3 ft) tall, borage bears star-shaped flowers with protruding black anthers in summer. They are usually bright sky blue, although they can sometimes be pink or white. The bush bears many sprawling, leafy branches with hollow stems, which can be quite fragile. The stems are covered with stiff white hairs and the greyish green leaves are also hairy.

GROWING METHOD

Planting. Sow seed directly into the garden in clumps and thin out the seedlings later, leaving 60 cm (2 ft) between plants. Seedlings do not transplant well once established. Successive sowings of seeds every 3–4 weeks after winter frosts have disappeared will extend the harvesting period. The plant self-sows readily and its spread may need to be controlled. Take tip cuttings from a mature plant in spring and pot them up, using a coarse sandy mix. Dampen the soil and cover the pot with a plastic bag supported on sticks or a wire frame. When cuttings have taken hold, plant them out in spring or summer.

Watering. Keep the soil moist at all times.

Fertilising. Apply complete plant food once each spring or use controlled-release granules.

Problems. Generally free of specific pest and disease problems.

HARVESTING

Picking. Pick the leaves as required while they are fresh and young. Harvest the open flowers during the summer months.

Storage. You must use the leaves fresh; you cannot dry and store them. You can crystallise the flowers and then store them in airtight jars.

Freezing. The leaves cannot be frozen. The flowers may be frozen in ice cubes.

USES

Culinary. Borage has a faintly cucumber-like taste: add young leaves to salads. Freeze flowers in ice cubes for cold drinks, or crystallise them and use to decorate cakes and desserts. *Note:* Borage may be a danger to health: it is now under study because of the presence of toxic alkaloids.

Gardening. An excellent companion plant in the garden, especially when it is planted near strawberries.

FEATURES

Caraway is a biennial plant growing to around 60 cm (2 ft) in height on slim, faintly striped stems. Its leaves are aromatic, finely cut and ferny, and in summer the plant produces heads of small white flowers. These are followed by ridged, dark brown seeds. The edible, carrot-like roots are white.

GROWING METHOD

Planting. Grow from seed sown in early spring or, where winters are not cold, in autumn, directly where the plants are to grow. Sow the seeds shallowly, 15–20 cm (6–8 in) apart, or thin to that spacing after germination. Mulch around the plants with compost, rotted manure or lucerne hay.

Watering. Water deeply during dry times.

Fertilising. Dig a ration of complete plant food into the soil before planting, and water plants with liquid organic or soluble fertiliser once or twice during late spring and summer.

Problems. No particular pest or disease problems, but to prevent an invasion of caraway seedlings, remove the seed heads before the seeds fall.

HARVESTING

Picking. Pick seed heads when thoroughly ripe but before the seeds have begun to fall. To dry them properly, place them in open containers in the sun. Pick the young spring leaves, the most palatable, as needed. Use the roots when young and small also. Pull up the whole plant in late spring.

Storage. Store dry seeds in airtight jars after separating them from the dried seed head. Store roots in the fridge for a few weeks. Eat the leaves while they are fresh.

Freezing. Caraway is not suitable for freezing.

USES

Culinary. Use the seeds in herbal tea and in baking, and add them to many other recipes, especially vegetable and fruit dishes and curries. Add the leaves to salads; steam or boil the roots and eat them as a vegetable.

Medicinal. All parts are good for the digestion and kidneys; chew the seeds after a heavy meal to relieve wind and bloating.

Gardening. Sowing a succession of caraway plants in heavy, not very friable soil improves its tilth.

Carum carvi

CARAWAY
APIACEAE/UMBELLIFERAE

CONDITIONS

Climate. Equally suited to cool or warm climates. In rainy tropical areas it is best grown in winter.

Aspect. Full sun, but will tolerate a few hours of afternoon shade. In windy areas, shelter is desirable.

Soil. Deeply dug, good quality, well drained soil allows the roots to grow straight and long. Soil that contains rotted organic matter is the most fertile.

Chamaemelum nobile syn.
Anthemis nobilis
CHAMOMILE
ASTERACEAE/COMPOSITAE

CONDITIONS
Climate. Grows in most climates, from hot to cool.

Aspect. Prefers full sun, but grows well in areas with partial shade.

Soil. Prefers a lime-rich soil.

FEATURES
This perennial herb is known as Roman chamomile and should not be confused with the erect and much taller growing annual form known as German chamomile (*Matricaria recutita*). Both forms have feathery foliage and flower from late spring to late summer. The daisy-like blossoms are white with a yellow centre, and they have many uses. Chamomile has an attractive apple-like fragrance and flavour.

GROWING METHOD
Planting. Plant the very fine seeds in spring in well fertilised beds. Or raise seedlings in trays of seed-raising mix and then prick them out into 8 cm (3 in) pots to harden and establish before planting them out. Dig and rake the area before transplanting the seedlings during spring. For a chamomile lawn, prepare the area over winter, then spread or sow the seed directly into a prepared lawn bed. Finely rake the bed to cover the seed then water it in. Keep the lawn weeded. Alternatively, take rooted cuttings or offshoots of the parent plant and set them out in well manured soil, 45 cm (18 in) apart. In cold areas mulch them heavily so they will survive severe frosts.

Watering. Keep the soil evenly moist; do not let it dry out.

Fertilising. Give light applications of blood and bone during spring and autumn.

Problems. No specific pests or diseases worry this herb.

Pruning. Chamomile lawns can be mowed and will regenerate quickly.

HARVESTING
Picking. Pick flowers as they appear during late spring and summer, just as the petals start to turn backwards from the central yellow disk.

Storage. Dry flowers on paper on racks in a cool, airy space, then store them in airtight jars.

Freezing. Flowers can be frozen for up to six months.

USES
Cosmetic. Use the flowers to make face masks and hair rinses.

Culinary. Chamomile is popular as a herbal tea.

Craft. Use the flowers in pot pourris.

Gardening. As a companion plant, chamomile keeps a range of other plants happy and healthy, especially cucumber, onions and other herbs.

FEATURES

This large perennial plant sometimes reaches over 1 m (3 ft) in height. It has intense sky blue, fine-petalled flowers, borne in summer, that open in the morning but close up in the hot midday sun. The broad, oblong leaves with ragged edges, reminiscent of dandelions, form a rosette around the bottom of the tall, straggly stems. The upper leaves are much smaller, giving a bare look to the top of the plant. Chicory is an attractive background plant but it sometimes needs support to remain upright. If cultivated by forced growth and blanching, the lettuce-like heart of the chicory plant is turned into the vegetable witlof, also known as Belgian endive.

GROWING METHOD

Planting. Plant seeds in spring, into drills or trenches 2–3 cm (1 in) deep, and thin the seedlings to 30 cm (1 ft) apart when they are established. Seeds may also be germinated in seed trays and seedlings transplanted into the garden during the months of spring. Divide the mature plants in autumn, then replant in spring. Sow seeds in autumn in hot, dry tropical areas.

Watering. Keep chicory well watered during spells of hot weather, especially in hot, dry areas without much natural rainfall.

Fertilising. Add compost to the garden bed in midsummer, but do not provide too much nitrogen or the leaves will grow rapidly at the expense of root growth.

Problems. No particular pests or diseases affect this plant.

HARVESTING

Picking. Pick young green leaves of chicory when they are required.

Storage. The leaves cannot be stored either fresh or dried. The root can be dried and then rendered into a powder.

Freezing. Not suitable for freezing.

USES

Culinary. Use young, freshly picked leaves, either in salads or in cooking. The strong, bitterish flavour is similar to dandelion. Flowers can be crystallised and used to decorate cakes and puddings. The root powder is used in beverages.

Cichorium intybus
CHICORY
ASTERACEAE/COMPOSITAE

CONDITIONS

Climate. Suitable for most climates but not usually long lived in the monsoonal tropics.

Aspect. Prefers full sun.

Soil. These plants require deep, rich, friable soil for best growth. Dig in plenty of organic matter in the form of compost or decayed animal manures before planting. Keep the garden beds free of weeds.

Coriandrum sativum

CORIANDER
APIACEAE/UMBELLIFERAE

CONDITIONS

Climate. Likes hot, dry climates resembling those of the eastern Mediterranean region and southern Europe but coriander will grow in cool, warm and tropical areas.

Aspect. Prefers a sunny position, or partial shade in very hot climates.

Soil. Well drained and mulched beds required to keep weed growth down. Coriander is a very fast growing but short lived herb which will grow in most soils that are not over-rich in fertiliser. Too much nitrogen lessens the flavour in the plant.

FEATURES

Also known as Chinese parsley or cilantro, this very quick-growing, bright green annual reaches a height of approximately 50 cm (20 in). Leaves on the lower part of the stem are oval with serrated edges but as they mature on the outside branches they become feathery and are divided into narrow segments. The small flowers are white to pink, mauve or reddish and are borne in short-stalked clusters in summer. The spherical seeds are brownish yellow in colour, about 3 mm (1/8 in) in diameter and have a musty odour.

GROWING METHOD

Planting. Successive sowings of seed several weeks apart will extend the cropping period. Autumn sowings in mild climates produce seedlings that fare much better than those germinated in spring, which may mature quickly and go to seed. Sow directly into garden beds, into holes 1 cm (1/2 in) deep and 20 cm (8 in) apart. Seedlings appear within 1–2 weeks, two from each seed. Thin plants to 10–15 cm (4–6 in) apart.

Watering. Water evenly and do not let the soil dry out during hot, dry spells.

Fertilising. No fertiliser is necessary.

Problems. Coriander is prone to bacterial wilt and downy mildew. The mildew may be sprayed; otherwise remove and burn affected plants.

HARVESTING

Picking. Pick fresh leaves as required; the smaller immature leaves have the better taste. Harvest seed when leaves and flowers turn brown and the seed is ripe. Pull out the whole plant, place it upside down in a paper bag and hang it in a cool, dry, airy space. The ripened seeds should fall into the bag.

Storage. Seeds are dried and stored in sealed jars or ground to a powder. The leaves cannot be dried satisfactorily.

Freezing. The leaves can be frozen for up to six months.

USES

Culinary. Leaves, seeds and roots are used for culinary purposes, especially in Asian cuisines. Both leaves and roots can be eaten fresh, the leaves having a pronounced sage flavour with citrus overtones and the roots having an additional nutty flavour. They also go well with meats and vegetables in cooking. Ground coriander seed is much favoured as a spice.

FEATURES

Also known as citronella grass, lemon grass is a perennial grass of tropical regions. The narrow, ribbon-like, leafy stalks grow in clumps that reach 1 m (3 ft) or more in height. The leaves swell slightly at the base to form a fleshy stolon or underground stem. The stem is white and is also edible. The edges of mature leaves are rough and can be quite sharp – it's easy to get cut fingers when harvesting them.

GROWING METHOD

Planting. Lemon grass rarely flowers. Plant commercially purchased root stock or propagate in spring. To do this, divide the mature plant, breaking off portions from the outer edge of the clump, and then replant.

Watering. Water well as this plant requires a great deal of water, especially during the earlier stages of its growth.

Fertilising. In spring and summer apply liquid or soluble fertiliser monthly.

Problems. Lemon grass is not attacked by any particular pests or diseases.

HARVESTING

Picking. Pick leaves or remove portions of the stem in summer as required.

Storage. Harvested portions will keep in the fridge for a few days. Lemon grass cannot be dried.

Freezing. Can be wrapped in plastic wrap and frozen for up to six months.

USES

Culinary. Lemon grass is widely used in the cuisines of Southeast Asia. The 'sweet–sour', lemony flavour of the leaves is used in herbal teas, or pieces can be tied together and used to flavour marinades and in cooking. The white, fleshy stem is chopped and used to flavour cooked dishes such as curries, fish or soups. If fibrous, it should be discarded after cooking.

Cymbopogon citratus
LEMON GRASS
GRAMINEAE/POACEAE

CONDITIONS

Climate. Lemon grass prefers to grow in warm or tropical regions but will grow in cooler areas if the frosts are not too severe and if the plant is heavily mulched in autumn to protect it throughout winter.

Aspect. Outside tropical areas, lemon grass needs a protected, sunny position. In cooler climates, it can be grown in a container in a greenhouse or on a sunny, protected deck – these conditions provide enough humidity to simulate its natural environment.

Soil. Rich, fertile soils. Add plenty of organic matter in the form of compost, leaves, straw or decayed animal manures to the soil before planting and mulch constantly throughout the season to retain moisture levels.

Eruca vesicaria subsp. *sativa*
ROCKET
CRUCIFERAE

CONDITIONS

Climate. Best suited to cool and warm climates but grows reasonably well in the tropical winter.

Aspect. During spring grow rocket in full sun but in summer and in the tropics, a cooler, partly shaded spot helps slow the plant's rush to seed and thus lengthens its useful life.

Soil. Grow in fertile, well drained soil enriched with rotted manure or compost. Rocket will grow in poor soils, too, but its leaves will be tough and more bitter.

FEATURES

Rocket is an annual with long, deeply lobed, dark green leaves, often tinted red, and simple, cross-shaped, creamy white flowers. The leaves have a pleasant, peppery, nutty flavour and are produced in a dense rosette at the base of the plant, from which rise the branching stems. The stems, which may reach 1 m (3 ft), bear flowers, followed by plump seed heads which shatter when dry, each dispersing hundreds of seeds. Rocket grows very fast and several crops may be raised during spring and summer.

GROWING METHOD

Planting. Sow seeds in early spring 2 cm (1 in) deep and thin the young plants to about 15 cm (6 in) apart. If sharp frosts are still likely then, sow indoors in trays or punnets of seed-raising mix placed in a sunny window. Plant out when the seedlings are big enough to handle and frosts are light or have passed. As rocket grows fast and young leaves are the most palatable, make new sowings approximately every four weeks. When the latest batch of seedlings is big enough to pick from, pull out the previous batch. You can continue sowing rocket until about mid-autumn. In the tropics, start sowing in late autumn and continue until the end of winter.

Watering. For the fastest growth and the sweetest, best tasting leaves, keep the plants well watered. Plants enjoy consistent moisture but not wetness around their roots, so make sure that the soil drains well.

Fertilising. Dig in a ration of complete plant food at sowing time and then water the plants every two weeks or so with a soluble, high-nitrogen fertiliser.

Problems. Snails and slugs may damage the leaves of freshly sown plants in early spring and autumn. Either pick them off by hand or lay snail bait. As rocket can quickly become an invasive weed it is important to prevent flowering except to provide seeds for resowing. On most plants, snap off flower stems as they rise or, better still, replace flowering plants with new, young plants.

HARVESTING

Picking. Start picking young leaves about five weeks after seedlings have emerged, sooner in summer when growth is faster. Seeds are harvested when the pods have plumped out and are beginning to look dry.

Storage. Seeds may be stored in airtight jars but leaves must be used fresh.

Freezing. Not suitable for freezing.

USES

Culinary. Young leaves give green salads an appealing piquancy. Add them late to stir-fries.

Medicinal. Rocket is said to be a stimulant and good for warding off colds.

FEATURES

Fast growing and spreading, this herbaceous perennial can reach a height of nearly 2 m (6–7 ft). An erect, finely foliaged plant with a strong aniseed aroma, it has a bulbous, fleshy base, hollow stems and delicate, thread-like, dark olive green leaves. Flattened heads of tiny, bright yellow flowers appear on the top of the plant in summer. Fennel is an extremely invasive plant that has been declared a noxious weed in some areas. It should only be grown where an unwanted spread can be easily controlled.

GROWING METHOD

Planting. Most easily grown from seed sown in spring or, in frost-free areas, autumn. Sow the seeds directly where they are to grow, 6 mm (1/4 in) deep and thin to about 30 cm (1 ft) apart. Vigorous young plants produce the sweetest and best flavoured 'bulbs', and you should dig out and replace plants every three years.

Watering. Keep well watered during spring and summer. Consistent moisture around the roots ensures sweet, succulent growth. Decrease water from about mid-autumn.

Fertilising. Additional feeding is not necessary if the soil is rich and fertile. If in doubt, apply complete plant food once in early spring.

Problems. No particular problems.

HARVESTING

Picking. Pick leaves any time from late spring to late summer. Seeds are harvested when ripe in late summer and as this time approaches, plants should be inspected regularly so that ripe seeds can be gathered before they start to fall. The bulbous bases can be dug up as required.

Storage. Store dried seeds in airtight jars. Use the leaves fresh as they lose flavour during drying.

Freezing. Wrap small bunches of leaves in a freezer bag or foil and freeze for up to six months.

USES

Cosmetic. Cold tea made from the seeds is a refreshing facial rinse that is said to reduce wrinkles and tone the skin.

Culinary. Seeds, which are an aid to digestion, are chewed raw or used whole or ground in recipes. Add the finely chopped leaves to many dishes, notably fish and carbohydrates such as pasta and potatoes, and to vinegars. Eat the fleshy, white base raw or cooked.

Medicinal. All parts of fennel are said to be beneficial to the digestion, good for the eyes and a mild appetite suppressant. Tea made from the seeds is a mild laxative. Chew the seeds to freshen stale breath.

Foeniculum vulgare
FENNEL
APIACEAE/UMBELLIFERAE

CONDITIONS

Climate. Grows in most areas but does best in cool to warm climates where frosts are not very severe. Not well suited to the high levels of summer rain and humidity in the tropics.

Aspect. Full sun is essential and shelter from blustery winds advisable.

Soil. Most vigorous on crumbly, sandy loam with plenty of rotted organic matter. Dig in 1 cup of lime per square metre (square yard) of soil before planting as fennel prefers slightly alkaline conditions.

Hyssopus officinalis
HYSSOP
LABIATAE/LAMIACEAE

CONDITIONS

Climate. Best in cool or warm areas. In the tropics, grow in pots sheltered from heavy summer rains.

Aspect. Full sun produces compact growth and the strongest flavour but hyssop tolerates shade for part of the day.

Soil. Likes light, fertile, well drained soils but will grow in any reasonably fertile soil as long as it drains freely.

FEATURES

A perennial to around 60 cm (2 ft) tall, hyssop has many erect stems clothed in narrow, lanceolate, sage green leaves. Spikes of small blue-violet, pink or white flowers appear in summer. The whole plant exudes a pungent aroma and the leaves have a bitter taste.

GROWING METHOD

Planting. Hyssop can be grown from seed, softwood cuttings or division of the roots. Sow seeds in spring into trays of seed-raising mix. Cover lightly, keep moist and when seedlings are big enough to handle prick out into small, individual pots to grow on. Plant out about 30 cm (12 in) apart when plants are about 20 cm (8 in) tall. Take 8 cm (3 in) tip cuttings in spring and insert into pots of sandy potting mix. Keep the mix moist and in bright, sheltered shade – roots will form within a month. To divide, lift an established plant in late autumn or early spring. Cut the root mass into several smaller sections and replant the sections immediately.

Watering. Keep soil moist, especially during the warmer months, but do not overwater. Hyssop is a resilient plant that can often get by on rain.

Fertilising. Complete plant food applied in spring when new growth appears is enough.

Problems. No particular problems.

Pruning. When new growth begins in spring, pinching out the tips of young stems will encourage the plant to become bushier and thus produce more flowers. In late autumn, the remains of the plant can be cut to ground level.

HARVESTING

Picking. Pick flowers for using fresh or for drying when they are in full bloom. Harvest individual stems as needed.

Storage. Store flowers and leaves dry. Cut bunches of flowering stems, tie them together and hang them upside down in a dim, airy place. When they are dry, crumble them into airtight jars.

Freezing. Not suitable for freezing.

USES

Culinary. One or two fresh leaves, finely chopped and added late, give an appealing piquancy to soups and casseroles while fresh flowers can be used to add flavour and colour to salads.

Medicinal. Tea, made from the dried stems, leaves and flowers, is taken to relieve the symptoms of colds; hyssop leaves are often a component in mixed herbal tonics and teas.

Cosmetic. Oil distilled from hyssop is used in perfumes and other commercial cosmetics. At home, it may be added to bath water, and cooled hyssop leaf tea is a cleansing, refreshing facial rinse.

Gardening. Hyssop is a decorative plant and very attractive to bees and butterflies. Use it in a border of mixed flowers or grow it as an edging to paths.

FEATURES

Orris root is a rhizomatous perennial iris. It consists of a fan-shaped clump of stiff, upright, sword-shaped leaves in grey-green with distinct parallel veins. The showy flowers appear in spring or summer, and are white flushed with mauve or soft lilac-blue. The plant grows to a height of approximately 45 cm (18 in). Once dried, the root exudes a strong aroma reminiscent of violets, a property not shared with other irises.

GROWING METHOD

Planting. Grow from divisions of the rhizome taken after bloom. Lift the plant and cut its creeping rhizome into sections. Each section should have its own fan of leaves and a growing point. The old centre of the clump, which has flowered, will never do so again and should be discarded. Cut the leaves in half crosswise, and then replant the rhizomes about 35 cm (14 in) apart into soil that has been well dug over. Lay them horizontally so that about half the rhizome is above ground level – deeper planting will cause the rhizomes to rot.

Watering. Keep soil evenly moist during the warmer months. Orris root is not particularly tolerant of prolonged dry conditions.

Fertilising. Dig in a lean ration of complete plant food at planting time, but no other feeding will be necessary. A thin mulch of very old, rotted manure or compost may be applied.

Problems. No particular problems.

HARVESTING

Picking. Dig out the root in early summer. A few pieces of young rhizome can be replanted to provide future crops and the rest can then be put aside for processing.

Storage. Clean the root and cut it into small segments. Dry it in the sun and then store it in an airtight jar in the fridge. The fragrance of the root does not develop fully for about a year.

Freezing. Not suitable for freezing.

USES

Craft. Orris root is mainly used to impart a heady violet scent to pot pourris. It also acts as a preservative in such dried material. Do take care, however, as orris root may cause sneezing, coughing and other allergic reactions in some sensitive people.

Iris x *germanica* var. *florentina*
ORRIS ROOT
IRIDACEAE

CONDITIONS

Climate. Best suited to cool climates. Can be grown in warm areas if they are not excessively hot, wet and humid in summer.

Aspect. Full sun is essential.

Soil. Plants do best in well drained, slightly alkaline soil to which a proportion of rotted organic matter has been added. Take care not to over-enrich the soil with either manures or fertilisers as these plants do not grow well with high levels of nitrogen.

Laurus nobilis
BAY TREE
LAURACEAE

CONDITIONS
Climate. Mediterranean-style climate with hot, dry summers and cool, wet winters.

Aspect. Prefers full sun in cool to warm zones but needs partial shade on very hot summer days if growing in tropical areas.

Soil. Moderately rich and well drained soil. For a potted tree, add lime if the soil is very acid, ensure that the pot is large enough for the root ball and add decayed animal manure or compost if necessary. Mulch the top soil.

FEATURES
An aromatic, evergreen tree 10–20 m (33–66 ft) high, the bay is often grown in containers where the height can be controlled. The trunk has smooth grey bark and the short stalks bear alternate, shiny, dark green elliptical-shaped leaves with wavy edges. The leaves, the edible part of the plant, are 3–6 cm (1–2 in) long and leathery in texture. The inconspicuous yellowish green flowers, which appear in spring, produce dark purple or black one-seeded berries.

GROWING METHOD
Planting. Fresh green shoots or tip cuttings taken in autumn and summer offer the best chance of success. Take an 8 cm (3 in) cutting from a mature plant and remove the upper and lower leaves. Dip the end in hormonal rooting powder to speed up root growth. Place the cutting in a small pot containing a mix of two-thirds coarse sand and one-third peat moss. Place the pot under a plastic bag, making a wire frame to hold the bag off the cutting. This mini-glasshouse provides a warm, humid environment. Cuttings may take nine months to take root before they can be planted in the garden.

Watering. Let the soil dry out between waterings, but during hot weather keep the moisture up, especially for potted specimens.

Fertilising. Apply complete plant food once in spring, and then mulch with rotted organic matter. Keep mulch away from the trunk.

Problems. Scale, a small wingless insect covered with a waxy substance, may suck the sap of the plant and cause stunted growth. Secretions attract ants, promoting sooty mould. Treat with insecticidal soap sprays.

Pruning. Prune only if you want to restrict the height or formalise the shape.

HARVESTING
Picking. Pick leaves early in the day throughout the year and then use fresh or dried as required.

Storage. Dry in a dark, airy room. Place leaves on a firm, flat surface and weigh them down to prevent curling. Leave for at least two weeks. Store dried leaves in sealed jars.

Freezing. Wrap the leaves in plastic wrap; freeze for up to six months.

USES
Culinary. Excellent as a flavouring in soups, stews, sauces and custards, bay is also used when cooking game, in terrines and in pickling brines. The leaves are an essential component of bouquet garni.

Gardening. This very slow-growing tree casts dense shade. It is sometimes pruned into formal shapes when grown in containers.

FEATURES

The many varieties of this fragrant perennial herb include *L. angustifolia* (a favourite subspecies is *L. angustifolia* 'Alba', white lavender), *L. dentata* and *L. stoechas*. The common names English, French and Italian lavender are used, but authorities disagree as to which species is which. Heights differ but all grow into evergreen, bushy shrubs with woody stems and hairy, silvery to grey-green, fragrant leaves. Edges are smooth or serrated, depending on variety. Long spikes of fragrant deep purple to pinkish flowers appear in late winter to summer.

GROWING METHOD

Planting. Seed has a long germination time and may not come true to strain: taking cuttings is the best way to get the lavender you want. Take 5 cm (2 in) tip cuttings with a heel or base of old wood in autumn or late winter. Trim off the upper and lower leaves and plant in a mixture of two-thirds coarse sand to one-third peat moss. Keep soil on the dry side until the cutting has taken root and new leaf shoots appear. Then pot on into a good quality potting mix. Plant in the garden in spring about 60 cm (2 ft) apart. Or pull a lower branch of a mature plant to soil level, slightly scratch the underside and peg it into the soil. Once the branch has taken root, cut it off and transfer it to its new spot.

Watering. Water only in dry weather as lavenders do not require a great deal of water.

Fertilising. Applications of a complete fertiliser (NPK 5:6:7) will improve fragrance. Less cold-resistant varieties may need winter mulching.

Problems. Roots are often attacked in this otherwise tough plant. Root knot nematodes can arrest the flow of nutrients and water to the plant. Companion planting with marigolds will keep nematodes down. Root rot can result from poor drainage, and diseased plants need to be removed. Leaf spot, causing yellowing leaves with whitish spots, indicates plants may be too close together and need more air circulation. Do not water over leaves.

Pruning. Keep plants pruned in their first year to discourage flowering: bushier plants result.

HARVESTING

Picking. Cut flowers in early spring before they open. Dry by hanging in bunches in a dry, airy, hot place.

Storage. Store dried leaves and flowers in airtight jars.

Freezing. Not suitable for freezing.

USES

Culinary. Use fresh or dried flowers and leaves to flavour sugars, jellies, ice creams and cheeses. Flowers can also be crystallised and used as decoration on cakes.

Craft. Use dried lavender spikes for their fragrance in pot pourris, perfumed sachets and dried arrangements. Lavender is also used to make essential oil and floral waters.

Lavandula sp.
LAVENDER
LABIATAE/LAMIACEAE

CONDITIONS

Climate. Best suited to cool or warm climates where most rain falls in winter. Not suited to the tropics or areas that are very humid.

Aspect. Prefers full sun. Flowering spikes need protection from severe winds.

Soil. Prefers well drained soil, but it need not be rich. If it is acid, add lime or dolomite.

Levisticum officinale
LOVAGE
APIACEAE/UMBELLIFERAE

CONDITIONS

Climate. Lovage is not suitable for hot tropical areas. It grows well in cool climates, tolerating extremes of frost.

Aspect. Prefers full sun or semi-shade.

Soil. Moist, fertile, well drained alkaline soil. Dig plenty of compost and decayed animal manure deep into the soil and if acidity is a problem, add some lime or dolomite into the top soil. In warmer areas, mulch the soil around each plant to keep it cool, moist and free of weeds.

FEATURES

A very tall perennial herb that reaches 1–2 m (3–7 ft), this plant looks quite spectacular when growing in the garden. Dark green to yellowish leaves become smaller towards the top of the plant and break into wedge-shaped, ridged leaflets. Greenish flowers appear in summer, and are then followed by 6 mm (1/4 in) long, light brown, grooved aromatic seeds. The hollow, ribbed stems of lovage look and taste like celery and there is a longish tap root that is much like a carrot. Lovage may die back to ground level over winter but it will regenerate in the following spring.

GROWING METHOD

Planting. Sow seeds in late summer through autumn directly into the garden, or plant seedlings approximately 30 cm (12 in) apart. Propagate mature plants that have been in the garden for at least two seasons by dividing the roots in autumn or spring.

Watering. Water well so that the soil is moist, especially in hot, dry weather.

Fertilising. Give an application of complete plant food once in early spring.

Problems. Aphids love lovage and can transmit viral diseases to the plant. Hose vigorously to break their cycle or treat with organic or recommended insecticidal sprays. Leaf miner maggots will tunnel into the leaves, causing white blotches. Remove infected leaves.

Pruning. For a bushier plant, prune the flowers in summer.

HARVESTING

Picking. Harvest any part of the plant as needed. Do not cut the central stem when picking leaves.

Storage. Dry stems, leaves and seeds and keep them in airtight jars.

Freezing. Blanch the leaves in boiling water and then quick freeze them wrapped in small lots or frozen within ice cubes. Can be frozen for up to six months.

USES

Culinary. The leaves, stems and seeds are substitutes for celery. Try leaves and stems in fresh salads and dried seeds in soups, casseroles, sauces and pickling mixtures, or savoury biscuits. Lovage is also used in teas, vinegars and butters.

FEATURES

A spreading perennial growing to 90 cm (3 ft) high, lemon balm has small, serrated, nettle-like leaves with a lemon scent. They are supported on squarish stems with spikes of inconspicuous white flowers borne in the axils of the leaves during summer. These plants are very sensitive to frosts and may die back during winter, but established plants will regenerate in spring. Position lemon balm anywhere in the garden and especially near trees or plants that require bees to pollinate blossoms.

GROWING METHOD

Planting. Balm can be propagated in three ways. Sow seeds directly into the garden in early to middle autumn, or germinate them first in seed boxes and then transplant them during early spring. The germination period is long, and in the garden seedlings may need protection throughout winter. Mulching will help. Root division of the parent plant in early spring is also successful. Space the divided roots at least 65 cm (26 in) apart. Cuttings 10–12 cm (4–5 in) long can be taken from new spring growth. Cut below a node of the parent plant and remove the top leaves of the cuttings. Plant them deeply in small pots containing a 3:1 mix of river sand and peat moss, and keep the soil moist.

Watering. Keep plants well watered in hot dry spells.

Fertilising. Apply complete plant food once in early spring when new growth begins.

Problems. The diseases most likely to strike are fungal. Brown leaves, or orange, powdery spots or pustules on the undersides of the leaves indicate rust infection. In moderately dry climates, powdery mildew may form a light grey powdery coating on leaves, flowers or young shoots, causing stunting or even defoliation of the plant. Treat both diseases with recommended fungal sprays. Spider mite is the most common insect pest. Spray with the appropriate insecticide.

Pruning. Keep straggly clumps in shape by pruning during spring for summer growth.

HARVESTING

Picking. Pick fresh leaves as required. Cut whole stems when flowers begin to emerge and then dry them. The leaves are most tender and full of flavour in spring.

Storage. Dry quickly by hanging cut stems in a cool, airy space. Rub dry leaves and flowers from the stems and store in airtight jars.

Freezing. Wrap in plastic wrap and freeze for up to six months.

USES

Culinary. Use fresh leaves and flowers in salads; you can also use the leaves in stuffings or sauces for poultry and fish. Lemon balm herbal teas are very popular and fresh leaves can also be used to flavour cool summer drinks.

Melissa officinalis
LEMON BALM
LABIATAE/LAMIACEAE

CONDITIONS

Climate. Balm comes from the hot regions of North Africa and southern Europe but is now cultivated successfully in warm zones and even some cooler areas. May be grown in the cooler months in the tropics.

Aspect. Prefers full sun or partial shade.

Soil. Soils should be rich in organic matter and kept moist and well mulched. Before planting, dig lime or dolomite into the beds.

Mentha sp.
MINT
LABIATAE/LAMIACEAE

CONDITIONS
Climate. Grows in most climates, even in arid areas if it is watered regularly.

Aspect. Prefers a semi-shaded position but will grow in full sun if the soil is kept moist. Mint can be grown indoors in a container.

Soil. Moderately rich and well mulched soil that retains moisture. Too much organic matter or fresh manures added to the bed will encourage rust diseases.

FEATURES
There are many varieties of mint, but all are perennials and they all have square stems and invasive, spreading roots. They can be prostrate or upright in nature. The simple, light to dark green or mottled leaves have toothed edges and their own individual fragrance, depending on the variety. The small flowers are purple, pink or white and come in whorls on terminal spikes. They appear in summer. Because of their invasive nature, mints are best grown in containers or in garden beds that have a solid border at least 50 cm (20 in) deep.

GROWING METHOD
Planting. Most mints can be raised from seed (although some varieties, such as spearmint, cannot be propagated this way), but root division during spring and summer is the easiest method of propagation. Lift runners, divide them and replant in rich, moist soil.

Watering. Keep the soil moist as mint must always have plenty of water.

Fertilising. No fertiliser is necessary if mint is planted in well mulched soil.

Problems. Mint flea beetle is a tiny, dark, oval pest that is continually on the move when disturbed. It eats holes in the leaves and its larvae will eat into the roots of the plant. To treat it, keep weeds down and spread lime around the bush. Spider mite can be treated with an appropriate spray. Discolouring of leaves may indicate mint rust – which can be treated with sulphur dustings – or a form of wilt that causes leaves to brown and drop. Treat the wilt by removing diseased plants and do not feed with high-nitrogen fertilisers.

Pruning. Frequent pruning of the stems forces lateral branching and healthier plants.

HARVESTING
Picking. Pick young, fresh leaves at any time. The younger the leaf, the more tender and tasty it will be.

Storage. Dry the leaves by placing them on a rack in a cool, airy space. When they are dry, crumble them and store in airtight jars.

Freezing. Fresh leaves can be chopped and frozen in small packages or in ice cubes.

USES
Culinary. Mints have a wide range of flavours, from the fruity taste of apple mint to the perfume-like one of the eau de cologne variety, making them very useful, especially in sauces or jellies. They can be used fresh in salads, drinks, vinegars or as a garnish to vegetables, often turning a bland taste into an exciting experience. Dried mints can be used in place of some of the salt in soups.

Gardening. Some organic gardeners promote the growth of mint around apple trees to ward off moths, but there is some doubt about its effectiveness.

FEATURES

This small evergreen tree reaches 5–6 m (17–20 ft) tall and has compound leaves about 2–5 cm (1–2 in) long. They are lanceolate to ovate in shape, and spicily aromatic when crushed. The small white flowers are produced during spring and summer in clusters at the ends of the branches and then are followed by dark red berries.

GROWING METHOD

Planting. Can be raised from seed sown in spring into 15 cm (6 in) wide containers of potting or seed-raising mix. When seedlings are about 20 cm (8 in) tall, either pot them up to grow bigger or plant them out into their permanent positions. Alternatively, take firm tip cuttings in late spring or early summer. Insert them into sandy potting mix and place the containers onto a heated seed-germinating pad. Keep the soil evenly moist.

Watering. Trees grow fastest and best in soils that are always moist, so give regular, deep soakings during extended droughts or if rain is unreliable.

Fertilising. If soil is deep and fertile, a yearly or twice yearly application of rotted organic matter beneath the foliage canopy will be sufficient. In poorer soils or the monsoonal tropics, give a ration of complete plant food once in spring and again towards the end of summer.

Problems. The fruit is attractive to birds, so there's a risk of self-seeding in frost-free areas.

Pruning. No pruning is necessary but the tree can be pruned at the start of spring in order to control its size.

HARVESTING

Picking. Harvest the leaves at any time as they are needed.

Storage. You can dry the leaves but this diminishes the flavour. The longer they are stored the less flavour there will be.

Freezing. Not suitable for freezing.

USES

Culinary. Fresh leaves are used to impart a curry-like flavour to soups, stews, pickles and marinades. They cannot be used as a substitute for curry powder, which is a different product altogether.

Medicinal. In India, all parts of the tree are used medicinally. Extracts are said to be effective for the relief of headaches, diarrhoea and intestinal worms.

Gardening. This attractive tree can also be grown successfully in a big tub.

Murraya koenigii
CURRY TREE
RUTACEAE

CONDITIONS

Climate. Grows best in warm and tropical regions. It tolerates light frosts but only if they are relatively infrequent.

Aspect. Prefers full sun but in tropical areas will tolerate afternoon shade. In windy areas, grow it in a sheltered spot.

Soil. Needs deep, fertile, moisture-retentive soil that drains freely after watering or heavy rain.

Nasturtium officinale
WATERCRESS
CRUCIFERAE

CONDITIONS
Climate. Warm moist climates are ideal. In warm climates grow watercress mostly in winter, in cooler zones grow through spring and autumn.

Aspect. Prefers a wet shady place that is protected from both strong winds and winter frosts. A pot or tub that can be kept damp is also suitable.

Soil. If growing watercress in a container, use very damp rich soil and top it up occasionally with well rotted garden compost. Do not let the water stagnate: drain off some once a week and top it up with fresh water each time. The water should be alkaline and at a temperature of around 10°C (50°F).

FEATURES
Although European in origin, watercress is now widely used in Asian cuisines. It is a low-growing perennial (to 20 cm or 8 in) with a spreading habit. Round dark green leaves composed of several leaflets have a peppery mustard flavour and are carried on fleshy stems. These either float or are submerged in shallow, moving water or root in rich wet soil. Clusters of small white flowers appear in early summer.

GROWING METHOD
Planting. Grow by root division of a mature plant. Place new pieces into a container with good quality potting mix and then lower it into a waterbed. Seeds can also be sown in spring by placing them on a constantly damp seed-raising mix. Transplant seedlings to a permanent position when they are about 8 cm (3 in) tall.

Watering. Requires a great deal of water.

Fertilising. Apply soluble plant food that is high in nitrogen every two weeks from spring to late summer.

Problems. Watercress is sometimes subject to fungal diseases, which cause rotting of the stems and death of the leaves. Remove infected plants.

HARVESTING
Picking. Pick leaves as required.

Storage. Freshly picked leaves will keep in fresh cold water or sealed plastic bags in the fridge for a couple of days.

Freezing. Not suitable for freezing.

USES
Culinary. Watercress is rich in vitamin C. Use it raw in salads, sandwiches or as a garnish. The Chinese tend to cook the herb, making delicious soups.

FEATURES

There are several varieties of catmint or catnip, all with slightly different growing habits, but in general this is a low-growing perennial, reaching between 30 and 90 cm (1–3 ft). Fine white hairs cover both the grey-green leaves and the stem, which is square as in all members of the mint family. The leaves are coarse-toothed and ovate, although the base leaves are heart shaped. The tubular summer flowers are massed in spikes or whorls. White, pale pink or purplish blue in colour, they are followed by very fine seeds. Cats find some species of catmint very attractive.

GROWING METHOD

Planting. Once established, catmint self-seeds readily, and can also be grown from cuttings taken in spring. Cut a 10 cm (4 in) piece from the parent plant, remove the tip and lower leaves, and place the cutting in a thoroughly moist soil medium. Cuttings take root in 1–2 weeks. They are very sturdy and can be planted out into the garden. Water in thoroughly. You can also divide mature plants into three or four clumps in early spring.

Watering. Keep moist at all times. Do not stand pots in water or the plants will drown.

Fertilising. For more leaf growth, feed catmint in spring with nitrogen-rich fertiliser such as poultry manure.

Problems. Catmint is basically pest-free.

Pruning. Prune back each year to keep bushes in shape.

HARVESTING

Picking. Pick fresh leaves as required. Cut leafy stems in late summer when the plant is in bloom and hang them to dry in a cool, shady place.

Storage. Strip leaves from dried stems and store them in airtight jars.

Freezing. Wrap leaves in plastic wrap and freeze for up to six months.

USES

Culinary. Once popular salad and herbal tea ingredients, the fresh young leaves are less of a favourite now.

Craft. Use dried flowers and leaves in pot pourri mixtures, and in toys for cats.

Nepeta x *faassenii, N. cataria*
CATMINT
LABIATAE/LAMIACEAE

CONDITIONS

Climate. Grows in most climates, but is not well suited to lowland tropical regions. In arid regions water regularly.

Aspect. Prefers full sun to partial shade. The fragrance is stronger in good sunlight.

Soil. Best in light, organically enriched sandy loams. Dig in lime or dolomite if the soil is too acid.

Ocimum basilicum, O. sanctum
BASIL
LABIATAE/LAMIACEAE

CONDITIONS
Climate. Warm to hot. Sensitive to cold and frost. In cold areas grow basil indoors in containers.

Aspect. Full sun to partial shade. Protect from winds. In tropical areas basil needs some shade.

Soil. Rich, moist, well drained soils that are not too acid. Mulch once the soil has warmed up.

FEATURES
Most basils, including sweet or common basil (*O. basilicum*), are annuals, but perennial varieties are also grown. They include lemon basil (*O. basilicum* 'Citriodorum'), bush basil (*O. basilicum* 'Minimum') and sacred or holy basil (*O. sanctum*). All basils have an overriding and specific aroma and taste, depending on the variety. Their colours range from yellow-green to dark green and purple, and the small white flowers that appear in summer produce tiny dark brown seeds. Basils grow into bushy plants, between 30 and 90 cm (1–3 ft) tall.

GROWING METHOD
Planting. Plant seed in late spring to early summer in warm zones, in cooler months in the tropics, and in summer when the soil has warmed in colder areas. Sow seeds directly into the garden, covering them with a light scattering of seed-raising mix. Firm down and moisten the soil. Thin out seedlings to 20 cm (8 in) apart. Or sow seeds in trays using a moist mixture of vermiculite and perlite or a good quality seed-raising mix. Soil temperature needs to be warm: 25–30°C (77–86°F). When large enough to handle, prick them out to pots and then transplant into open beds or larger pots from mid-spring onwards.

Watering. Water regularly as basil likes moisture.

Fertilising. If growing in containers, feed occasionally with a nitrogen-rich liquid fertiliser.

Problems. Remove beetles and slugs by hand or set shallow beer traps in damp soil.

Pruning. Keep the centres pinched to inhibit flowering and promote a bushier plant.

HARVESTING
Picking. Pick fresh leaves at any time or harvest and dry them during late summer. Cut whole sprigs after the flower buds have formed but before they open.

Storage. Preserve leaves and sprigs in oils or vinegars, or dry leaves and store them in airtight jars. Place bunches in water and store them for a few days in the fridge.

Freezing. Wrap the sprigs in plastic wrap. They can be frozen for up to six months.

USES
Culinary. Basil is a very popular culinary herb, especially in Italian, Mediterranean and Thai cuisines. Use the leaves and flowers in salads or as an aromatic garnish, or in combination with other herbs in tomato, vegetable and meat dishes. Preserve leaves and sprigs in oils, vinegars or butters, to which they add their own particular flavour.

Medicinal. Basil tea is a useful remedy for travel sickness.

Craft. Basil is much prized for its fragrance, and is used in pot pourris and sachets. The flowering stems are sometimes used in small bouquets and other floral arrangements.

Gardening. Basil is a popular companion plant with organic gardeners, who believe that planting it next to tomatoes and capsicum will improve their growth.

FEATURES

This species includes annual, biennial and perennial plants with many upright leafy stems. From late spring and right through the summer, each of these stems is topped with a cluster of golden yellow (sometimes pink, red or white), sweetly fragrant flowers which open towards the end of the day. The foliage, which is bluish green, forms a rosette around the base of the plant. Evening primrose is native to dry areas in the central and eastern United States. It should be planted with caution as it self-seeds most prolifically and can spread quickly in favoured locations.

GROWING METHOD

Planting. Grows from seed sown in autumn or early spring directly where it is to grow. Thin seedlings out so that there is at least 30 cm (12 in) between them.

Watering. Do not overwater. Once established, plants are drought tolerant and can usually get by on rain in areas where it falls regularly.

Fertilising. No fertilising is necessary. Over-rich soils can lead to excessive foliage growth and weak or deformed stems.

Problems. No particular problems.

Pruning. Pruning is not necessary, but snap off flower stems after the blooms have faded but before the seeds ripen. This plant self-seeds freely and can create a major weed problem. Allow one plant to seed in order to regenerate the plants, but collect the seed before it falls so that you can sow it where you want it.

HARVESTING

Picking. All parts of the plant are edible. Leaves may be picked any time, while seeds are harvested when ripe in autumn. The small roots may also be dug in spring or autumn.

Storage. Store the seeds in airtight containers. Use other parts of the plant fresh.

Freezing. Not suitable for freezing.

USES

Culinary. Use the fresh leaves in salads, or lightly steam or stir-fry them. Eat the seeds raw or use them in recipes.

Medicinal. Tea made from the leaves is good for coughs and colds, and is a tonic for the liver, kidneys and intestines. An oil contained in the seeds has traditionally been credited with amazing therapeutic powers.

Gardening. Evening primrose looks wonderful in a moonlit garden; it is a pretty plant and a good partner for other meadow flowers such as California poppies and paper daisies.

Oenothera sp.
EVENING PRIMROSE
ONAGRACEAE

CONDITIONS

Climate. Evening primrose grows in cool, warm and hot, arid places.

Aspect. Full sun is essential.

Soil. Not very fussy about soil and grows in most places as long as the drainage is good. This plant thrives in average garden soils.

Origanum marjorana syn.
Marjorana hortensis
MARJORAM
LABIATAE/LAMIACEAE

CONDITIONS

Climate. Grows in warm zones; must be well drained in areas of summer rain. Doesn't like frost but does well in containers indoors in cooler areas. In the tropics grow as a cool season annual.

Aspect. Prefers full sun.

Soil. Quite rich soils containing plenty of compost and decayed animal manure. Add lime or dolomite if the soil is too acid. Shallow cultivate to keep the soil free of weeds.

FEATURES

This variety of marjoram, known as sweet or knotted marjoram, is the one most commonly grown in herb gardens. A tender, bushy perennial herb, it is often grown as an annual as it does not survive cold winters. It can grow to 60 cm (2 ft) or more, producing small oval leaves covered with fine hair. The leaves are light green on top and grey-green underneath, and are borne on short stalks. During summer very small white to lilac flowers appear in clusters, first in knot-like shapes, and produce tiny light brown seeds.

GROWING METHOD

Planting. Seeds are slow to germinate and are usually planted in seed boxes. Pot on into small containers after the first few true leaves have formed, and then put into the garden in spring when the seedlings are established. Plant in small clumps 15 cm (6 in) apart. Propagation by cuttings is also possible, during autumn. Take 8 cm (3 in) pieces of woody stem from the parent plant, trim the leaves from the cuttings and strike them in a mixture of two-thirds coarse sand to one-third peat moss. Transplant in spring when the root structure is established and new growth appears on the stems. You can also divide the roots of a mature plant in autumn.

Watering. Water adequately but do not overwater.

Fertilising. Little additional fertiliser is needed in well mulched soil. Apply liquid organic fertiliser or seaweed-based conditioner every six weeks.

Problems. Damping off of seedlings is one problem of this herb: they become water-soaked, shrivel and die. Keep seed beds warm and use good quality, sterile seed mix. Bad drainage will bring on this disease, and root rot in older plants. Pests include aphids and spider mite. Hose down, or treat with insecticide.

Pruning. Flowers can be pruned at knot stage to maintain the shape of the bush.

HARVESTING

Picking. Pick leaves for culinary use at any time. Harvest leaves to be dried and unopened knot-like flowers in summer, and hang them to dry in a cool, shady spot.

Storage. Remove leaves and buds from the stems and store them in airtight jars.

Freezing. Chop finely, mix with a little water and freeze in ice cubes.

USES

Culinary. The taste resembles that of a mild oregano, for which it can be substituted. It is often used in bouquet garni. Use the fresh leaves and flowers in salads, stuffings for meat and poultry, or in marinades. The flavour blends with most vegetable dishes and can also be used to flavour vinegars and oils. Dried, it makes a refreshing herbal tea.

Craft. Marjoram adds fragrance to pot pourris.

FEATURES

Oregano is very closely related to marjoram and is often confused with it. Three varieties of this summer flowering perennial are widely grown. Common or wild oregano (*O. vulgare*) is a small shrub growing to 30 cm (12 in) high, with woody stems and oval, soft hairy leaves and tiny white flowers. Golden oregano (*O. vulgare* 'Aureum') is very decorative in the garden but will tend to spread if uncontrolled. The leaves are golden yellow in colour and the flowers are pink. Greek or white oregano (*O. vulgare* 'Viride') is taller than the other varieties, reaching 50 cm (20 in). Its leaves are dark green and covered with a white hairy bloom. They have a very pungent flavour. The flowers are white.

GROWING METHOD

Planting. Sow seeds in spring, in damp, warm seed-raising mix. For the best results, temperatures need to be above 20°C (68°F). Transplant seedlings into the garden when well established. More often, propagate by root division in late spring as it spreads by underground stems, or propagate by layering. Scarify the undersurface of the branch, peg it down and cover with soil. Keep damp until roots form, cut it off and replant. Replace plants every couple of years as the stems become woody.

Watering. Keep plants well watered and do not let the soil dry out.

Fertilising. Apply liquid organic fertiliser or seaweed-based soil conditioner every six weeks.

Problems. Treat aphids, leaf miner and spider mite with appropriate insecticidal sprays. Hosing leaves may bring temporary relief but if infestations are bad, remove and burn the diseased plants. Remove plants affected by root rot, which is caused by bad drainage; rotate plants every three years.

Pruning. Prune after flowering to keep plant compact.

HARVESTING

Picking. Pick fresh leaves throughout the growing season as required. Cut whole stems before flowering and hang them up to dry in a cool shady spot.

Storage. Strip dry leaves from the stems and store them in airtight jars.

Freezing. Wrap in plastic wrap; oregano can be frozen for up to six months.

USES

Culinary. Oregano is widely used as a flavouring, especially in Mediterranean-style cooking, in sauces, soups and casseroles, as well as in vinegars and butters.

Gardening. Oregano plants make excellent groundcovers.

Origanum vulgare
OREGANO
LABIATAE/LAMIACEAE

CONDITIONS

Climate. Prefers warm, relatively dry climates where most rain falls in winter. In areas of summer rain, soil must be very well drained. In the tropics grow it as a cool season annual. It does not like frost but grows satisfactorily in cooler regions as a container herb.

Aspect. Needs full sun or partial shade.

Soil. Likes well drained, not too rich garden soil. Mulch to keep soils moist in hot, dry weather.

Petroselinum sp.
PARSLEY
APIACEAE/UMBELLIFERAE

CONDITIONS
Climate. Parsley likes a warm to coolish climate. Grow these plants as a cool season annual in the tropics or in a container in areas where there are frosts.

Aspect. Parsley prefers full sun or possibly part shade.

Soil. Parsley plants need only a moderately rich, well drained soil.

FEATURES
Parsley grows from a strong tap root with erect, 30 cm (12 in) tall stems bearing divided, feather-like small leaves which may be flattish or curly depending on the variety. Tiny yellowish green flowers arranged in clusters are borne on tall stalks in summer, and produce small, brown oval and ribbed seeds. Common varieties of this biennial or short lived perennial plant include curly parsley (*P. crispum*), flat-leaved or Italian parsley (*P. crispum* var. *neapolitanum*), and Hamburg or turnip-rooted parsley (*P. crispum* var. *tuberosum*).

GROWING METHOD
Planting. Grow from seed planted during the warmer months when the soil is warm – above 10°C (50°F). Germination takes 6–8 weeks, so seeds are usually brought on in seed boxes before they are planted out. Before planting, create optimum conditions by soaking the seeds in warm water for 24 hours and pouring boiling water over the soil to raise the temperature. Transplant the seedlings out, 25 cm (10 in) apart, after they have grown several true leaves. If parsley is grown in a container, the pot should be at least 20 cm (8 in) deep, and the longer tap root of Hamburg parsley will require an even deeper one. Once parsley plants are established in the garden, the mature plants can be left to self-sow when they go to seed during the summer months in their second year of growth.

Watering. Keep the soil moist and do not let it dry out in dry weather.

Fertilising. Side feedings of a nitrogen-rich liquid fertiliser will promote more leaf growth.

Problems. The main pests are parsley worm, root-knot nematode and carrot weevils, which devour the foliage, stunt the growth and burrow into the top and root. Practise crop rotation and destroy affected plants. Watch for white fungal growth near the base of the plant and a brownish crust on the soil, indicative of crown rot. Treat as for pests.

Pruning. Parsley can be kept productive by frequent pruning and by nipping out the seed stalks whenever they appear.

HARVESTING
Picking. New growth comes from the centre of the stem, so always pick parsley from the outside of the plant. Pick this vitamin-rich, nutritious herb as needed.

Storage. Broad-leaved Italian parsley, with its stronger taste, gives a better result when dried than the other varieties.

Freezing. Curly parsley freezes well. Wrap it first in plastic wrap and put it in the freezer for up to six months.

USES
Culinary. Parsley is used in salads, as a garnish and in cooking. Hamburg parsley is used like a root vegetable. Fresh parsley is a breath freshener.

FEATURES
A dainty, feathery-looking annual that may reach a height of 60 cm (2 ft), anise has rounded, mid-green leaves with distinctly toothed edges. The flat heads of white flowers appear in late spring or summer, followed by the small licorice-flavoured seeds – aniseeds.

GROWING METHOD
Planting. When spring has turned warm, sow seeds where they are to grow about 1 cm (1/2 in) deep and 15 cm (6 in) apart. For its seeds to ripen properly, anise requires a long hot summer, so in cooler areas sow them indoors in late winter or early spring into trays of seed-raising mix. Place in a sunny spot on a heated seed-raising pad and keep lightly moist. Prick seedlings out into small pots and place these on the heated pad. Plant out only when the weather has turned warm.

Watering. Never allow the soil to dry out. To avoid flattening the stems, water the soil not the leaves.

Fertilising. If soil is friable but poor, dig in complete plant food when planting. Mulch when seedlings reach 20 cm (8 in).

HARVESTING
Picking. Place the ripe seed heads in the sun to dry out. Pick the fresh leaves as they are needed.

Storage. When the heads are dry, rub the seeds to separate them from the husks. Store seeds in airtight jars.

Freezing. Not suitable for freezing.

USES
Culinary. The seeds give a pleasant licorice taste to many cooked foods, including cakes and pies, stewed fruits and vegetable dishes. Use fresh leaves in salads or add them late to casseroles, stews and soups.

Medicinal. A good tonic for the digestive system. Regular intake of aniseed is said to help prevent colds and to banish bad breath. Taken before bed, aniseed encourages sound sleep.

Craft. Aniseed is used in pot pourris and pomanders.

Gardening. Anise will attract bees and butterflies to your garden.

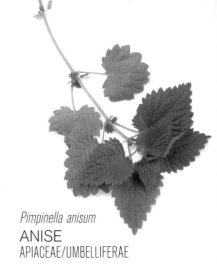

Pimpinella anisum
ANISE
APIACEAE/UMBELLIFERAE

CONDITIONS
Climate. Will grow in all areas, but in the monsoonal tropics is best raised in the cooler, drier months.

Aspect. Prefers full sun, sheltered from strong winds.

Soil. Light, sandy, well drained soil enriched with rotted organic matter.

Polygonum odoratum
VIETNAMESE MINT
CONVALLARIACEAE/LILIACEAE

CONDITIONS

Climate. Grows best in a warm or tropical climate as it is not hardy in temperatures that are much below freezing.

Aspect. Plant in bright dappled shade or where it receives shade during the hotter part of the day in summer. It grows in full sun if kept well watered.

Soil. Fertile, well drained soil that contains enough rotted organic matter to retain the moisture. It enjoys good conditions and can get out of hand very quickly if regular care is not taken to control excess growth.

FEATURES

Vietnamese mint is a very aromatic, creeping perennial that may grow to nearly 1 m (3 ft) tall in ideal conditions. The reddish stems are jointed at leaf junctions, and wherever they touch the ground, roots will form. The lanceolate leaves are about 8 cm (3 in) long, olive green with a brownish red marking on the upper side. Small, pink flowers are produced at the ends of the stems in spring and summer.

GROWING METHOD

Planting. As Vietnamese mint stems root where they touch the ground, new plants are easily created by detaching the newly rooted section from the parent plant and replanting it. Cuttings also root very easily if struck in late spring and summer. The cutting can be taken from the parent plant and then inserted into the ground directly where it is to grow.

Watering. Although Vietnamese mint that has withered from lack of water will recover when rewetted, it grows fastest and best where it has ample water always.

Fertilising. During spring and summer, water it occasionally with soluble fertiliser that contains a high proportion of nitrogen or sprinkle it with a ration of complete plant food once in spring and again in summer.

Problems. No particular problems apart from the plant's ability to spread fast.

HARVESTING

Picking. Pick individual leaves or stems as required. Vietnamese mint is best used fresh.

Storage. As this plant grows so fast, there is no need to store it.

Freezing. Not suitable for freezing.

USES

Culinary. A popular herb in Vietnamese and other Southeast Asian cuisines, Vietnamese mint is added during cooking and is also a salad ingredient. It has a peppery taste which is pleasant in small amounts.

FEATURES

This spreading, succulent annual is very adaptable, growing as a weed in many parts of the world. Purslane forms a mat-like growth, which makes it a useful groundcover in areas where it will not spread unduly. It has bright, light green, spoon-shaped leaves on trailing, fleshy stems that are reddish in colour. The small bright yellow flowers are produced at stem junctions during the spring and summer months. They will open only when the plants are in sunlight.

GROWING METHOD

Planting. Sow the seeds directly where they are to grow in early spring or, in cooler areas, after all danger of frost has passed. In tropical areas, sow them during the autumn months. Purslane can also be started from cuttings that are taken any time from mid-spring onwards. Make the cuttings about 5 cm (2 in) long, strip off the lower leaves and insert the cuttings into small containers of very sandy potting mix or seed-raising mix. Keep the containers warm and moist, and put them in a bright but not sunny spot until the roots have formed. The plants can then be planted out into their permanent positions in the garden.

Watering. Having water-storing leaves and stems, purslane is well able to cope with dryness, but for the best quality leaves, keep the soil evenly moist during spring and summer.

Fertilising. Fertilising will not be necessary if purslane is grown in fertile soil. Elsewhere, water the plants once a month with a high-nitrogen soluble fertiliser.

Problems. No pest or disease problems, but flowers should be routinely removed to minimise unwanted spread by seed.

HARVESTING

Picking. Let the plants grow until they are about 10 cm (4 in) across and then pick the stems and leaves as they are needed. Plants regrow quickly.

Storage. Cut purslane stems may be stored in the fridge for a few days.

Freezing. Not suitable for freezing.

USES

Culinary. Leaves and stems contain large amounts of iron and have a fresh, acid taste. Eat them raw in salads, or lightly stir-fry or steam them as a vegetable.

Portulaca oleracea
PURSLANE
PORTULACACEAE

CONDITIONS

Climate. Purslane can be grown almost everywhere, from cool zones to tropical climates, as it is very forgiving.

Aspect. Prefers full sun but will tolerate shade for part of the day.

Soil. Plants will produce succulent leaves more quickly if they are grown in fertile, sandy soil that contains some rotted organic matter.

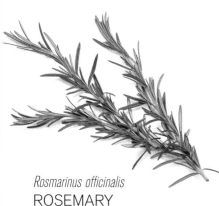

Rosmarinus officinalis
ROSEMARY
LABIATAE/LAMIACEAE

FEATURES

A perennial, evergreen woody shrub, rosemary has thin, needle-like leaves, glossy green above and whitish to grey-green and hairy below. They have a fragrance reminiscent of pine needles. In spring, small-lobed flowers appear among the leaves. They are white or pale blue to pinkish, depending on the variety. There are several varieties of rosemary, ranging in habit from the upright (*R. officinalis*) to the dwarf (*R. officinalis* 'Nana') and the prostrate (*R. officinalis* 'Prostratus'). Other popular varieties are 'Blue Lagoon' rosemary (*R. officinalis* 'Collingwood Ingram') and pink rosemary (*R. officinalis* 'Rosea'). Rosemary bushes can be between 50 cm (20 in) and 2 m (6–7 ft) high, depending on the variety.

CONDITIONS

Climate. Grows well in warm, relatively dry climates with most rain in winter. This is a good herb to grow in containers, and it also grows well in seaside positions where not much else will grow, as it will withstand salt and wind. Tolerates cooler climates, but best grown there in containers.

Aspect. Likes full sun and a reasonably dry position.

Soil. Needs well drained soil to lessen the risk of root rot, and is more fragrant in alkaline soils. If acidity is a problem, dig in 200 g per square metre (7 oz per square yard) of lime or dolomite before planting.

GROWING METHOD

Planting. Propagate mainly from cuttings and layering. Seeds are not often used because they have long germination times and tend not to come true to type. Take 10 cm (4 in) long cuttings in late spring (and early autumn in warmer climates), trim off the upper and lower leaves, and place the cuttings in small pots containing a moist mixture of two-thirds coarse sand and one-third peat moss. Cover with a plastic dome and set aside in a semi-shaded position until roots and new leaves form.

Watering. Prefers soil to be on the drier side; give average garden watering.

Fertilising. Fertiliser is not needed.

Problems. Look out for mealy bug, scale, spider mite and whitefly. Treat with appropriate insecticidal sprays. Botrytis blight, a fungal growth affecting all parts of the plant, and root rot can be treated by improving drainage and removing yellowing leaves and dead flowers or badly infected plants. Frequent summer rainfall can cause the shrub to rot.

Pruning. Prune to keep bushes compact. 'Blue Lagoon' has a very straggly growing habit.

HARVESTING

Picking. Fresh leaves or sprigs 5–10 cm (2–4 in) long can be picked as required.

Storage. Dry sprigs in a cool dry place, strip leaves from stems and store in airtight jars.

Freezing. Store sprigs in plastic bags and freeze for up to six months. To use, crumble before they thaw.

USES

Cosmetic. Rosemary hair rinses help control greasy hair.

Culinary. Use fresh, dried or frozen leaves in cooking, marinades and salad dressings. The leaves are used in vinegars, oils, teas and butters. Fresh flowers are good in salads or as decorations for puddings and desserts.

Craft. It is used in pot pourris and herb wreaths.

FEATURES

Broad-leaved sorrel, *R. acetosa*, is an upright clumping perennial with spear-shaped, lemon acid-tasting leaves, growing 60–90 cm (2–3 ft) tall. French sorrel, *R. scutatus*, has heart-shaped leaves with a more delicate lemon flavour; it is lower growing, to about 50 cm (20 in). Small green flowers appear on long stalks in summer.

GROWING METHOD

Planting. Sow seed directly into the garden during spring. Thin seedlings to 30 cm (12 in) apart. Mature plants can be divided in autumn or early spring. To do this, dig up older plants, trim the leaves and stems, and replant the divided portions 30–40 cm (12–16 in) apart.

Watering. Water regularly. If the soil is left to dry out, the leaves wilt and burn off.

Fertilising. Give an application of high-nitrogen liquid or soluble fertiliser monthly.

Problems. Snails and slugs attack leaves. Pick them off by hand or set stale beer traps among the beds (see page 45). If leaf miners attack the plant, remove and destroy the infected leaves.

Pruning. If you are not growing plants for seed, pinch out the seed-bearing stalks as they appear.

HARVESTING

Picking. Leaves can be picked throughout the growing season as required. Always pick from the outside of the clump.

Storage. Freshly picked leaves will keep in the fridge for a few days if they are stored in a plastic bag.

Freezing. Pack leaves in plastic wrap and freeze for up to six months.

USES

Culinary. Sorrel used to be cooked and eaten like spinach. Today, because it is known to contain a lot of oxalic acid, the small lemony-flavoured leaves are only used in such dishes as salads or soups.

Rumex acetosa, R. scutatus
SORREL
POLYGONACEAE

CONDITIONS

Climate. Prefers moist, warm climates but grows in cooler regions; tolerates some dryness. Grow as a cool season annual in the tropics.

Aspect. Prefers sun or semi-shade but needs protection from winter frosts.

Soil. Needs light, average soil. To promote strong leaf growth, add animal manures to the soil and mulch well. Tolerates slightly acid soils.

Ruta graveolens
RUE
RUTACEAE

CONDITIONS

Climate. Grows in cool or warm climates, especially well in areas where most rain falls in winter. Dislikes summer humidity.

Aspect. In cooler areas where summers are mild, full sun is essential. In warmer areas, rue will tolerate some, but not full, shade.

Soil. Deep, well drained but rather poor, sandy or gravelly soil. Over-rich soils lead to lax, rampant growth and loss of compactness.

FEATURES

Rue is a rounded, shrubby perennial with many stems rising from a woody base. It can grow to about 1 m (3 ft) tall with a similar spread. The leaves are strongly aromatic and the colour varies: it may be green, blue-green or variegated. The foliage is finely divided and makes an attractive background for the small, spicily fragrant, yellowish flowers which appear in late spring or summer.

GROWING METHOD

Planting. Sow seeds in spring in trays or punnets of seed-raising mix. Keep moist and place in bright dappled shade until germination is complete. Gradually expose to greater amounts of sun before planting into the final position. Alternatively, new plants can be grown from cuttings taken towards the end of summer. Select growth that has matured but is not yet woody, and place 10 cm (4 in) cuttings into pots of very sandy potting mix. Keep the mix moist and place pots in bright shade until roots have formed. Where stems of mature plants touch the ground, they will often form roots. These rooted 'layers' can be detached from the parent plant, dug up and relocated.

Watering. Water deeply every two weeks from mid-autumn to mid-spring as this simulates the plant's natural conditions. Water in summer only in really dry conditions.

Fertilising. No fertilising is needed.

Problems. Usually no pest and disease problems but high summer heat, rain and humidity can lead to fungus diseases of the leaves and root rot. The plant's sap can severely irritate sensitive skins. Wear gloves whenever the plant is handled and do not let it touch your hands, face or body.

Pruning. Untidy plants may be pruned hard in early spring. Using sharp secateurs, cut back to a main framework of branches. New growth will restore the plant's rounded, bushy habit. Less untidy plants may be made more compact by a light, all-over shearing in mid-spring.

HARVESTING

Picking. Rue has toxic properties and must be used with extreme caution. Leaves may be picked at any time to make an insecticidal infusion.

Storage. Bunch leafy stems and dry them in a dark, airy place for later use.

Freezing. Not suitable for freezing.

USES

Gardening. Rue is a decorative plant that infuses the garden with its herbal aroma, especially on hot days. It is a good companion for other Mediterranean plants such as lavender and echium. An insect repellent for use on ornamental or productive plants can be made from the leaves.

FEATURES

Sage is a small, woody perennial shrub growing to about 75 cm (30 in). The long, oval, grey-green leaves, velvety in texture, have a slightly bitter, camphor-like taste. The flowers, borne on spikes in spring, are coloured from pink to red, purple, blue or white, depending on the variety. There are many varieties of this beautiful and hardy herb. The most popular edible types are common or garden sage (*S. officinalis*), purple sage (*S.* x *superba*), pineapple sage (*S. elegans* syn. *S. rutilans*) and golden or variegated sage (*S. officinalis* 'Variegata'). Other sages are grown purely for their decorative qualities in the garden, chief among them being clary sage (*S. sclarea*). Sage becomes woody after about four years.

GROWING METHOD

Planting. Plant seeds in late spring in seed-raising boxes, and when seedlings are 8–10 cm (3–4 in) tall, plant them out into the garden, spacing them 45 cm (18 in) apart. Cuttings, 10 cm (4 in) long, can be taken in late autumn or spring. Remove the upper and lower leaves, and plant the cuttings in small pots containing a soil mix of two-thirds coarse sand and one-third peat moss. Water, then cover the pots with a plastic bag to create a mini-greenhouse. Plant out when the cutting has developed roots and new leaves. Sage may also be layered – scarify the lower side of a branch and peg it into the soil to take root.

Watering. Give a deep soaking once a week.

Fertilising. At planting, apply complete plant food. Give an application each spring.

Problems. Slugs can be a problem. Pick them off by hand or set a stale beer trap in a saucer with the rim just at soil level. Spider mites will need to be sprayed with an insecticide. If the plant suddenly flops over for no apparent reason, this is probably due to bacterial wilt affecting the vascular system. Remove affected plants before the disease spreads. Root rot can be avoided by providing good drainage.

Pruning. Prune off flowers to stop the plant from setting seed.

HARVESTING

Picking. Leaves or flowers can be picked at any time as required. For drying purposes, harvest leaves before flowering begins.

Storage. Dry leaves on racks in a cool, airy place and then store them in airtight jars.

Freezing. Chop leaves, pack in plastic wrap and freeze for up to six months.

USES

Cosmetic. Sage hair rinses, used regularly, will darken grey hair.

Culinary. Fresh or dried leaves are used extensively as a flavouring in stuffings, marinades and cooking. The individual fruity flavour of pineapple sage complements citrus fruits and the edible flowers look decorative in salads or as a garnish.

Salvia sp.
SAGE
LABIATAE/LAMIACEAE

CONDITIONS

Climate. Sage plants tolerate most climates, except for the monsoonal tropics. In areas of extreme heat or cold, the plants are best grown in containers.

Aspect. Most varieties prefer a sunny, sheltered, well drained position.

Soil. Rich, well drained, non-clayish soil. If necessary, raise the beds to at least 20 cm (8 in) above the surrounding garden level. Prepare the beds by digging in 250 g (9 oz) of lime or dolomite, followed by plenty of organic matter, such as compost and decayed animal manure.

Sanguisorba minor syn.
Poterium sanguisorba
SALAD BURNET
ROSACEAE

CONDITIONS

Climate. Warm to cold regions are best. Burnet is not suited to the tropics.

Aspect. Salad burnet likes a sunny, well drained position.

Soil. Most soil types are suitable. Add lime or dolomite if the soil conditions are acid. Ensure soil is well drained at all times.

FEATURES

This small but bushy perennial herb grows in a clump about 50 cm (20 in) high. The roundish grey-green, toothed leaves are borne on a central stem which droops down close to the ground. Flower stems, growing to about 60 cm (2 ft) high, appear in summer and produce pinkish red oval flowers. Burnet is an attractive border plant and it can also be grown successfully in pots.

GROWING METHOD

Planting. Salad burnet readily self-sows. Germinate seed in seed-raising boxes, cover the seed lightly with mix and keep the soil damp. When the seedlings are 5–10 cm (2–4 in) tall, plant them into the garden or containers, spaced 30–40 cm (12–16 in) apart. Propagation by division of the parent plant during autumn or spring is also possible.

Watering. Water thoroughly in hot weather but do not overwater in winter as the plant tolerates much drier conditions then.

Fertilising. Apply complete plant food once each year in early spring and water in well.

Problems. Burnet suffers from root rot if the soil is not well drained. If conditions are too damp in winter, crown rot will develop and the plants will turn yellow and die.

Pruning. Removal of flower stalks will stimulate new leaf growth.

HARVESTING

Picking. Pick the leaves when they are still quite young and tender.

Storage. Cannot be successfully stored.

Freezing. Cannot be frozen.

USES

Culinary. Use burnet only when fresh. The leaves have a cucumber scent and flavour, and are much prized in salads or with fresh vegetables. They can also be chopped and included in cooked soups or sauces. Freshly picked sprigs look effective as a garnish in summer drinks.

Gardening. As a companion plant, burnet does very well if grown close by beds of thyme and mint.

FEATURES

A deciduous shrub or small tree, elder or elderberry is usually less than 6 m (20 ft) tall with rough, corky bark and compound leaves composed of five or so toothed dark green leaflets. Heads of creamy white, scented flowers appear in summer, leading to shiny blue-black berries in autumn. The flowers attract bees while the berries are eaten by birds.

GROWING METHOD

Planting. Sow from seed in spring, or dig and detach suckers, with their own roots, from the parent plant. This can be done at any time, but spring is generally best. Elders can also be propagated by cuttings. Take hardwood cuttings in winter or tip cuttings in spring. Root either type in containers of very sandy potting mix. Pot them up to grow larger and then plant them out into their permanent positions. If you are planting a group or row, leave at least 3 m (10 ft) between them to allow room for the suckers to develop.

Watering. Elders like moisture at their roots at all times, especially in summer. If rainfall is reliable and reasonably regular, mature plants usually need little extra water.

Fertilising. In average garden soils no special fertilising is required, especially if you mulch beneath the plants with rotted organic matter. If the soil is not particularly fertile, a ration of complete plant food once in early spring is sufficient.

Problems. No particular problems.

Pruning. No pruning is necessary.

HARVESTING

Picking. Pick the flower heads in the morning but only when all the flowers on each head have bloomed. Dry them in a cool, dark, airy place. Pick the berries when they are ripe.

Storage. Dried flowers can be removed from their stems and stored in airtight containers. Ripe berries can also be dried and similarly stored.

Freezing. Berries that have been cooked for a few minutes may be frozen for later use.

USES

Cosmetic. Cold elderflower tea splashed daily onto the face tones and soothes the skin.

Culinary. You can make fresh flowers into elderflower wine and jams or jellies. The berries can also be made into jams or jellies, and the juice can be fermented into elderberry wine. Berries should not be eaten raw.

Medicinal. Tea made from young leaves and taken in small doses is a diuretic, while the juice of cooked berries is taken for headaches.

Gardening. Elderberries, with their dense growth and suckering habit, make a good privacy screen and reasonable windbreak. Use as an understorey shrub beneath tall, open trees.

Sambucus nigra
ELDER
CAPRIFOLIACEAE

CONDITIONS

Climate. Best in cool climates. Where autumn nights are sufficiently cold, elder leaves colour well before falling. Grows well enough in warm areas but does not produce much in the way of autumn colour there.

Aspect. A sunny position is best although the plant will tolerate bright dappled shade or a few hours of full shade each day.

Soil. Friable fertile soil that drains well yet stays moist is best, but elder accepts a wide range of soil types.

Santolina chamaecyparissus
COTTON LAVENDER
ASTERACEAE/COMPOSITAE

CONDITIONS
Climate. Cotton lavender suits both cool and warm climates, and tolerates the heat of arid areas if watered as needed.

Aspect. Full sun is essential.

Soil. Good drainage is essential but it does grow well in poor, rather dry soils. If conditions are too rich it loses its dense, compact appearance and becomes straggly and lax. Cotton lavender will tolerate alkaline soils.

FEATURES
Grey, rounded and cushiony, cotton lavender is a low ground-covering shrub that usually grows about 30 cm (12 in) tall, sometimes taller. When crushed, the toothed leaves give off a strong aroma reminiscent of lavender but with a delightful difference. In summer, dull yellow flowers appear on leafless stems and make a striking contrast to the soft grey leaves.

GROWING METHOD
Planting. In late spring, take 8 cm (3 in) long cuttings of stems that have lost their sappy freshness but have not yet become woody. Insert the cuttings into small containers of sandy potting mix, and keep the mix moist and the container shaded until roots develop after 4–6 weeks. Harden off the cuttings by moving the container into full sun in stages so as not to burn the leaves that have become used to shade. When fully hardened, plant out the new plants about 30 cm (12 cm) apart.

Watering. Cotton lavender does best when the most rain falls from mid-autumn to mid-spring, with dry summers. Water to simulate these conditions. Once established, cotton lavender is tolerant of dry weather.

Fertilising. No fertilising is needed.

Problems. High summer rainfall and humidity can cause the plant to rot.

Pruning. Shear the plant all over once or twice during the summer months and once again more heavily in autumn. This will keep it neat and very bushy.

HARVESTING
Picking. Sprigs of leaves may be picked at any time as they are required.

Storage. Tie sprigs of the leaves together and hang them upside down in a dark airy place to dry. Then you can store the dried sprigs in an airtight container.

Freezing. Not suitable for freezing.

USES
Craft. Dried leaves can be used in pot pourris and herbal sachets.

Gardening. Cotton lavender is mostly used today as an edging plant along paths or driveways, or to border herb or vegetable gardens or other formal plantings. It can also be used as an unusual large-scale groundcover, especially if used on dry, sunny banks.

FEATURES

Summer savory (*S. hortensis*) is an annual plant growing to about 50 cm (20 in). It has small, narrow greyish leaves that turn slightly purple during summer and early autumn. The leaves are attached directly to a pinkish stem, and small white flowers appear on the plant in summer. The winter savories, both the upright (*S. montana*) and the prostrate (*S. montana* 'Repens') varieties, are perennial forms and have low-growing (they may reach 40 cm or 16 in) or sprawling habits. Glossy, dark green lanceolate leaves grow from woody stems in summer, and white to lilac flowers are grouped in terminal spikes.

GROWING METHOD

Planting. Sow seeds of summer savory directly into their final garden position in spring, after the weather has warmed up. Lightly cover them with soil and keep the soil around them damp. When seedlings are established, thin them to 45 cm (18 in) apart and support each plant by mounding soil around the base. Winter savory is best propagated by cuttings and root division during spring or autumn. Remove the upper and lower leaves of 8–10 cm (3–4 in) long cuttings and plant the trimmed stem in a mixture of two-thirds coarse sand and one-third peat moss. Water the container and cover it with plastic supported on a wire frame. Plant the seedlings out when new leaves appear and a root structure has developed. Pot up pieces of the divided root of the parent plant and transplant them later into the garden.

Watering. Water regularly, although summer and winter savories can bear dry conditions.

Fertilising. Summer savory needs to be given side applications of liquid fertiliser every two or three weeks during the spring and summer growth cycle.

Problems. Savories are not worried by pests or diseases to any great extent, with the exception of root rot, which can sometimes affect the winter varieties. Good drainage is essential for these plants, and it is prudent to rotate crops every three years.

Pruning. Prune winter savory in autumn after flowering (as a protection against winter cold) and again in early spring; use the cuttings to grow new plants.

HARVESTING

Picking. Pick fresh leaves of both summer and winter varieties at any time.

Storage. Dry leaves in a cool, airy space and then store them in airtight jars.

Freezing. Pack sprigs in plastic wrap and freeze for up to six months.

USES

Culinary. Summer savory has a peppery flavour and is called the 'bean' herb, as it complements beans and other vegetables. It is also used in herb vinegars and butters. Winter savory has a stronger aroma and more piney taste: use it with game meats and terrines. Either type can be used to make savory tea.

Satureja sp.
SAVORY
LABIATAE/LAMIACEAE

CONDITIONS

Climate. Grows best in warm climates. Winter savory can withstand much colder temperatures than the summer variety. Neither variety of savory is suited to growing in the tropics.

Aspect. Both varieties of savory prefer to be grown in full sun.

Soil. Savories like well drained, alkaline soils. If necessary, dress beds with lime, 200 g per square metre (7 oz per square yard). Summer savory prefers slightly rich soil and makes an ideal herb to grow in containers; winter savory favours a less rich, rather sandy soil.

Symphytum officinale
COMFREY
BORAGINACEAE

CONDITIONS
Climate. Prefers moist climates of warm and cool areas. Doesn't grow well in hot, dry inland areas.

Aspect. Prefers full sun but tolerates partial shade.

Soil. Comfrey needs moist, rich soils. Prepare beds with plenty of compost and animal manures.

FEATURES
This large, coarse, hairy perennial grows to 1 m (3 ft) or more high. It has dark green, lanceolate leaves, which reach 25–30 cm (10–12 in) long, and clusters of five-lobed flowers in yellow, white or mauve in summer. The sticky qualities of its rhizome, which is black outside and has juicy white flesh within, gave rise to its nickname of slippery root; its other name, knit-bone, comes from its use in healing. The plant dies down over winter but makes a strong recovery in spring and can be quite invasive in the garden, overrunning other plants once it takes hold. Confine it to distant parts of the garden where it can form an attractive backdrop to other plants.

GROWING METHOD
Planting. Comfrey can be propagated from spring plantings of seed, by cuttings at any stage of its life cycle or by root division in autumn.

Watering. Water well as this fleshy herb requires a great deal of water.

Fertilising. Requires little fertiliser or other maintenance once established.

Problems. No specific pests or diseases.

Pruning. Cutting the flowers will encourage more leaf growth on this plant.

HARVESTING
Picking. Pick the leaves in the spring, summer and autumn.

Storage. Dry the leaves and store them in airtight containers.

Freezing. Can be frozen for up to six months.

USES
Culinary. Culinary use is not recommended as controversy surrounds the use of young leaves in salads. Dried leaves are sometimes used to make a herbal tea.

Medicinal. The plant contains unusually high concentrations of vitamin B12, but a great deal would need to be eaten daily to have any beneficial effect; some studies suggest that certain alkaloids in the plant can cause chronic liver problems.

Gardening. Comfrey is best used as a liquid manure: steep fresh leaves in water for several weeks. Leaves can also be used to promote decomposition in the compost heap, so plant it close by.

FEATURES

A perennial, feverfew has aromatic, finely cut leaves and clusters of small, white, daisy-like flowers in spring (summer in cool areas). The plant is densely foliaged and can grow to 60 cm (2 ft). Leaves are usually a fresh, light green but a golden foliaged form is also available.

GROWING METHOD

Planting. Easily grown from seed sown in early spring. Press seeds just beneath the surface where the plants are to grow. Established plants can be dug up in winter and divided. Each division should have its own roots and the divisions should be replanted immediately. Soft-tip cuttings taken in mid-spring will also root easily. Make cuttings about 8 cm (3 in) long and insert them into small pots of very sandy potting mix. Place in a warm but shady and sheltered spot, and keep moist. Roots should form in about three weeks.

Watering. Do not overwater. Feverfew does not thrive on neglect but neither does it need frequent watering. Excessively wet conditions will cause the plant to rot.

Fertilising. A ration of complete plant food applied once each spring will meet the plant's needs. Alternatively, feed monthly with liquid or soluble plant food and water in.

Problems. Slugs, snails and caterpillars can strip the foliage or eat young plants entirely. Lay snail bait during spring and autumn; pick off and squash caterpillars whenever you see them. For major infestations of caterpillars, spray plants with products containing *Bacillus thuringiensis*, a biological control that affects only caterpillars.

HARVESTING

Picking. All the upper parts of the plant are useful medicinally and whole plants may be harvested any time they are in full bloom. Fresh, young leaves can be harvested any time but remember that plants need their leaves to live and you should grow enough plants so that you do not concentrate on just one or two for picking.

Storage. Dry the upper parts, including leaves, stems and flowers, in a cool, dark, airy place. When dry, coarsely chop and store in an airtight jar.

Freezing. Freshly picked leaves can be wrapped in foil and frozen for up to six months.

USES

Cosmetic. Feverfew makes a useful moisturiser.

Medicinal. Tea made from the dried upper parts relieves indigestion and period pain. Eating one or two fresh leaves every day may help prevent the onset of migraines in sufferers but in some people this causes mouth ulcers.

Craft. Flower stems placed in linen closets will discourage moths.

Gardening. Feverfew is attractive and massed plantings make a good display. It is also good for bordering paths. It attracts bees and is often planted near fruit trees to assist pollination.

Tanacetum parthenium syn.
Chrysanthemum parthenium
FEVERFEW
ASTERACEAE/COMPOSITAE

CONDITIONS

Climate. Best in cool to warm areas but it grows in the tropics as an annual in cooler, drier months.

Aspect. Full sun is essential in cooler areas. In warmer districts feverfew prefers light shade on summer afternoons, but plants will grow lax and flower poorly in areas that are too shady.

Soil. Average, well drained garden soil is preferred. In over-rich soils, plants produce too much soft leafy growth.

Tanacetum vulgare
TANSY
ASTERACEAE/COMPOSITAE

CONDITIONS
Climate. Tansy grows in cool and warm areas but is not well suited to the monsoonal tropics.

Aspect. Full sun, part shade or bright, dappled shade are equally suitable for tansy, although full sun produces more compact growth and many more flowers.

Soil. Any well drained soil will do. Tansy is an extremely adaptable plant, able to grow almost wherever its seed falls.

FEATURES
Growing over 1 m (3 ft) tall, tansy is a sprawling perennial with grey-green, finely divided, ferny foliage and heads of yellow button-like flowers in summer and autumn. The leaves are aromatic and bitter to the taste, and the whole plant dies back to ground level over winter. It spreads out by means of creeping roots and can become quite large over time. In smaller areas it will need to be reduced regularly.

GROWING METHOD
Planting. Dividing the roots of an established plant is the easiest way to start a new plant quickly. Lift the parent in early spring and cut or pull the creeping roots into sections, each with its own roots. Replant immediately into the permanent site. Tansy may also be started from seed sown in spring or early autumn or from cuttings of semi-ripe stems that are taken in late spring and rooted in a moist, sandy potting mix.

Watering. Water sparingly but deeply. In coastal areas, tansy can usually get by on rain.

Fertilising. No fertilising is needed.

Problems. No particular problems.

Pruning. Cut the plants to the ground in middle to late autumn (early winter in warm areas). New growth will appear in spring.

HARVESTING
Picking. Pick leafy stems any time during the warmer months. Cut flower stems when they are freshly opened rather than when they are old.

Storage. Both the leaves and the flowers can be stored dry. To dry either, tie bunches together and hang them in a dim, well ventilated place or lay them out on drying racks. When the leaves are dry, remove them from their stems and store them in airtight jars. Take the dried flowers off the stems and store the flowers in airtight jars.

Freezing. Not suitable for freezing.

USES
Cosmetic. Tansy leaves can be used to make a delightful skin freshener.

Medicinal. Although tansy can be taken for medicinal purposes, it must only be administered by a trained herbal practitioner. Tansy has toxic properties and can be easily taken to excess.

Gardening. Tansy is a lovely, silvery green plant with very attractive flowers and an aroma that is very pleasant in the garden. Grow it in borders of mixed flowers or in big containers that prevent its unwanted spread.

FEATURES

A perennial plant often seen as a weed in lawns or neglected places, dandelion produces a flat rosette of deeply lobed, bright green leaves from a big, fleshy tap root. Bright yellow flowers are produced in spring and summer on hollow, leafless stems and develop into puffy, spherical seed heads that shatter when ripe, the individual seeds floating away on the breeze. Dandelion has a milky sap and its hollow flower stems differentiate it from other weeds.

GROWING METHOD

Planting. Sow seeds in spring directly where the plants are to grow, with a bed in an established vegetable patch being the most suitable site. Plants may also be grown in containers that are deeper than they are wide so as to accommodate the long tap root. Although they are perennials, individual dandelion plants should be dug and discarded every two or three years. Replace them with fresh seedlings.

Watering. Keep the soil evenly moist.

Fertilising. If plants are grown in a bed that has had rotted manure dug into it, no further fertilising is required. For containers, add controlled-release fertiliser to the potting mix at planting time and feed the growing plants monthly with liquid or soluble fertiliser.

Problems. No particular problems.

Pruning. Remove flower stems as they rise or, if the pretty flowers are wanted, deadhead as they fade to stop unwanted seed formation, as dandelion becomes an invasive weed.

HARVESTING

Picking. Pick fresh spring leaves while they are small and sweet. Bigger, older leaves are very bitter. You can reduce the bitterness by blanching – that is, excluding light. Do this by covering the plant with an upturned tin or flower pot, being sure that all holes are covered. Young leaves are ready for picking when they have lost all or most of their green colour. Harvest roots only in late autumn or winter or they will lack flavour and body.

Storage. The leaves must be used fresh. Store the roots by roasting them first and then grinding the results into an airtight jar.

Freezing. Roasted, ground roots will stay fresher and more flavoursome if stored in the freezer like fresh coffee.

USES

Culinary. Young sweet leaves are highly nutritious and can be used in salads, stir-fries or to make teas. The roots, which are cleaned, chopped and roasted until dark brown, are ground and used as a coffee substitute.

Medicinal. The sticky, white sap of the dandelion is used to remove warts. Dandelion coffee is sleep inducing and a detoxicant said to be good for the kidneys and liver.

Taraxacum officinale
DANDELION
COMPOSITAE

CONDITIONS

Climate. Grows best in cool to warm climates, especially the higher rainfall areas. Not well suited to tropical regions.

Aspect. Full sun is essential.

Soil. Not particularly fussy, but you will get the biggest and best roots and less bitter leaves by growing plants in good quality, friable, well drained soil.

Thymus sp.
THYME
LABIATAE/LAMIACEAE

CONDITIONS

Climate. Warm, dry climates best suit thyme, although low, creeping varieties grow better than the bushier types in colder areas.

Aspect. Prefers full sun or partial shade and a light, well drained soil.

Soil. Does not need very rich soil but adding some compost will help to keep the soil friable. The soil should not be too acid: if necessary, add lime to the garden bed at the rate of 120 g per square metre (4 oz per square yard).

FEATURES

Thyme is one of the most common of garden herbs, and many varieties are grown. Most thymes are low, creeping plants although some will grow to 25–30 cm (10–12 in). The shape of the bush and the colour and aroma of the leaves all depend on the variety. Not all thymes are used in cooking, the most commonly used varieties including lemon-scented thyme (*T.* x *citriodorus*), caraway thyme (*T. herba-barona*), common garden thyme (*T. vulgaris*), orange thyme (*T. vulgaris* 'Fragrantissimus') and silver posie thyme (*T. vulgaris* 'Silver Posie'). Thyme plants are perennials but usually need replacing every two or three years.

GROWING METHOD

Planting. Sow seeds in spring or autumn in clumps in flat trays containing damp seed-raising mix. Mist spray the trays until the seeds germinate, which is usually within a week. When seedlings are 10 cm (4 in) tall, place the trays outside for a week to harden the seedlings and then transplant them into the garden. Dividing mature plants is by far the most common method of propagation. During spring or summer, gently lift the parent plant, cut it into two or three sections, each with a good root formation, and then place them elsewhere in the garden. Layering is also a satisfactory method of propagation.

Watering. Do not overwater. Thymes prefer a dryish soil. Water adequately in dry spells.

Fertiliser. No fertiliser needed.

Problems. Spider mite, which feeds by sucking juice, can affect this herb. Treat with a recommended insecticidal spray. Root rot will set in if the soil is not well drained and is allowed to become waterlogged.

Pruning. Prune or clip to prevent woodiness.

HARVESTING

Picking. Fresh leaves and flowers can be picked as required or the whole plant can be cut back to within 5 cm (2 in) of the ground in summer and the leaves dried.

Storage. Leaves are dried on the stem by hanging branches in a warm, airy place. Branches are then stripped and the leaves stored in airtight jars.

Freezing. Pack in small airtight containers or plastic wrap; thyme can be frozen for up to six months.

USES

Culinary. Thyme is a classic component of the French bouquet garni. Varieties of thyme add special, individual flavours to many dishes. Both leaves and flowers can be eaten fresh in salads or used as garnishes or as a flavouring to honey, vinegars, stuffings, butters or teas.

Gardening. Thymes can be grown for their decorative effect as their low, matting habit makes them excellent edging or rockery plants.

FEATURES

A trailing perennial that can be trained to reach up to 2 m (6–7 ft), nasturtium is nevertheless usually grown as an annual, especially in colder areas and in the tropics. The wide leaves are roundish and dark green to variegated in colour and have a peppery taste. The funnel-shaped, five-petalled and spurred flowers appear in late spring and summer, and range from creamy white through yellow to salmon, brilliant orange and red. Some varieties have double flowers and all have a slight perfume. The edible buds each produce one seed. This plant grows well in containers.

GROWING METHOD

Planting. Sow seeds from midsummer through to spring in hot and tropical climates, from spring through to summer in warm zones and during spring in colder areas. Sow several seeds of the trailing varieties together in clumps set about 80 cm (30 in) apart. Plant dwarf varieties 40 cm (16 in) apart. Sow the seeds 2 cm (1 in) deep directly into the garden bed or containers where they are to grow and keep the soil just moist.

Watering. Do not water excessively, especially when plants are well established.

Fertilising. More flowers and seeds will be produced if you hold back on the fertiliser and compost. Fertilising encourages the growth of leaves.

Problems. Sap-sucking aphids love nasturtiums. Vigorously hose the pest off or treat the plant with an appropriate spray. Bacterial wilt and leaf spot are common diseases. Don't cultivate while plants are wet and remove all diseased plants from the garden.

HARVESTING

Picking. Pick any part of the plant as required.

Storage. Leaves and flowers do not store well and should be used immediately. Buds and seeds can be pickled in vinegar, stored in airtight jars and used at a later date.

Freezing. Not suitable for freezing.

USES

Culinary. All parts of this herb are edible. You can use the fresh leaves and flowers in salads or the flowers alone as a garnish. Use the pickled buds and seeds as a substitute for capers.

Gardening. Because they are so attractive to aphids, nasturtiums are an excellent companion plant for vegetables such as cabbages, broccoli and other *Brassica*. The aphids will flock to the nasturtium and leave the vegetables alone.

Tropaeolum majus
NASTURTIUM
TROPAEOLACEAE

CONDITIONS

Climate. Native to South America and now cultivated in most climates. Grow as a cool season annual in the monsoonal tropics and as a summer annual in colder areas.

Aspect. Prefers full sun although dwarf varieties will grow in semi-shade. Leaf growth is more pronounced in shady situations.

Soil. Nasturtiums do not like an over-rich soil but good drainage is necessary.

Viola odorata
VIOLET
VIOLACEAE

CONDITIONS

Climate. Violets grow in cool or warm climates but dislike the tropics or hot, dry summers.

Aspect. Sun in winter and bright dappled shade in summer are ideal. Where summers are mild, violets will tolerate full sun. They do not tolerate hot, dry winds. The flowers are disappointing if violets are grown in too much shade.

Soil. Violets need deep soil rich in rotted organic matter, preferably from composted fallen leaves. Soil must drain freely but it must also remain moist between showers or watering.

FEATURES

Violets are low-growing perennials just 15 cm (6 in) tall with a wider spread. The dark green leaves are roundish or kidney-shaped with scalloped edges. Small, very sweetly fragrant flowers appear on short stalks in winter and early spring. They are usually violet in colour but there are also mauve, yellow and white forms. Violets spread rapidly by creeping roots.

GROWING METHOD

Planting. Violets are easily established by division. Lift immediately after flowering and separate the cylindrical runners. Each division should have its own roots but these will usually form later if they are absent. Plant so that the runners are firmly in contact with the soil but not buried. Scatter seed where it is to grow or, for better germination, onto trays of seed-raising mix. Cover lightly, keep moist and place trays in a bright but shady and cool place. Transplant seedlings when they are big enough to handle.

Watering. Once established, violets can usually get by on rain where it falls regularly, if soil conditions suit them. If they never go dry for long periods, violets will flourish.

Fertilising. Place a mulch of rotted manure around plants, but not over the root crown, each spring (this can be hard in a densely planted area), or sprinkle a ration of complete plant food over the plants in spring. Once or twice during summer, water over with a liquid, organic fertiliser or seaweed-based soil conditioner.

Problems. Lay bait for slugs and snails, which chew holes in the leaves and destroy flowers. Spider mites and aphids can also damage plants by sucking sap. You can buy predatory mites to help control the spider mites; aphids are easily controlled with low-toxicity pyrethrum, garlic or fatty acid sprays. If plants fail to flower, the cause may be too much shade or too much high-nitrogen fertiliser.

Pruning. No pruning is necessary, but if flowers fail to form, cut all the leaves off in early winter to encourage spring bloom.

HARVESTING

Picking. Pick the flowers as soon as they open and pick the leaves any time.

Storage. Flowers may be crystallised for later use.

Freezing. Not suitable for freezing.

USES

Culinary. Use crystallised flowers to decorate cakes or eat them as a sweet treat.

Medicinal. An infusion of the leaves and flowers may relieve the symptoms of colds.

Craft. Violets are used in pot pourris.

Gardening. Violets are a very desirable groundcover in partly shaded areas. Posies of cut flowers will fill a room with fragrance.

FEATURES

A clump-forming perennial, ginger is a native of tropical lowland rainforests. It has many erect stems that grow to about 1.5 m (5 ft) tall. Lanceolate leaves, mid-green and about 20 cm (8 in) long, are produced all along the stems. Unremarkable flowers appear in summer, after which the top growth begins to die back.

GROWING METHOD

Planting. Plants can be started from sections of fresh root ginger bought from a fruit market. Cut the rhizome in sections about 8 cm (3 in) long, ensuring that each has a pointed growth bud. Allow the cut ends to dry for a few days before planting horizontally 8–10 cm (3–4 in) below the surface. Water in thoroughly. In tropical areas plant in autumn but otherwise mid-spring is better. Mulch the planted bed with compost, rotted manure, lucerne hay or other old organic matter. Don't plant the rhizomes too closely together, especially in the tropics, as ginger is a spreading plant that needs space.

Watering. At planting time, water in deeply. In tropical areas where winters are dry, continue to water deeply once a week. Out of the tropics, keep the soil lightly moist, gradually increasing the water as temperatures rise. In summer, the plant cannot be overwatered if drainage is good. After the plant has flowered, start to reduce the watering.

Fertilising. As well as the fertiliser applied at planting time, ginger should be fed with liquid or soluble plant food monthly from mid-spring to late summer. Replacing the mulch as it is washed into the soil also helps feed the plant.

Problems. No particular problems.

Pruning. In autumn, old stems can be cut out at ground level to make room for vigorous new growth.

HARVESTING

Picking. Ginger is harvested in autumn. Dig up and detach the rhizomes, replanting a few to produce next year's crop.

Storage. Rhizomes can be wrapped tightly in foil and stored in the crisper bin of the fridge for a few weeks, or they may be pickled or crystallised for long-term storage.

Freezing. Not suitable for freezing.

USES

Culinary. Ginger is widely used in Asian, African and Caribbean cuisine. It is an essential ingredient in everything from curries, soups and stews to salads and vegetable dishes. Crystallised, it is enjoyed as a sweet; dried, powdered ginger is added to cakes, biscuits and other foods.

Medicinal. Fresh juice directly applied is said to relieve the pain of burns.

Zingiber officinale
GINGER
ZINGIBERACEAE

CONDITIONS

Climate. A tropical climate is best but ginger will grow anywhere that is frost-free.

Aspect. In the tropics, part or dappled shade is best. In warm areas more sun is needed, but ginger still appreciates shade on hot summer afternoons. Shelter from strong winds is essential.

Soil. Deep, friable, well drained soil that is rich in rotted organic matter and a little on the alkaline side (dig in 1 cup of lime to the square metre, or square yard, at planting time). Dig the bed over deeply, adding rotted manure or compost and complete plant food as you go. The finished bed should be light, fine and crumbly.

index

Page numbers in *italics* indicate a recipe. **Bold** face indicates an entry in the directory.

a

Abelmoschus esculentus   146
Acacia decurrens   122
acacias   78
Achillea millefolium   75, 115, **196**
Acorus calamus   154, 185
Aesculus hippocastanum   57
agar-agar   127
aïoli   *137*
air drying   58, 60–2
air fresheners   185
Ajuga reptans 'Catlin's Giant'   100
Alexandrian School   108
alfalfa (*Medicago sativa*)   79
all-purpose cleaner   *193*
Allium cepa   146–7, 187
      drying   58
Allium sativum   35, 80, 136–7, **197**
Allium schoenoprasum   16, 23, 24, 45, 79, **198**
allspice   53
aloe vera (*Aloe barbadensis*)   160, **199**
Aloysia triphylla   18, 35, **200**
Alpinia galanga   136, **201**
Althaea officinalis   116, 121
Althaea rosea   116
Anethum graveolens   23, 38, 45, 53, 60, **202**
angelica (*Angelica archangelica*)   68, 127, **203**
      seeds   38, 60
anise (*Pimpinella anisum*)   50, 90, **231**
aniseed   53
annatto   128
annual sweet pea (*Lathyrus odoratus*)   78
Anthemis nobilis   43, 46, 154, 161, 174, 187, **210**
Anthriscus cerefolium   34, 46, 140, **204**
Apium graveolens   34, 53, 81, 132, **205**

apothecary's garden   90, 98
apothecary's rose (*Rosa gallica officinalis*)   34, 109, 119
aquatic plants   29–31
Armoracia rusticana   35, 60, 81, 139, **206**
aromatherapy   123, 155
arrowroot   128
Artemisia   82, 83, 85, 99
Artemisia abrotanum   189
Artemisia absinthium   83, 85, 99, 121
Artemisia dracunculus   37, 141, **207**
arthritis herb (*Hydrocotlye asiatica*)   109, 121
artichoke   99
arum lily   29
Arum maculatum   171
Asclepius   107
Asian herbs   130–1
aspect, of garden   16, 18
Atriplex patula   10
autumn crocus (*Crocus sativus*)   184, 185
avens (blessed herb) (*Geum urbanum*)   10, 177
Avicenna   115
Ayurvedic medicine   13

b

bagna cauda   129
bai toey   147
barberry seeds 'Zareshk'   53
barrier crops   79–81
basil (*Ocimum basilicum*)   23, 34, 49, 81, 175, **226**
      cuttings   56
      varieties   140
bath bags   164
bath oil   162–4
bay tree (*Laurus nobilis*)   34, 47–8, 128–9, **218**
      drying leaves   62
bees, and colour blue   168, 171
beetroot (*Beta vulgaris*)   84
bergamot (*Monarda didyma*)   34, 114, 172
      oil   12, 62
berries, mashing   40, 41
Beta vulgaris   84
birds   74, 171

Bixa orellana   128
black walnut (*Juglans nigra*)   85
black willow (*Salix nigra*)   57
bog garden   31
bog sage (*Salvia uliginosa*)   175
borage (*Borago officinalis*)   64, 77, 160, **208**
botany   13
botrytis blight   36
bouquet garni   129
box-leafed honeysuckle (*Lonicera nitida*)   94
braised fennel   *133*
Brassica sp.   144
      companions   27, 70, 72, 81
bubble bath   *163*
buckwheat (*Fagopyrum esculentum*)   79
Buddleia   171
bugbane (*Cimicifuga*)   171
butterflies   79, 171
butterfly bush (*Buddleia*)   171

c

cabbage, companions   27, 72, 81
calendula   80
Capsicum frutescens   131
caraway (*Carum carvi*)   46, 53, **209**
cardamom (*Elettaria cardamomum*)   19, 52
cardoon (*Cynara cardunculus*)   129
carrots, companions   81
Carum carvi   46, 53, **209**
Castanea sativa   43
catmint (*Nepeta* x *faassenii*)   **225**
celery (*Apium graveolens*)   34, 53, 81, 132, **205**
chamomile (*Chamaemelum nobile*)   43, 46, 154, 161, 174, 187, **210**
chamomile face mask   *164*
Chelsea Physic Garden   90
chervil (*Anthriscus cerefolium*)   34, 46, 140, **204**
chestnut (*Castanea sativa*)   43
chickweed (*Stellaria media*)   33
chicory (*Cichorium intybus*)   **211**
chilli 'Habanero' (*Capsicum frutescens*)   131
chilli and soap spray   *191*
chilli tea   *192*
chive tea   *191*

chives (*Allium schoenoprasum*)   23, 24, 45, **198**
  barrier plant   79
  in cold climate   16
chocolate mint (*Mentha piperita* cv.)   28, 48
chocolate root (*Geum rivale*)   177
Christmas rose (*Helleborus argutifolius*)   121
chrysanthemum greens   132
Cichorium intybus   **211**
Cimicifuga   171
clary sage (*Salvia sclarea*)   157
Claviceps sp.   116
climbers   97
cloves   185
coast rosemary (*Westringia*)   96, 175
Coleus amboinicus   25
collards   81
colour schemes   98–9, 100, 101
comfrey (*Symphytum officinale*)   74, 75, 140, 186,
  242
common mint   23, 26
companion planting   25, 48, 70–3, 75, 81
  checklist   86–7
  unsuccessful   85
Compositae family   6
composting   26–7, 74–5
Confucius   117
container gardening   21–2, 43, 45–51
coriander (*Coriandrum sativum*)   34, 46, 87, 124,
  131, **212**
  kitchen herb   140
  seeds   38, 47, 53
cosmetics   152–5, 160–1
cotton lavender (*Santolina chamaecyparissus*)   82,
  94, **240**
creeping thyme (*Thymus serpyllum*)   178
Crocus sativus   184, 185
crop rotation   73, 84
Cryptotaenia japonica   21, 50
Cucurma domestica   18
culinary herbs   124–51
  cooking tips   126
  storage   126
Culpeper, Nicholas   8, 10, 112, 114

cumin seeds   53
curry leaf tree (*Murraya koenigii*)   **223**
curry plant (*Helichrysum angustifolium*)   84, 178
cuttings   55–7
Cycas sp.   148
Cymbopogon citratus   46, 47, 130, 142, **213**
Cynara carduculus   129

d

dame's violet *see* eveweed (*Hesperis matronalis*)
damping off disease   35
dandelion (*Taraxacum officinale*)   32, 132, 184, **245**
Daucus carota   74
dessicants   58, 68–9
Dianella sp.   187
digestive herbs   10
Digitalis purpurea   114
dill (*Anethum graveolens*)   23, 45, **202**
  seeds   38, 53, 60
Dioscorides   9, 108
dogbane (*Plectranthus ornatus*)   84, 182

e

Earl Grey tea   12
eau de cologne   *159*
eau de cologne mint (*Mentha x piperita* var. *citrata*)
  28
echinacea (*Echinacea purpurea*)   104, 111, 120
Echinops, cuttings   57
Echium wildpretii   97
edging   101
eelworms *see* nematodes
elderberry (*Sambucus nigra*)   117, 133, 160, 186,
  239
elderflower cordial   *133*
Elettaria cardamomum   19, 52
Eruca vesicaria subsp. *sativa*   36, 47, **214**
Eryngium foetidum   24, 130
Eryngium maritimum   57
essential oils   13, 62, 126, 156–9, 171
  effect on pests   79–80
  home enfleurage   157
  vaporisation   158

evening primrose (*Oenothera*)   34, 173, **227**
everlasting pea (*Lathyrus latifolius*)   78
eveweed (*Hesperis matronalis*)   57

f

fabric dyes   182–4, 186–7
Fagopyrum esculentum   79
fairy moss (azolla)   30
fennel face cleanser   *165*
fennel (*Foeniculum vulgare*)   8, 133, 165, **215**
  seeds   53, 60
fenugreek seeds   53
fertilising   20, 73
feverfew moisturiser   *165*
feverfew (*Tanacetum parthenium*)   34, 83, 120, 122,
  123, **243**
fiddlehead fern   133
fig (*Ficus carica*)   107
finocchio   133
five-in-one herb (*Coleus amboinicus*)   25
Flanders poppy (*Papaver rhoeas*)   106
fleabane   185
floral and herb pot pourri   *181*
Florence fennel (*Foeniculum vulgare* var. *azoricum*)
  133
flower stems, wiring   64
flowers
  edible   6, 58, 60, 134–5
  harvesting   63
  language of   11
  night-flowering   171
fly deterrents   *192*
Foeniculum vulgare   8, 53, 60, 133, 165, **215**
Foeniculum vulgare var. *azoricum*   133, **215**
foliage, decorative   60, 99, 101
foliar feeding   20
foxglove (*Digitalis purpurea*)   114
Fragaria vesca   161
fragrance   28, 98, 172–7
frangipani (*Plumeria rubra*)   152
French marigold (*Tagetes minima*)   72, 73, 80, 81
fungal disease   34, 35, 36, 37

g

galangal (*Alpinia galanga*)   136, **201**
garden design   88–9, 97–101
garlic (*Allium sativum*)   35, 80, 136–7, **197**
garlic spray   *192*
Gerard, John   10, 109, 113–14
germination   44
Geum rivale   177
Geum urbanum   10, 177
ginger (*Zingiber officinale*)   68, 138, **249**
gingerbread men   *138*
ginseng (*Panax ginseng*)   13, 138–9
glass jars, sterilising   167
golden feverfew (*Tanacetum parthenium* 'Aureum')   161
gooseberry (*Ribes uva-crispa*)   112
Grasse   155
green wattle (*Acacia decurrens*)   122
groundcovers   97
growing tips   24–5
growth suppressors   85
gula melaka   148
gumbo   146, 149

h

hair rinses   158, *167*
Hanging Gardens of Babylon   8, 104
harvesting   24, 58, 60
heartsease (*Viola tricolor*)   54
hedging   94
    fragrant   174–7
    pruning   175
Helianthus tuberosus   139
Helichrysum angustifolium   84, 178
Helichrysum petiolare   161
heliotrope (*Heliotropium arborescens*)   178
Helleborus argutifolius   121
Helleborus orientalis   113
herb carpets   173–4
herb gardens   13
herb globes   22
herb and lavender pot pourri   *180*
herb mixes for meat   67

herb pillow   *190*
herb Robert   35
herb teas   126
herb vinegars   64–5
herbal medicine   13, 104–23
    Aboriginal   122
    Chinese   13, 117–18
herbals   10, 108–9, 111–13, 114
herbs   6, 13
    cultivation history   8–12
    medicinal qualities   13
    need for light   24
    for pots   45–51
    scented   168–71
    shade-loving   25
    summer/winter   173
Hesperis   173
Hesperis matronalis   57
Hibiscus sabdariffa   134
Hill, Thomas   93
Hippocrates   9, 107–8
hollyhock (*Althaea rosea*)   116
holy basil (*Ocimum sanctum*)   49, 131, 140, **226**
honeysuckle (*Lonicera periclymenum*)   10
horehound   35, 101
horse chestnut (*Aesculus hippocastanum*), cuttings   57
horseradish (*Armoracia rusticana*)   35, 60, 81, 139, **206**
horseradish cream   *139*
humus *see* composting
Hydrocotlye asiatica   109, 121
Hypericum sp.   187
hyssop (*Hyssopus officinalis*)   94, **216**

i

Indian borage   25
Indian ginseng   109
indigo   184
insecticides   *190–2*
insects   24, 171
    beneficial   74, 81
    repelling   27, 34–5, 45, 72, 76, 80, 84, 170

interplanting   77
Iris germanica   159
Iris x *germanica* var. *florentina*   180, **217**
Isatis tinctoria   184
Italian lavender (*Lavandula stoechas*)   48, 170
Italian parsley   50

j

Jamaica flower (*Hibiscus sabdariffa*)   134
Japanese parsley (*Cryptotaenia japonica*)   21, 50
Jekyll, Gertrude   12, 100
Jerusalem artichoke (*Helianthus tuberosus*)   139
Juglans nigra   85
Juglans sp.   85
juniper berries   52, 186

k

kitchen gardens   96, 98
knot gardens   91, 93–5
kuzu (*Pueraria lobota*)   142

l

lads love   84
Lamiaceae/Labiatae (mint) family   6, 175
Lathyrus latifolius   78
Lathyrus odoratus   78
Laurus nobilis   34, 47–8, 62, 128–9, **218**
Lavandula angustifolia   64–5, 94, 156
Lavandula stoechas   48, 170
Lavatera plebia   116
lavender bag   *189*
lavender ice cream   *135*
lavender (*Lavandula*)   48, 88, 154, 160, 162, **219**
    drying   60, 64, 65
    in food   134–5
    pest control   82, 83
    problems   35
    propagation   55
    pruning   21
lawns, fragrant   46, 173–4, 175
layering   54
leaf cuttings   57

leaf perfumes   170, 173-4
Lee, Ann   119
legumes   78
lemon balm (*Melissa officinalis*)   35, 171, **221**
lemon basil   130
lemon grass (*Cymbopogon citratus*)   46, 130, 142,
   213
   propagating   47
lemon savory (*Satureja biflora*)   168
lemon verbena (*Aloysia triphylla*)   18, 35, **200**
lemon-scented pot pourri   *181*
Lenten rose (*Helleborus orientalis*)   113
Levisticum officinale   35, **220**
licorice plant (*Helichrysum petiolare*)   161
lime (*Tilia* sp.)   163
Lonicera nitida   94
Lonicera periclymenum   10
lords-and-ladies (*Arum maculatum*)   171
lotus root   142
lotus root and vegetable stir-fry   *143*
Louisiana iris   31
lovage (*Levisticum officinale*)   35, **220**
lucerne   26, 78, 79

m

madder   182
mandrake (*Mandragora officinarum*)   9
Maranta arundinacea   128
marigolds (*Tagetes* sp.)   80, 160, 187
marinated sardines   *151*
marjoram (*Origanum marjorana*)   23, 35, 140-1,
   228
marshmallow (*Althaea officinalis*)   116, 121
mastic   143
meat tenderiser   51
Medicago sativa   79
Melissa officinalis   35, 171, **221**
Mentha piperita cv.   28, 48
Mentha spicata   170
Mentha x *piperita* var. *citrata*   28
menthol   28
mesclun   143
mignonette (*Reseda*)   173

milfoil yarrow (*Achillea millefolium*)   75, 115, **196**
milk thistle (*Sonchus oleraceus*)   32
millet (*Panicum miliaceum*)   144
miniature waterlily (*Nymphaea tetragona*)   30
mint garden   28
mint (*Mentha*)   23, 48-9, 141, **222**
   in cold climate   16
   companion plants   25, 27, 70
   family   6, 175
   pest repellant   27, 82, 83
   problems   36
   propagation   54
mint rust   36, 48-9
mintbush (*Prostanthera*)   96
mistletoe (*Viscum album*)   9
Monarda didyma   12, 34, 62, 114, 172
monastery gardens   9-10, 110, 111
moth deterrents   188, 189
moth sachet   *189*
mulberry (*Morus nigra*)   8
mulch   25-6, 75
   organic   25, 75, 78
Murraya koenigii   **223**
musk   154
musk rose (*Rosa moschata*)   154
mustard   144-5
   seeds   52, 144

n

Nasturtium officinale   33, 37, 49, **224**
nasturtium (*Tropaeolum majus*)   32, 60, 81, **247**
   problems   36, 80
native hollyhock (*Lavatera plebia*)   116
nematodes   72, 73, 80-1
Nepeta x *faassenii*   **225**
nettle (*Urtica* sp.)   145
nigella seeds   53
nitrogen   20, 26
nitrogen fixers   78
nurse crops   77
nutmeg   53, 154
nutrient retrievers   79
Nymphaea tetragona   30

o

oatmeal   164
Ocimum basilicum   23, 34, 49, 56, 81, 140, 175,
   226
Ocimum basilicum 'Red Rubin'   38
Ocimum sanctum   49, 131, 140, **226**
Oenothera   34, 173, **227**
okra (*Abelmoschus esculentus*)   146
onion chives (*Allium schoenoprasum*)   45, 131
onions (*Allium cepa*)   146-7, 187
orach (*Atriplex patula*)   10
oregano (*Origanum vulgare*)   23, 36, 49, 140-1,
   249
   dividing   55
   dried   124
organic gardening   73, 77
Origanum marjorana   23, 35, 140-1, **228**
orris root (*Iris* x *germanica* var. *florentina*)   180, **217**
oyster fern (*Osmunda cinnamomea*)   133

p

Panax ginseng   13, 138-9
pandanus leaves   147
Panicum miliaceum   144
Papaver rhoeas   106
Papilionaceae family   78
parsley (*Petroselinum* sp.)   23, 50, 140, **230**
   germination   44, 50
   problems   36
parterres   93-4, 96
paw paw mask for oily skin   *166*
pea family   78
   pH range   20
pearl onions   147
peat moss   26
Pelargonium   96
peppercorns (*Piper nigrum*)   52, 148
peppermint oil   162
perennial chamomile (*Chamaemelum nobile*)   43,
   64
perennial coriander (*Eryngium foetidum*)   24, 130
perfume   152, 155, 156, 158

pest control   27, 45, 73, 76, 80-3, 170
    spatial interaction   76
    trap plants   72, 81
pest/disease checklist   34-7
pesto   *140*
Petroselinum sp.   23, 50, 140, **230**
pH   20
phosphorus   20
physic gardens   109-10
pigweed (*Portulaca oleracea*)   32, 149, **233**
Pimpinella anisum   50, **231**
pink thyme (*Thymus* x *citriodorus*)   178
Piper nigrum   52, 148
Pistacia lentiscus   143
plant selection   19
plantain (*Plantago lanceolata*)   33
Plectranthus ornatus   84, 182
Plumeria rubra   152
pollination   170-1
Polygonum odoratum   130, **232**
pomanders   188, *188*
pomegranate seeds   53
ponds   29, 30
poppy seeds   52
Portulaca oleracea   32, 149, **233**
pot pourri   62, 178-81
potagers   76, 92
potassium   20
preservation   58-60
    air drying   58, 60-2, 64-5
    freezing   58, 60, 63
    oil/vinegar/alcohol   66
    oven drying   61
    salt/sugar   67, 68
    using dessicants   58, 68-9
    using glycerin   69
pricking out   42
propagation   38, 45-51
    cuttings   55-7
    division   55
    layering   54
    self-seeding   54
    see also seeds
Prostanthera   96

Prunella vulgaris   118, 120
Pueraria lobota   142
purple sage (*Salvia officinalis* 'Purpurascens')   51, 79
purslane (*Portulaca oleracea*)   36, 149, **233**
pyrethrum (*Tanacetum cinerariifolium*)   120

q
Queen Anne's lace (*Daucus carota*)   74

r
rack of lamb in herb crust   *141*
Reseda   173
Rhizobium   78
Rhus eoriaria   151
Ribes uva-crispa   112
roasted Jerusalem artichokes   *139*
rocket (*Eruca vesicaria* subsp. *sativa*)   36, 47, **214**
root cuttings   56-7
root rot   36, 37
root-knot nematodes   35, 36
roots
    fragrant   177
    harvesting   68
    pest control   80
Rosa filipes 'Kiftsgate'   101
Rosa gallica officinalis   34, 109, 119
Rosa moschata   154
rose hip seeds   41
rose petals   135
rose sugar syrup   *135*
rose-scented geranium   190
rose-water   135
rose-water and glycerine hand lotion   *166*
rosemary (*Rosmarinus officinalis*)   23, 50, 82, 154-5, 178, **234**
    drying   62
    hedging   94
    kitchen herb   141
    problems   36
    propagation   55
rue (*Ruta graveolens*)   9, 37, 83, 189, **236**
Rumex acetosa   37, 50-1, 150, 186, **235**
rust   34, 35

s
Sackville-West, Vita   12, 100, 101
saffron (*Crocus sativus*)   135, 184
sage (*Salvia officinalis*)   23, 51, 120, **237**
    drainage   21
    drying   62
    kitchen herb   141
    medicinal uses   113
    problems   37
    pruning   21
sage tea   113
sago (*Cycas* sp.)   148
sago pudding   *149*
St Anthony's fire   112, 116
St John's wort (*Hypericum*)   187
salad burnet (*Sanguisorba minor*)   37, **238**
salad leaves   149
salade lyonnaise   *132*
Salix nigra   57
Salvadora persica   154
Salvia officinalis   51, 113, **237**
Salvia officinalis 'Purpurascens'   51, 79
Salvia sclarea   157
Salvia uliginosa   175
Sambucus nigra   117, 133, 160, 186, **239**
Sambucus sp.   117
Sanguisorba minor   37, **238**
Santolina chamaecyparissus   82, 94, **240**
Saponaria officinalis   90
sassafras (*Sassafras albidum*)   149
Satureja biflora   168
savory (*Satureja* sp.)   37, **241**
scented cream   *166*
scented rush (*Acorus calamus*)   185
scented-leaf geraniums (*Pelargonium*)   96, 178
sea holly, cuttings   57
seed pods   52-3
seed trays   42, 43
seed-raising mix   43, 44
seedlings   44, 45
seeds   38-42, 52-3
    harvesting   38, 68
    scarification   40

sowing 41, 42, 44
    stratification 40
self-seeding 54, 80
selfheal (*Prunella vulgaris*) 118, 120
sereh powder 142
sesame seeds (*Sesamum orientale*) 52, 150
Shakers 119
Sissinghurst gardens 100, 101
skordalia *137*
snails/slugs 24, 34, 35, 45
    beer bait 45
soap cleaner *193*
soapwort (*Saponaria officinalis*) 90
soil
    improvement 24, 26–7, 73
    pH 20
    temperature 26
    types 16, 18
Sonchus oleraceus 32
sorrel (*Rumex acetosa*) 37, 50–1, 150, 186, **235**
southernwood (*Artemisia abrotanum*) 189
Spanish thyme 25
spearmint (*Mentha spicata*) 27, 170
spices 47, 52, 135
spruce 85
star anise, seeds 52
Stellaria media 33
still rooms 10
stinking Benjamin (*Trillium erectum*) 171
storage 58, 60
strawberry plants, with borage 77
strewing herbs 185
sumac (*Rhus eoriaria*) 151
summer savoury 80, 81
sunflower seeds 68
sweet flag (*Acorus calamus*) 154, 173, 177
sweet (Genoa) basil 12, 140
sweet peas 11, 78
sweet rocket (*Hesperis*) 173
sweet violet (*Viola odorata*) 6
Symphytum officinale 74, 75, 140, 186, **242**

t

Tagetes minima 72, 73, 80, 81
Tagetes sp. 80
tamarind (*Tamarindus indica*) 151
Tanacetum cinerariifolium 120
Tanacetum parthenium 34, 83, 120, 122, 123, **243**
tansy (*Tanacetum vulgare*) 72, 80, 83, **244**
tansy-leaf skin freshener *166*
Taraxacum officinale 32, 132, 184, **245**
tarragon (*Artemisia dracunculus*) 37, 141, **207**
tea tree oil 193
Thai basil (*Ocimum basilicum* 'Anise') 130
Thai mint 131
theme gardens 98
thyme (*Thymus*) 23, 51, 141, 155, 174, **246**
    dividing 55
    problems 37
    sowing seeds 41
Thymus carnosus 174
Thymus 'Mount Tomah' 51
Thymus serpyllum 178
Thymus x *citriodorus* 178
Tilia sp. 163
tip pruning 21
tomatoes, companions 27, 73, 81
topiary 96
tower of jewels (*Echium wildpretii*) 97
Townsend, Charles 'Turnip' 84
trap plants 72, 81
Trillium erectum 171
Tropaeolum majus 32, 36, 60, 80, 81, **247**
turmeric (*Cucurma domestica*) 18
tussie mussies 11

u

Umbelliferae family 6
Urtica sp. 145

v

valerian (*Valeriana officinalis*) 68, 108, 120
vanilla (*Vanilla planifolia*) 53, 151, 158
    essence 66
    sugar 53
variegated apple mint 27
Vietnamese mint (*Polygonum odoratum*) 130, **232**
Villandry gardens 93, 94
Viola odorata 6, **248**
Viola tricolor 54
violas, drying 60
violets 11, 37, **248**
    drying 64
    propagation 55
Viscum album 9

w

Walling, Edna 174
walnuts (*Juglans* sp.) 85
water crystals 22
water features 29
watercress (*Nasturtium officinale*) 33, 37, 49, **224**
watering 22
waterlilies (*Nymphaea* sp.) 29–31, 173
weeds, edible 32–3
Westringia 96, 175
white yarrow (*Achillea millefolium*) 115, 121
wild strawberry (*Fragaria vesca*) 161
wise women 10, 115–16
witchcraft 10, 116–17
woad (*Isatis tinctoria*) 184
woodbine 10
worm farms 26
wormwood (*Artemisia absinthium*) 83, 85, 99, 121

y

yarrow (*Achillea millefolium*) 60, 115, **196**

z

Zingiber officinale 68, 138, **249**

Acknowledgments

The publisher would like to thank Renaissance Herbs, Warnervale NSW, ph (02) 4392 4600 for generously supplying herbs and for allowing photography in the nursery; and 'Kennerton Green', Mittagong NSW, ph (02) 4871 1110 for allowing photography in the grounds.

Photographic credits

Ben Dearnley/Jared Fowler 127–9, 132–51.

Joe Filshie 7, 9, 14–15, 17, 18 (L), 19 (R), 21 (R), 27, 28 (btm L), 30–1 (centre), 39, 43 (top), 48–9, 50 (R), 51, 54 (btm), 59, 62 (btm), 69, 71, 72–3 (centre), 76, 78 (R), 80 (R), 89, 90 (L), 91–2, 94 (btm), 95–9, 113 (R), 114, 126 (L), 157 (top), 158 (L), 165, 169, 171, 172–3, 175 (top), 189 (btm), 200, 205, 209, 211, 215–16, 224–5, 227, 233, 235–6.

Andrea Jones 163.

Chris L Jones 50 (L), 107.

Meredith Kirton 93.

© Murdoch Books Photo Library 12 (btm), 68, 75, 90 (R), 94 (top), 115 (R), 126 (R), 155 (btm), 158 (R), 164 (R), 170 (R), 184 (btm), 188, 192, 196–9, 202–4, 206–8, 210, 212–14, 217–23, 231–2, 238–45, 247–9.

Lorna Rose 8, 10, 12 (top), 13, 47 (top), 55, 72 (L), 73 (R), 77 (L), 79, 100–1, 109 (R), 110, 113 (L), 119, 122–3, 153–4, 159, 177, 185, 189 (top), 190, 193.

Sue Stubbs 4, 11, 18 (R), 19 (L), 20, 21 (L), 23–6, 28 (top and btm R), 29, 30 (L), 31 (R and btm), 32–3, 40–2, 43 (btm), 44–6, 47 (btm), 52–3, 56–7, 60–1, 63 (L), 64, 64–5 (centre), 66–7, 74, 77 (R), 78 (L), 80 (L), 81–5, 87, 102–3, 105–6, 108, 109 (L), 111, 112, 115 (L), 116–18, 120–1, 125, 130–1, 155 (top), 157 (btm), 160–2, 164 (L), 166–7, 170 (L), 174, 175 (btm), 176, 178–81, 183, 184 (top), 186–7, 191, 194–5, 201, 226, 228–30, 234, 237, 246.

Mark Winwood 22, 54 (top), 62 (top and centre), 63 (top R and btm), 65 (R, top to btm), 156.

The publisher would like to thank the following for allowing photography in their gardens:

Dell Adam: 55.
'Ashfield', Sandy Bay, Hobart TAS: 59.
Avon Valley Historical Rose Garden, York WA: 154.
Sarah Baker and John Spence, Leichhardt NSW: 74 (R).
'Buskers End', Bowral NSW: 79.
Calthorpes House, Canberra ACT: 159.
Ray, Myrtle and Ron Charteris, members of Brisbane Organic Growers Inc.: 77 (L).
Dr G Cummins, Pymble NSW: 177.

Michelle Cutler and William Tocher, Tascott NSW: 62 (btm).
Kath and Peter Edwards, Cammeray NSW: 100.
'Elmwood', Exeter NSW: 69.
'Evandella', Hunters Hill NSW: 54 (btm).
Flower Power, Enfield NSW: 7, 17, 126 (L).
D D Franklin: 113 (R).
J Hancock, Erskineville NSW: 48 (top), 80 (R).
Diana Hill and David Potter, Ashbury NSW: 21 (L), 29 (L), 30 (L), 77 (R), 112, 157 (btm), 175 (btm).
'Hillview', Exeter NSW: 185.
Howell Garden, Rosevears TAS: 114.
Jill and John Hughes, Littlerose Nursery, North Canterbury, New Zealand: 109 (R).
'Kennerton Green', Mittagong NSW: 13, 30–1 (centre), 43 (top), 71, 72–3 (centre), 76, 78 (R), 89, 91–2, 94 (btm), 95–9, 172–3, 175 (top).
Meredith Kirton and Michael Bradford, Putney NSW: 29 (L), 31 (R), 56–7, 174.
Robert and Carmela Machin, Putney NSW: 28 (top).
'Moidart', Bowral NSW: 31 (btm), 106.
Mount Tomah Botanic Gardens, Mount Tomah NSW: 113 (L).
Paula Pellegrini, Randwick NSW: 11, 60 (L), 63 (L).
Sue and Robert Read, Pennant Hills NSW: 20, 24 (R), 25, 44, 61, 64, 74 (L), 170 (L).
Renaissance Herbs, Warnervale NSW: 9, 14–15, 18 (L), 19 (R), 21 (R), 27, 28 (btm L), 39, 48 (btm), 49, 50 (R), 51, 90 (L), 158 (L), 165, 169, 171, 189 (btm), 200, 205, 209, 211, 215–16, 224–5, 227, 233, 235–6.
Linda Ross, Kurrajong NSW: 40–2, 81, 84 (R), 87, 125, 191.
Royal Botanic Gardens, Sydney NSW: 8, 47 (top), 72 (L), 189 (top).
Dora Scott, Wahroonga NSW: 123.
Cec and Rita Sullivan, 'Lindfield Park', Mt Wilson NSW: 45 (btm).
Tasman Bay Roses, Motueka, New Zealand: 119.
'The Rose Garden', Watervale SA: 101.
Villandry, France: 93.
'Wildflower World', Auckland, New Zealand: 110.
Woodlyn Nurseries, Fiveways VIC: 73 (R).

Although every care has been taken to trace and acknowledge copyright, the publisher apologises for any accidental infringement where copyright has proved untraceable. The publisher would be pleased to come to a suitable arrangement with the rightful owner in each case.